Ain't That a Knee-Slapper

Ain't That a Knee-Slapper

Rural Comedy in the Twentieth Century

Tim Hollis

University Press of Mississippi
Jackson

www.upress.state.ms.us

Designed by Todd Lape

Page ii: No one is quite certain what rural-themed film featured the scene in this movie still. The standing actor is George Cleveland, later Gramps of the Lassie TV series. Whatever its origin, it is a terrific representation of the strain of general store/cracker barrel humor that would run through many rural comedies to come.

The University Press of Mississippi is a member of the Association of American University Presses.

All illustrations are from the author's personal collection.

Manufactured in the United States of America

First printing 2008
∞
Library of Congress Cataloging-in-Publication Data

Hollis, Tim.
Ain't that a knee-slapper : rural comedy in the twentieth century / Tim Hollis.
p. cm.
Includes bibliographical references and index.
ISBN 978-1-934110-72-0 (cloth : alk. paper) — ISBN 978-1-934110-73-7 (pbk. : alk. paper) 1. Rural comedies—United States—History and criticism. I. Title.
PN1992.8.R87H65 2008
891.4—dc22 2007040488

British Library Cataloging-in-Publication Data available

Contents

Ain't That a Knee-Slapper

Introduction

What This Book Ain't

Before we dive headfirst into this lengthy discussion about the history of rural humor, or country comedy, or whatever you may choose to call it, we really should make plain what the book does not cover. Ready?

You will notice that the subtitle designates it as rural comedy in the twentieth century. That means that for the sake of space, we are not concerning ourselves here with the vast history of hick humor that predated the modern mass communication era. Rural comedy has been an American tradition for longer than there has been an America. Probably the nation's first homespun humorist was Benjamin Franklin, whose Poor Richard character of almanac fame was the archetypical wise fool. He first appeared in 1733, and his almanac crammed full of his witty observations on life ("He that falls in love with himself will have no rivals") was published each year through 1758.

After the business of the revolution was out of the way, other American writers took up the cause of making the hayseed seem wiser than his citified cousins. In 1846, James Russell Lowell introduced his character of Hosea Biglow in the pages of the *Boston Courier*. In 1860, the *Cleveland (Ohio) Plain Dealer* produced Artemus Ward, a pen name for Charles Farrar Browne. Ward's supposed writings were laced with humorous misspellings, simulating uneducated speech. Also shortly before the Civil War, Henry Wheeler Shaw created another rural humorist, Josh Billings, publishing humorous essays that kept a kindly tone toward the subjects of their satire. They were collected into books with such titles as *Josh Billings and His Friends* (1865), *Everybody's Friend* (1874), and *Josh Billings Struggling with Things* (1881).

All of these rustics paved the way for the nation's premier humorist of country life, Samuel (Mark Twain) Clemens. Unlike Josh Billings, Twain did not believe in playing nice all the time; literary critics have noted that his satire tended to become more mean-spirited as he got older. However, his works were among the first to mine humor out of the rural areas of the United States other than New England. (Interestingly, considering that characters such as Hosea Biglow and Josh Billings were presented as New England farmers, the first rural comedians on radio would also adopt that background.)

Also during roughly the same period as Twain's influence, jokes about the supposed backwardness of the state of Arkansas began to emerge, initiating a trend that would persist more than a century later. The various purveyors of this new kind of hick hilarity included former Little Rock newspaper editor Opie Read, who moved to Chicago and published a humor magazine, *The Arkansas Traveler,* as well as several books on the subject of his onetime home state. Another of these authors was the party responsible for the publication known as *On a Slow Train through Arkansaw* (1903). In 1942, *Time* magazine reported, "The two-bit joke book was the making of author Thomas W. Jackson and the unmaking of Arkansas." The article went on to quote a typical example of the alleged humor contained in the book:

> *Arkansas Native*: All we need in this state is a little more rain and a little better society.
>
> *Visitor*: That's all Hell needs.

The book's success inspired blatant imitations, including *I Blew in from Arkansas* (1908) and *Through Arkansas on a Hog* (1908). Is it any wonder that as the years went by, people in Arkansas came to resent nearly any comedian who dared make wisecracks at the state's expense? Yet as we shall see, the gags just kept on coming, right up to and including the 1990s.

So rather than trying to analyze rural humor's long literary roots, this book begins with the birth of commercial radio in the mid-1920s. As it moves through the eras of silent movies, sound movies, television, and animated cartoons, another genre reluctantly had to be discarded. This book concerns itself only with rural humor that is placed in the time frame of when the production in question first appeared. More plainly, although productions such as Walt Disney's *Davy Crockett* epics and the 1964–70 NBC-TV series *Daniel Boone* (both of which starred Fess Parker, not coincidentally), as well as numerous film and television adaptations of Mark Twain's works, had elements of comedy, they were set in the distant past and thus have been eliminated from this discussion for sheer space purposes.

Do not be looking for social criticism on the merits—or lack thereof—of perpetuating the image of the lazy, drunken hillbilly long after other ethnic stereotypes had been well and truly put to bed. Our purpose is to document what was done, not necessarily why it was done. These pages will show how character types and plots—as well as actors and writers—run through many different branches of rural comedy. We will also see that while most people associate the terms *rural* and *hillbilly* with *southern*, many examples of such characterizations come from outside the southeastern quadrant of the country.

Well, as more than one comedian in this book would remark, "Let's stop spittin' on the handle an' start plowin'." Kick off your shoes and grab a tall, cold bottle of Mountain Dew ("It'll tickle yore innards"), and come 'n' listen to our story 'bout a man named Jed . . . and Lum . . . and Abner . . . and Snuffy . . . and Andy . . . Oh, you get the idea.

Chapter One

Let's See What's Going on Down in Pine Ridge

As we tune our vintage 1920s crystal set radios, we search in vain for some sort of programming to emerge from the mishmash of static and whine coming through our headphones. The world of commercial radio has changed little during the first five or six years of its existence: no one quite seems to know just what sort of programming the listeners—presuming there *are* listeners out there somewhere—actually want to hear. Music always seems to be a safe bet, whether classical, popular, or that emerging new brand out of the hill country known as hillbilly music. Programming that depends heavily on the spoken word is less common, possibly because the primitive conditions for transmission and reception make it doubtful that anyone can understand two or more consecutive sentences.

That was the status of radio in the middle of its first decade. Prior to the formation of the giant broadcasting networks, NBC and CBS, local stations provided whatever entertainment they felt was appropriate for their respective markets. Although most if not all of the early radio stations were based in large cities, station officials always seem to have believed that much of the audience lived in the surrounding countryside. Rural families, with less everyday contact with the great outside world, especially relied on radio for entertainment and news, and the stations did not hesitate to play to the room, as it were. By the mid-1920s, such weekly "hillbilly music" extravaganzas as Chicago's *WLS Barn Dance* and Nashville's *WSM Barn Dance* (soon to become known as the *Grand Ole Opry*) were firmly established, but they were primarily showcases for instrumental performances, with almost no vocals or other essential verbal communication that could be obscured by static.

The concept of radio programming took a dramatic turn in January 1926, thanks to Chicago's station WGN. According to radio veterans, since WGN was owned by the powerful *Chicago Tribune* (the call letters stood for World's Greatest Newspaper), company executives decided that the station would be programmed as if it were a newspaper, with the day divided up into segments that roughly paralleled a single edition of the *Tribune.* To correspond to comic strips, WGN initially wanted to produce a radio version of Sidney Smith's popular strip *The Gumps.* The two novelty singers assigned to the new show, Freeman Gosden and Charles Correll, quickly convinced management that they knew little about domestic humor, which was the mainstay of the Gump family's funny papers existence. What Gosden and Correll did know from vast professional experience was blackface comedy, so they concocted a show called *Sam 'n' Henry* that would run in nightly ten-minute episodes and carry a continuing story line.

Broadcasting historian Elizabeth McLeod has made a very valid point that applies to our discussion here. "While Sam and Henry are primarily remembered as 'black characters,'" she wrote, "it is often forgotten that they were also 'rural characters'—born and raised in a small town outside Birmingham, Alabama—and much of the early humor in *Sam 'n' Henry* stemmed from the characters' adjustments to the complexities of city life." (If this sounds like the show was prefiguring a theme that would later manifest itself in a hit TV show called *The Beverly Hillbillies,* well, you're just too smart for us.) When Gosden and Correll had the opportunity to jump from WGN to another Chicago station, WMAQ, they found it necessary to change their characters' names, inasmuch as WGN owned *Sam 'n' Henry*. The new title was *Amos 'n' Andy*.

Another historian of the show, Melvin Patrick Ely, has pointed out that both sets of characters derived much of their humor from their intellectual shortcomings: "Amos and Andy, even when they pooled their powers, could barely manage to write a letter and fared even worse when confronted by an arithmetic problem." Ely does not mention that such obtuseness was characteristic of all rural, unsophisticated characters, be they black or white. In fact, when the situation came up at all in their scripts, Sam and Henry and Amos and Andy were more likely to be belittled for their rural origins than for their racial background. Ely cites the example of one of the first *Sam 'n' Henry* episodes, in which the pair are hired for a job at a construction site. When they botch things up, the (white) foreman snarls, "A couple more dumbbells—where are you two rubes from?" Significantly, he does not use any of the accepted racial slurs that would have been more common at the time.

Although the story of *Amos 'n' Andy* could fill an entire book—and, in fact, has filled at least a couple of them—what is important here is that their innovative show demonstrated just how powerful and addictive the radio medium could be. Within a year of *Sam 'n' Henry*'s debut, other radio comedies had begun to spring up throughout the country, and just as the early radio musical programs had been aimed toward rural listeners, this would prove to be fertile soil for comedians as well.

Considering that most people, if they even think about it at all, probably equate "rural humor" with stereotypes of the American South, it is ironic that the first shows to bring this genre to radio listeners were based in locales that were both geographically and philosophically thousands of miles from the southern mountain country. McLeod's exhaustive research into pre-1935 radio has pinpointed a 1927 series, *Luke Higgins's Main Street Stories,* as the primary progenitor of the rural situation comedies. Broadcast from WOR in Newark, New Jersey (but considered a part of the New York City market), *Luke Higgins* starred young actor George Frame

Brown. Whereas Gosden and Correll had impressed their audience with the fact that the two of them combined to portray all the various character voices in *Sam 'n' Henry/Amos 'n' Andy,* Brown went one better, providing all the voices in *Luke Higgins.* The show was set in the "typical" upstate New York town of Titusville, where the kindly and gently humorous old geezer Higgins ran his general store, a sitcom setting that would become quite familiar to both radio and TV audiences of many comedy series to come.

According to McLeod, when Brown got the offer to move *Luke Higgins* to the fledgling NBC network in mid-1928, he was informed by WOR that the station owned the title and character, and, just as had happened with *Sam 'n' Henry,* he would not be allowed to continue using the names after he defected to NBC. Brown changed his lead character's name to Matt Thompkins, the name of his setting to Thompkins Corners, and the title of the show to *Real Folks,* which made its NBC debut in August 1928. Matt Thompkins continued as the owner of a general store, and the show was successful enough to secure sponsorship by the Cheseborough Company (manufacturers of Vaseline) for the next four years, with a final season sponsored by Log Cabin Syrup. By April 1932, when *Real Folks* and Matt Thompkins shuffled off to wherever canceled radio serials go, an astounding number of other rural-themed serials had invaded the airwaves. As was the case with *Luke Higgins* and *Real Folks,* most were based on New England characterizations.

This is where the story becomes a bit entangled, as many of these series shared the same writers and actors and were broadcast concurrently. Trying to put them into some semblance of order, McLeod has determined that in 1928, ex-Broadway playwright William Ford Manley created a weekly anthology show known as *Soconyland Sketches.* (For the uninitiated, *Socony* was an acronym for Standard Oil Company of New York, and the scripts in this series attempted to re-create various historical events from the area served by that conglomerate.) While *Soconyland Sketches* did not set out to have continuing characters, one of its most popular episodes was repeated several times. "Sebago Lake" was a humorous yarn in which an uptight New York businessman took a springtime fishing trip to

Maine and discovered that life could be a whole lot more peaceful than he ever imagined. (Like many themes throughout rural comedy, this one would resurface numerous times in the future, most notably in a memorable episode of TV's *Andy Griffith Show.*) While the hypertension-hindered businessman was supposed to be the primary character, the show was stolen by one of Manley's repertory company actors, Arthur Allen, as the philosophical fishing guide who taught the city slicker a thing or two about real living. Allen would have a lot to say in the world of rural New England humor over the next few years.

Our convoluted story now introduces Phillips H. Lord, a native of Maine galvanized into action by radio programming that he felt lacked a good deal of authenticity when it came to depicting his home turf. As a rebuttal, in 1929 he sold NBC a series that came to be known as *Sunday Evening at Seth Parker's.* McLeod described this series as "an odd combination of dialect humor, rural drama, and soft-soaped religion," with Lord himself as the kindly old Seth Parker, master of ceremonies. While this series was still running, Lord branched out into other forms of Yankee humor, creating *Uncle Abe and David* in 1930. For the first time, William Ford Manley's star player, Arthur Allen, was teamed with another Maine native, Parker Fennelly, and the two actors would find themselves linked as a radio comedy team for many years. *Uncle Abe and David* was yet another series set in a small-town general store—this time in Skowhegan, Maine—but McLeod reports that halfway through the show's nearly two-

Arthur Allen (*left*) and Parker Fennelly were first teamed in 1930 for the radio show *Uncle Abe and David*. The following year, they became the lead characters in *The Stebbins Boys*, for which this publicity photo was taken.

year run on NBC, Uncle Abe and his nephew, David, sold the store and moved to New York City, putting them firmly in the poor-fish-out-of-water genre being done more successfully on *Amos 'n' Andy.*

In June 1931, the formidable Lord/Allen/Fennelly trio was responsible for yet another series in this vein, *The Stebbins Boys.* In the small town of Bucksport Point, Maine, the two elderly brothers—Allen as John Stebbins and Fennelly as Esley Stebbins—were in business together in (would you believe it?) a general store. Although Lord is generally considered the mastermind behind this series, the extant scripts from its run were written by Henry Fisk Carlton, so the exact division of duties among these various parties is uncertain at best. The scripts give a terrific idea of the sort of humor that prevailed in this type of series, however.

In a story line from the week of Christmas 1931, John and Esley are taking care of a thirteen-year-old orphan girl, Sarah Browning, only to find that some of the more unscrupulous characters in town have their eyes on her inheritance. Chief among these misguided miscreants is Hobble B. Stevens Esq., who quickly spirits young Sarah away on some pretext or other. (Like some of the aforementioned story lines, the character of Hobble Stevens would be reborn several times over the ensuing fifty years—ever heard of a couple of charlatans named Mr. Haney and Boss Hogg?)

One of the most humorous scenes comes when the two Stebbins brothers decide to celebrate Christmas Eve by surprising Sarah at Stevens's house. They have ordered a Santa Claus costume from a mail-order catalog, but they find that looking like jolly old St. Nicholas is a harder job than the description of the costume would indicate:

John: Which one o' these is the coat an' which is the pants?
Esley: I don' know—figger it out fer yerself—come on—
John: Wal, I figger mebbe this is the coat. Slide into it.
Esley: It's a mite long, ain't it?
John: Ye sure that wa'n't the costume meant fer Mrs. Santy Claus?
Esley: What'd ye mean?

John: The thing looks like a skirt to me the way it trails on the ground.

Esley: I'm goin' to try on the whiskers. Now—how's that—how does it look now?

John: Ye look like the bearded lady at the circus with that red skirt draggin' on the ground.

Esley: Pshaw now, John, git serious. We've got a job on our hands. Think of how pleased little Sarah is goin' to be when I come in!

John: Mebbe she'll jump through the window in fright—you look more like one o' them hop-goblins ye read about than Santy Claus.

Esley: I know what's the trouble—I ain't got the cap on.

John: Wal, here ye be. Good-bye, Esley.

Esley: Why do ye say good-bye?

John: I jes' noticed the size of it. When ye git that thing on, I ain't goin' to be able to see ye at all.

While all of these goings-on were going on in Bucksport Point, Phillips Lord was not neglecting the nation's regular Sunday night visits with *Seth Parker*. In a promotional stunt that would have made P. T. Barnum proud, in 1933 Lord purchased a three-masted schooner that he promptly named the *Seth Parker*. His idea was to take the sailing ship on an around-the-world cruise, during which he would broadcast his dialogue for the weekly show via shortwave radio while the rest of the cast remained in New York. It was an idea that would not be unheard of in today's world of reality shows, but it spelled the end of Lord's career as radio's patron saint of rural New England comedy. In early 1935, the noble *Seth Parker* was wrecked off the coast of Fiji during a tropical storm. Word trickled out that the shipwreck was caused not only by the inclement weather but by the copious amounts of alcohol being consumed during the cruise, compounded by who knows what all brands of other debauchery. Fans of *Sunday Evening with Seth Parker* felt betrayed by their not-so-saintly hero, and the kindly old New Englander disappeared from the airwaves just as quickly as his schooner had disappeared beneath the ocean waves.

(We should not feel too sorry for Phillips Lord, however, as his career was soon literally coming on like gangbusters. Returning to New York, Lord hit on the idea of dramatizing true crime stories instead of gentle rural comedies, and the noisy opening credits of his resulting *Gang Busters* series not only gave rise to that figure of speech but made him such a giant figure in radio history that everyone soon forgot Seth Parker.)

Just to prove that general store settings were not confined exclusively to New England, we now turn to a series based in Chicago that would have far-reaching effects on the world of radio. Husband-and-wife team Jim and Marian Jordan had struggled through the vaudeville ranks for several years before they eventually landed at WMAQ and made the acquaintance of an aspiring writer, Don Quinn. The Jordans had enjoyed some minor success in Chicago radio, but nothing that would make them household names. Realizing that three heads are often better than two, the couple huddled with Quinn and came up with a show that would be called *Smackout.*

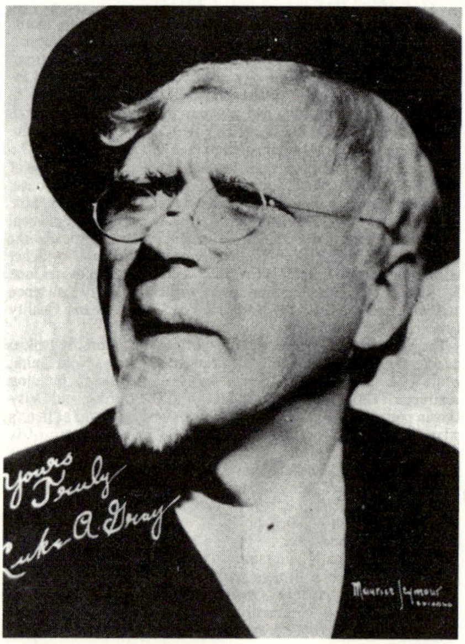

Jim Jordan played Luke Gray, the prevaricating old keeper of the general store, on *Smackout* in 1931. Four years later, Jordan and his wife, Marian, became radio legends with their show, *Fibber McGee and Molly*.

What in tarnation kind of title was that, you ask? Well, it does require some explanation. In the show, Jim Jordan would play the starring role of Luke Gray, the grizzled old proprietor of (what else?) a general store in the tiny community of Smackout Corners, otherwise known as "the Crossroads of the Air." In their exhaustive biography of the Jordans, historians Tom Price and Charles Stumpf have elaborated on the character of Luke: "His favorite pastimes were whittling and pitching horseshoes, which he would much rather do than tend the store. Frequently, Luke would deny that the store was open, and almost always told customers that he was 'smack out' of whatever it was they were asking for. . . . However, he was always well-stocked with a goodly supply of tall tales, such as the one about the time he taught some woodpeckers to tap out messages in Morse Code, and another one about the time he grew square tomatoes to use in bacon, lettuce and tomato sandwiches."

In addition to playing Luke, Jordan appeared under his own name, enlivening the episodes by singing while his "girlfriend" Marian accompanied him on the store's piano. The talented twosome provided the voices of all the other characters in Quinn's scripts as well. Jim's larynx contained such personalities as Augie Pigmeyer, the German immigrant farmer; village idiot Perky McSnark; local con man Squire Lovejoy; and Luke's old crony, Mort Toops. Not to be outdone in the multiple voices department, Marian loaned her versatile tones to a little girl named Teeny who "bothered the whey out of" crusty old Luke, Mrs. J. High-Hat Upson, Widow Wheedledeck, and Bertha Boop. Someone once estimated that between the two of them, the Jordans had given voice to approximately 150 different characters during the program's four-and-a-half-year run.

Although NBC broadcast *Smackout* on a sustaining basis—radio terminology for a show that has no sponsor—the series was popular enough that it might eventually have secured a permanent place in radio history. The Jordans would indeed do that, but only indirectly because of *Smackout.* We will check back in with them in a few pages and see if they are still running that general store.

All of the rural sitcoms we have examined up to this point were more or less popular for a time, but they did not prove to have much long-lasting sticking power. In practically every case, they survive only as brittle script pages (when even that much of them exists) and occasionally in fragmentary recordings, as in the case of *Smackout.* Another comedy series, however, emerged in the midst of all these others and would prove to be the most famous and long-running of the crowd. It got its start even more inconspicuously than the now-forgotten *Seth Parker, The Stebbins Boys,* and their ilk.

Situated in the Ouachita Mountains of western Arkansas was the small town of Mena, significant only because it marked the halfway point of the Kansas City Southern railroad (which connected

Kansas City with the Gulf coast at Port Arthur, Texas). Chester Lauck and Norris Goff were the sons of two of Mena's more prosperous families: the Laucks had interests in both the banking and lumber businesses, while the Goffs operated a successful wholesale grocery house. Both Chester and Norris—nicknamed Tuffy for his prowess on the football field—helped out in their families' endeavors, but they reportedly spent nearly as much time goofing around as they did working. They discovered an uncanny knack for playing off of each other and anticipating each other's responses, and they mastered a wide variety of ethnic dialects for entertaining their fellow townspeople with their comedy.

Early in 1931, radio station KTHS in Hot Springs, Arkansas, initiated a series of programs in which various communities throughout the listening area would send local talent to represent them on the air. The manager of KTHS, Cam Arnoux, had already made a reputation for himself that, if not exactly national, was at least widespread throughout the Southeast. Because KTHS was an NBC network affiliate, Arnoux no doubt hoped that his statewide talent search might produce something that could be parlayed into a hit, but he likely did not expect it to come out of Mena. On Saturday, April 18, 1931, KTHS presented the program put together by the Mena Lions Club, which consisted of a string band for the musical portion and those two local cutups, Lauck and Goff, handling the speaking parts.

Just what happened on that historic occasion has become such a part of radio legend that some of the key facts have most likely been obscured. Lauck and Goff frequently related how they had worked up what they thought was a boffo blackface routine but found when they got to the station that several other blackface acts had already been presented on previous shows. On the spot, they decided to switch to two rural characters based on the folksy types they had encountered when pounding a beat through the Ouachitas on behalf of the family banking and wholesale grocery enterprises. Needing something to call each other, Lauck decided to become Lum Edwards, and Goff chose the name Abner Peabody. Thus, the team of Lum and Abner took to the air for the first time.

When Chester Lauck and Norris Goff first appeared as Lum and Abner on station KTHS in Hot Springs, Arkansas, on April 26, 1931, they quickly became household names throughout the powerful station's coverage area.

Or did they? Contemporary newspaper coverage of the occasion plus interviews with surviving family members many years later confirm that Lauck and Goff hardly got any dialogue on the air during that April 18 program. For some reason, the station lost power just as their routine began. (Lauck's widow later said, "We thought it was because they were so bad.") An apologetic Arnoux and his staff invited the Mena contingent to return on Sunday, April 26, to complete their program. In the decades to come, April 26 was consistently given as the debut of *Lum and Abner*, leading to a supposition that perhaps the aborted April 18 routine was a blackface one, giving Lauck and Goff eight days to come up with their replacement hick characters. We will never know for sure, but what is certain is that Lum and Abner—whenever they finally appeared—were immediate hits with the KTHS listeners.

The station gave them a regular Sunday evening slot beginning in early May, and the publicity campaign that followed was positively massive for what amounted to a local program. Oscar Plaster, a Mena photographer, produced the first photo showing Lauck and Goff in character as their rustic counterparts. Since both men were less than half the age of the characters they portrayed, looking the part called for some drastic makeup attempts, including a feather affixed to Goff's chin to represent Abner's goatee. Lauck, for his part, grayed his naturally wavy hair and put on a gigantic handlebar mustache to pass for Lum. While their makeup would improve in coming years, becoming more and more professional, the basic look established in that May 1931 publicity photo would remain with Lum and Abner throughout the rest of their careers.

While much is known about the early publicity surrounding *Lum and Abner*, things are quite understandably a bit dimmer when it comes to determining just what sort of show they put on during their time with KTHS. Since the pair habitually did not use a script in those early days, ad-libbing their way through the allotted airtime, nothing along that line survives to help. The only slight indication of the direction the show was taking came from a brief article in their hometown newspaper, the *Mena Star*, which reported on their upcoming May 17, 1931 broadcast: "The Mena entertainers are proving so popular that they were announced to appear again next Sunday, at which time they will tell about going to court at Little Rock, where they also expect to attend one of those 'girlie' shows they have heard about, and which will be done if possible without the knowledge of Mrs. Lum and Mrs. Abner."

From this, we can gather that perhaps the show was already beginning to take on its serialized, continuing story line format, but from the remark about taking in a girlie show in Little Rock, it sounds as if the characters were perhaps a bit more rough around the edges than the upstanding citizens they would later become. Also quite telling is the reference to "Mrs. Lum and Mrs. Abner." While Lauck and Goff were happily married to their Arkansas sweethearts until death did them part, for the balance of the radio show's run, Abner was portrayed as the long-married suffering husband, with Lum as a "bashful bachelor" who courted a long line of ladies but could never get up the nerve to ask any of them to marry him. A script from January 1932 contained one of the last references to the fact that Lum had once been married, and after that, it must have been assumed that so few people had heard the early broadcasts that they could pretend Mrs. Edwards had never existed.

After only a few weeks of Lum and Abner's KTHS appearances, Cam Arnoux encouraged Lauck and Goff to take their act to Chicago and try for some network exposure. In those days, the usual procedure was to sell a show idea to an advertising agency, which would buy it for one of their clients. The clients, in turn, would then purchase airtime on a network. Being relatively unfamiliar with how things were done, Lauck and Goff finagled an appointment with the Quaker Oats Company (through Goff's connections in the wholesale grocery business). Not only did they audition *Lum and Abner* for the company, but Quaker bought the show as a temporary replacement for its popular *Gene and Glenn* series, which was soon to go on summer vacation. The Arkansas pair first spoke to a nationwide audience over NBC on July 27, 1931.

In interviews conducted many years later, Lauck and Goff claimed that in the beginning they did not specify Arkansas as the setting for their show. Their original intent was to make it as generic as possible so that any listeners who had ever lived in a small town could identify with it. There is some evidence that their earliest shows referred to Lum and Abner's hometown as Shady, but before too many months had elapsed, they had changed the name to Pine Ridge because it sounded more evocative of the mountain country.

The pair also claimed that when they made their network debut, they used a dialect that was much more authentic than the one with which listeners later became familiar. However, they found that when they accurately mimicked the speech patterns of the old-timers in their native Ouachitas, the general public had difficulty understanding what they were saying. They had to "tone it down," as they put it, to make the dialogue comprehensible to a wider audience. Other changes were made because of evolving attitudes toward what was and was not appropriate for radio. In some of the early *Lum and Abner* episodes, Lum was heard to express astonishment with the oath, "By the great I Am." NBC obviously considered this a little too close to swearing, and before too long, Lum and Abner had each developed a meaningless all-purpose expression, "I grannies" for Lum and "I doggies" for Abner. They never tried to explain what either saying meant, although "I doggies" was probably the origin of Jed Clampett's more famous "Well, doggies" of thirty years later.

The most amazing thing about the first year and a half of *Lum and Abner*'s broadcast life, especially considering what had gone before it, is that the pair did not originally run a general store as part of the story line. With everyone from Uncle Abe and David to the Stebbins brothers sticking their hands into the cracker barrel, one would think that Lum and Abner would have immediately jumped on that concept as well, but in the beginning Lum was presented as the town's justice of the peace, while Abner was the local constable. Not until January 1933 did they add a grocery store to their list of temporary sidelines, and since the business was to be operated on a basis of "strictly credit, no cash" (so as to keep Abner from making mistakes giving change, they explained), they held a contest for their listeners to submit names for the new mercantile establishment. Several listeners, mindful of the typical method of

Lum and Abner opened their Jot 'Em Down Store in January 1933, making them the latest—but not the last—in a long line of rural comedians to get laughs out of that type of setting.

keeping up with running accounts in country stores, suggested the name Jot It Down Store. Lauck and Goff hesitated to recognize multiple listeners, so instead they chose the entry submitted by young Paul Fiocca of Ohio: Jot 'Em Down Store. It would become one of the most famous businesses in all of radioland.

As the months turned into years, Lauck and Goff followed the Gosden and Correll tradition of playing virtually all the different roles in the show themselves. Beginning in the late 1930s, some of radio's finest character actors would be added to the cast to play various parts from time to time, but the core group remained the Lauck and Goff voices. In addition to Lum, Chet Lauck played Cedric Weehunt, whose strength as a character transcended what could have been a one-joke role as the village idiot. Lauck was also the crabby old town patriarch, Grandpappy Spears, who participated in highly argumentative and occasionally violent checker games with Abner. A more rarely heard Lauck characterization was Snake Hogan, the town bully and bad man.

Norris Goff was no slouch himself in the multiple roles department. Besides Abner, his major character was Squire Skimp, the con man extraordinaire who might have even been able to pull a fast one or two on *Amos 'n' Andy*'s Kingfish. During the first decade of *Lum and Abner*, Goff also used his natural speaking voice to play Dick Huddleston, the genial owner of the larger general store across the street from the Jot 'Em Down Store. This was a rare example of the show using a real person's name, as Dick Huddleston was a good friend of the Lauck and Goff families who owned a general store in the small community of Waters, eighteen miles east of Mena. Another major Goff character was not added to the show until 1941, the milquetoast Mousey Gray, who turned out to have a mean right hook when irritated.

The early *Lum and Abner* story lines presented a somewhat darker—and probably more realistic—view of life in the rugged Arkansas hills than the more idyllic portrayal of Pine Ridge that emerged later. Although comedy was always present, it was frequently set among events that were not so humorous. Characters would threaten each other with firearms, and several of the most prominent Pine Ridge citizens—including Abner, who served for a time as the town's mayor—were described as being unable to read or write.

One thing that did not change over the years was Lum and Abner's inability to fill out any sort of questionnaire without making it into a mishmash of misunderstood information. In a typical exchange from 1932, Lum was trying to apply to a matrimonial bureau:

Lum: What nationality? Meanin I reckon if you're a Indian or Irishman or German or what.

Abner: You ain't nuthin air you.

Lum: Nope, I'm jist a Arkansawer. I reckon though I ort to put somethin down ther to make it look right.

Abner: Put down ther that yer a Chinese.

Lum: I don't look like no Chinese. I'll jist say I'm a Arkansawer. Now let's see. Next un here is Race.

Abner: Race?

Lum: Yea, jist plain race. RACE question mark.

Abner: What kind a race they talkin bout, foot racin or horse racin?

Lum: I don't know. I'm jist goin to set down "no" here.

But by far, the most common source of humor on the show would originate when Lum would illustrate the point he was trying to make by using some familiar proverb or aphorism (which he called his "old Eddards sayins"). Inevitably, Abner would take the expression literally and Lum would have to spend the rest of the episode trying in vain to explain what he had meant.

Lum: Yeah, well jist recollect that old Eddards sayin', a barkin' dog seldom bites.

Abner: Huh?

Lum: I say a barkin' dog seldom bites.

Abner: I don't know 'bout that, Lum. Old Lead, that dog of mine, barks at everthing that comes on the place and anybody that don't think he'll bite jist orter try to come in that yard of a night.

Lum: Well, that's a old sayin' of mine. If that dog of yours barks, he won't bite.

Abner: That's jist all you know about it. I know I've saw him. He might nigh takened a leg offen Mose Moots here a while back.

Lum: Well, your dog is a exception then.

Abner: No, he ain't nuthin' but a hound but he'll bark and bite both, I know that.

Lum: Well, what I meant by barkin' is braggin'.

Abner: Oh, well no. Lead don't brag none. He cain't even talk. Yeah, you're right about that alright, if a dog could talk he wouldn't have to bite, he could jist tell fokes to stay outa the yard.

Actually, routines such as this one were probably remnants of Lauck and Goff's beginning as would-be blackface comics. A team known as Moran and Mack, the "Two Black Crows," had enjoyed some minor success on radio and bigger recognition for their phonograph records, in which they too would dismember slogans such as "A rolling stone gathers no moss" or "The early bird gets the worm." The punch line for the latter routine, "Aw, who wants a worm anyhow?" became a running gag among other comedians and especially in animated cartoons. Lauck and Goff may originally have been following the same pattern and simply saw no reason to change it once they moved into rural dialect.

Within just a few months of the beginning of *Lum and Abner*'s network run, other radio comedies with surprisingly similar themes and characters began to appear. Perhaps because the creators of these programs felt that the networks were already drowning in corn, what with *Lum and Abner* coexisting with the ongoing New England rural comedies, at least two of the major Lum and Abner clones were syndicated programs, with recorded episodes bicycled from one radio station to the next in the form of sixteen-inch transcription disks.

One of these two series reached the airwaves as early as May 1932. *Eb and Zeb* was sponsored by the Shell Oil Company and starred Al Pearce as Eb Peters and Bill Wright as Zeb Winterbottom, two old geezers who (surprise!) ran a general store in the tiny burg of Corn Center, California. These two hayseeds had first been heard as a recurring skit on *Blue Monday Jamboree*, a weekly variety show from KFRC in San Francisco that became a West Coast phenomenon in the late 1920s. Unlike most such comedy teams, where the characters had clearly defined personalities and roles, little distinguished Eb from Zeb or vice versa. Even their voices were much alike, except for Eb's peculiarity of whistling his *S*s when he spoke.

The story lines for *Eb and Zeb* were much more loosely constructed than those of *Lum and Abner* or any of the other rural comedies. Although the plot ostensibly continued from day to day, it would frequently be interrupted or abandoned for an entire episode just so the characters could exchange vaudeville-style jokes with each other, as in the program's first episode:

Eb: Zeb! When in tarnation did ye git back?

Zeb: About a half hour ago on the 4:20 train.

Eb: 4:20 train?

Zeb: Yessir.

Eb: Why, hit ain't even three o'clock yit.

Zeb: I know, but this was yistidy's train!

Zeb explained that while he was on a trip to the city, he hired an efficiency expert to return to Corn Center with him and help figure out ways to make their store more profitable:

The publishers of this shortwave hobbyists' magazine certainly realized the close relationship between radio and country store humor. Could these characters have been the stars of *Eb and Zeb*?

Zeb: He's a durn smart feller—but then, I tole ye about him in the letter.

Eb: What letter?

Zeb: Why, that letter I writ ye last week.

Eb: Did you write that letter?

Zeb: Certainly I writ it—didn't ye see my name signed to it?

Eb: Nope, I didn't read it. I kept it fer a spell then sent it back.

Zeb: Sent it back? Why, ye poor fish, wha'd ye do that fer?

Eb: 'Cause hit said ta do it right ther on the corner of the envelope. Said, "Return to sender in five days."

With Shell Oil footing the bills, *Eb and Zeb* was able to employ a larger supporting cast than most shows of its type. While both Pearce and Wright played additional roles, more often than not the supporting parts were taken by now-unidentified radio actors. In keeping with the loosely structured plots, some of these characters appeared only occasionally, when a certain joke's punch line needed to be set up. On the female side were Miz Newbride, who existed solely to deliver jokes about inexperienced newlyweds; Hortense Schulzenheimer, who filled the need for a pseudosophisticate to argue with and be exasperated by the rustic store owners; and movie producer Heebie B. Beebie, who came to Corn Center to film a rural epic.

The primary male supporting character was Hector Smith, a smart-aleck wisecracker with a slurring speech impediment, played by Pearce. This figure obviously came in handy because entire episodes could be filled by having him match wits with Eb and Zeb (even though they all seemed only half prepared). Later in the decade, after Pearce became the host of his own highly successful comedy-variety radio series, the basic Hector voice would return as Pearce's most famous recurring character, timid door-to-door salesman Elmer Blurt, who always knocked and then muttered, "Nobody home, I hope I hope I hope I hope."

Eb and Zeb were perhaps the only radio comedy characters in competition with their own sponsor. In an effort to find some way to get passing traffic to stop at their general store, the duo met Mr. Sharp, a representative of the fly-by-night (and fictional) Longshot Oil Company, who convinced them to install one of his gasoline pumps in front of their store:

> *Sharp*: What you fellows need is a Longshot gas pump.
> *Eb*: Ye mean Longshot gas will make automobiles stop?
> *Sharp*: It certainly will—and what's more, they STAY stopped. And the nice thing about this pump is that any part of it can be replaced if it breaks down—as you'll soon find out.

Many gags dealt with the advisability of buying only gasoline with a proven brand name—a not-so-subtle plug for Shell, naturally.

Because radio recordings from the early 1930s are comparatively scarce, it is uncertain just how long the *Eb and Zeb* series ran. The 1932–33 set included at least 256 episodes, but the characters were revived periodically for many years thereafter. When *Al Pearce and His Gang* became a popular weekly prime-time variety series from 1933 to 1947, Pearce and Wright frequently dragged their two rube voices out of mothballs for isolated skits, much as they had begun with on *Blue Monday Jamboree,* rather than the continuing story lines of old.

The other syndicated series that in hindsight appears to have ridden on Lum and Abner's well-worn coattails was *The Misadventures of Si and Elmer.* Whereas the similarities between *Eb and Zeb* and *Lum and Abner* are mostly cosmetic and stem primarily from the general store setting, *Si and Elmer* took the idea of Pine Ridge plagiarism a few steps further.

The show was the creation of Perry Crandall, whose entire known career was built around the syndicated radio shows market. The first episode introduced Crandall as Si Perkins and William H. Reynolds as Elmer Peabody (yes, he shared Abner's last name, which might not have been a coincidence), two old loafers who have grown tired of hanging around the general store in Punkinville and have taken a mail-order course in becoming private detectives. Their personalities were established immediately; whereas Eb and Zeb were virtual clones of each other, Si and Elmer were quite easy to tell apart (although Elmer shared Eb's penchant for whistling *S*s). Unfortunately, Crandall and Reynolds seem to have created their personalities by taking Lum and Abner's primary characteristics and exaggerating them to the point of obnoxiousness.

For example, Lum was always a semiconceited braggart, forever ready to claim that he was a descendant of the famed "King Eddardses" or an expert at running a bank or a restaurant or whatever other business venture the pair attempted. Abner was more cautious, frequently pleading with Lum to abandon his latest wild scheme before they both ended up in jail, the poorhouse, or the cemetery. Elmer may have shared Abner's last name, but his personality was 200 percent Lum. His bragging and bullying of his partner were more distasteful than humorous. Si, for his part, was a whining hypochondriac who was often on the verge of tears as he complained about his "misery" acting up again. Si evidenced none of Abner's backbone, and listeners were left to wonder why the two quarreling old coots even bothered to put up with each other.

Lest it sound as if the show were a total disaster, let's be fair and acknowledge that it carried some story lines that were every bit as gripping as those heard on better-known serials. Because Si and Elmer were self-professed detectives, they encountered situations that were somewhat grimmer than their radio cousins who hung out around general stores. Potential murderers, dead bodies, and other harrowing escapades awaited in nearly every episode. Unlike *Lum and Abner* and *Eb and Zeb,* which generally unfolded in "real time" (that is, each episode represented fifteen minutes of a day, and the next episode took place twenty-four hours later), *Si and Elmer* followed a pattern, later common among daytime soap operas, in which the events of a single hour in the story could consume four or five consecutive shows.

This approach enabled Crandall and Reynolds to set up some suspenseful situations that would not have been as effective had they been split up over a series of daily events. Probably their greatest story line involved the "midnight murder train" that was reported roaring past a nearby railroad workers' camp every night at the same time. The only problem was that the tracks were not completed, and no one ever saw the train, but every time its sound was heard, another worker or railroad official mysteriously disappeared, never to be seen again. After much bungling, Si and Elmer managed to solve the mystery, but while it lasted, it could make the hairs on the back of one's neck stand up. (Out of consideration for those who might want to experience this series for themselves, we hereby refrain from revealing the outcome of the story.)

These midget mysteries also provided plenty of opportunity for humor, of course. During one story, the bucolic buddies were helping the local sheriff investigate threats against millionaire Stephen Gregory. Checking Gregory's house for clues, the threesome made their way through the library:

Sheriff: Now, be careful in here, you fellers . . . some of these books in Mr. Gregory's library are rare first editions over a hundred years old.

Si: Huh, with all o' his money hit looks like he could afford ta buy some new ones.

Another way that *Si and Elmer* more closely resembled *Lum and Abner* than some of the other shows, *Eb and Zeb* included, was that Crandall and Reynolds played all the supporting roles themselves. The pair was quite versatile, with dialects other than Si and Elmer's rural twang and whistling *S*s, but this also meant that their fictional setting of Punkinville was much more of an ethnic melting pot than Pine Ridge ever was. In the surviving recordings, we hear Irish characters, black characters, Hispanic characters, and even an effeminate sissy character named Clarence. (Elmer mutters, "One of these days I'm goin' to fergit he's a lady and sock him one.") In the true hallmark of a low-budget show, Crandall even served as the show's announcer. As another blatant lift from *Lum and Abner*, he used his natural voice to play the role of genial Punkinville storekeeper Steve (no last name given), who could well have been the twin brother of Pine Ridge's Dick Huddleston.

Meanwhile, undaunted by imitators trespassing on their turf, Lum and Abner themselves just kept growing in popularity. By early 1933, when the Jot 'Em Down Store was introduced and given its name, they were based in Cleveland, Ohio, and had added a new feature to their format. On Monday through Thursday, the show carried its established continuing story line in fifteen-minute installments; on Friday, the program became a half-hour variety show known as the "Friday Night Sociable." It supposedly took place in the Pine Ridge schoolhouse, where Lum would leave the telephone off the hook so "all the fokes out ther on the party line" could listen in on the doings.

Lum and Abner's comedic exchanges were kept to a minimum on the "Friday Night Sociable," with the emphasis put on whoever the week's visiting performers might be. Some of them were strictly local Cleveland talent, while others were nationally famous radio notables, including singers Frances Langford and Annette Hanshaw and announcer Graham McNamee. In addition to Lauck and Goff,

Lum and Abner broadcast their "Friday Night Sociable" from WTAM in Cleveland, Ohio. The young guitar player at far right is Louis Marshall Jones, who picked up an idea or two from seeing Lauck and Goff don their old-age makeup for the studio audience's benefit.

the only regulars were the members of a musical aggregation that was aggregated for the show, the Pine Ridge String Band.

The leader of the String Band was Warren Caplinger, who had already made a reputation for himself in early country music (or "hillbilly music") circles. Those circles were not unbroken, however, and when it was announced that Lum and Abner needed a band for their show, Caplinger was not opposed to assembling one from scratch. One of the young hopefuls he auditioned and hired was guitar and banjo player Louis Marshall Jones, along with Jones's friend, Joe Troyan, who specialized in the harmonica and did animal imitations. The band not only played on Lum and Abner's regular Friday night broadcasts but also accompanied the comedy team when they made personal appearances in theaters throughout the area. This is where young Louis Jones received an inspiration.

Naturally, Lauck and Goff did not need to don makeup during the radio broadcasts to look like the two old duffers they portrayed. Theater appearances were different, however, and part of

Shortly after leaving *Lum and Abner*, Louis Marshall Jones (*right*) came up with his own old-man makeup and was known as Grandpa Jones from that time forward. Here he enjoys a comedy routine with his two stage partners, Bradley Kincaid (*left*) and Bashful Harmonica Joe Troyan.

their act involved them doing comedy routines as Lum and Abner, then ducking backstage to remove their makeup and returning to let the audience see what youthful, good-looking men they were in real life.

When the *Lum and Abner* series finished its run in Cleveland and was to return to Chicago in early 1934, discontinuing the "Friday Night Sociable" format, the String Band broke up. The members all went on to other pursuits, with Jones and Troyan hooking up with country singer Bradley Kincaid for stage and radio work. Jones later recalled that on the radio, listeners thought his voice sounded much older than he really was and were constantly writing in to ask, "Just how old is that old fellow on your show, anyway? He sounds like he's eighty." With this misconception already planted in the audience's mind and remembering Lauck and Goff's makeup tricks, Louis Marshall Jones devised some old-age makeup of his own, becoming known professionally as Grandpa Jones from that point on. Yes, we will be checking in with Grandpa again a few pages hence.

The mid-1930s were glory days for *Lum and Abner.* In 1934 they secured Horlick's Malted Milk as their sponsor, and while Horlick's four-year association with the show would not be their longest-running sponsorship—that would come later, during the World War II years—the fact that company founder William Horlick was a personal fan of the show helped immeasurably with the publicity it received. Horlick's issued more tie-in *Lum and Abner* premiums

Some of the local radio comedy programs that took their cue from the popularity of *Lum and Abner* were (*clockwise from top left*) *Rufie and Goofie* (Dallas–Fort Worth), *Herb and Hank* (Rochester, New York), *Pa and Ma Smithers* (Wichita, Kansas), and *Cat Mountain Boys* (Birmingham, Alabama).

than any other sponsor the show would have, and by the time of the show's fifth anniversary on April 26, 1936, the real-life Dick Huddleston had petitioned the U.S. Postal Service to change the name of the post office at Waters to Pine Ridge, Arkansas, so his general store's location would better fit with that of its fictional radio counterpart. All of the attendant publicity helped make *Lum and Abner* one of radio's hottest shows during the period.

Many other local stations saw what was happening down in Pine Ridge and decided to try their own hands at developing comics. Even Mena thought it could make lightning strike twice: local performer Haskell Gordon teamed up with Paul Duncan on radio station KGFF in Shawnee, Oklahoma, to star in *Ike and Eli.* (No, the lightning stayed in the clouds where it belonged and did not strike again.) KFBI in Wichita, Kansas, presented *Pa and Ma Smithers,* described as "sketches which portray an old couple living on the outskirts of Tinkerville. Pa (Dan Hosmer) writes the skits, while Ma (Christine Crans) helps with suggestions." *Herb and Hank* was a feature of WHAM in Rochester, New York. WHO in Des Moines, Iowa, presented *Lem and Martha* plus the humorous commentary of "Tillie Boggs, Sunset Corners spinster." *Rufie and Goofie* goofed around on WFAA in Dallas, while WSGN in Birmingham featured the *Cat Mountain Boys,* with yet another general store setting. WGIL in Galesburg, Illinois, brought forth *Elmer and Orphelia,* with Ken Schleifer and Betty Harler in the title roles. And as if the gang of comedians who hung out in the old hayloft known as the *National Barn Dance* over WLS in Chicago were not enough (don't worry, we'll get around to them in the next chapter), the same station presented *Wilbur and Ezra,* which an April 1932 radio magazine described in mighty familiar terms: "Wilbur and Ezra are two beloved old bachelors living in a one-room walk-up. The sketch is built around the adopting of a baby by these two yokels, and while the dialect is of the rural type, the situation and lines are too humanly interesting and genuinely entertaining to limit its scope to country listeners."

Meanwhile, out in Kansas City, Missouri, KMBC had begun *Happy Hollow,* described as "a down-home program featuring tra-

At KMBC in Kansas City, Missouri, familiar-looking characters gather around the general store on the *Happy Hollow* series. One of the writers and occasional performers was Paul Henning, who put that experience to good use when he created *The Beverly Hillbillies* in 1962.

ditional music, country humor, and the corn-fed wisdom of 'Uncle Ezra.'" Unfortunately, little but this brief blurb has survived to indicate just what the show and its format were all about, but some publicity photos released during its run show yet another general store setting and characters who would have been at home in any of the other existing rural comedies. Probably the most notable thing about *Happy Hollow* is that one of its cast members hired in 1933 was Paul Henning. Beginning as an actor and singer, Henning soon realized that his greater talent lay in script writing. Almost three decades later, Henning had a lot to do with bringing rural comedy into the even wider world of television—but discussing that now would be sorta like puttin' the mule in back o' the wagon, so we'll catch up with Henning a few chapters down the road.

And speaking of catching up with people, what about that even earlier general store show, *Smackout*, and its stars? Jim and Marian Jordan had continued holding down the counter as Luke Gray and his plethora of rural associates until one day the wife of an executive who handled the Johnson's Wax advertising account happened to catch one of their episodes. The waxworks, based in

Racine, Wisconsin, had been looking for a new act to sponsor, and after some tinkering with the format, on April 16, 1935, the Jordans appeared on behalf of Johnson's Wax as the title characters of *Fibber McGee and Molly.*

Now, the McGees were hardly the same type of rural characters as the ones we are discussing in this book, but at least in the beginning they were heavily derived from the cast of *Smackout.* The original Fibber McGee was a close country cousin to Luke Gray, with a cracker-barrel drawl, while Molly spoke with a heavy Irish accent. As months and then years went by, both voices modulated into the Jordans' own natural speaking tones, and the show became a domestic situation comedy that was rural only in the broadest sense of the word, inasmuch as their hometown of Wistful Vista was not a large city but a small midwestern hamlet.

A 1935 radio fan magazine described how the recently countrified couple made a point of dressing the part for their live studio audience, even though the listeners over NBC could not see them: "In the front row of Studio 8-H sits a couple looking like a pair of sightseers from the country. . . . You might take them for curious intruders, were it not for the scripts in their hands. She wears a frowsy cotton print dress, fitting her like a sack. He, with battered straw hat, ill-fitting horn-rimmed spectacles, one-button striped suit, is the conventional 'rube,' right down to his bright orange colored shoes."

The Jordans, alias the McGees, must have wanted to hedge their bets as to which of their series would have the most success. They continued presenting *Smackout* on weekdays for the first four months of *Fibber McGee and Molly.* Once it became obvious that the public was taking the McGees to heart, *Smackout* was blacked out and soon forgotten. *Fibber McGee and Molly* became a vital part of the world of radio in the 1940s, when the medium hardly resembled itself in its days of *The Stebbins Boys* and *Seth Parker.* Rural comedy never went completely out of style, however, and in our next chapter we shall see how the end of a depression, the duration of a world war, and the emergence of a modern postwar world affected those hicks from the sticks.

Chapter Two

Radio Rules the Roost

While it may seem that the airwaves were so crowded with rural comedy teams of the *Lum and Abner, Eb and Zeb,* and *Si and Elmer* tradition that you couldn't stir 'em with a stick, the fact is that many other types of drawling, overall-clad, pigtailed comedians existed. Actually, the idea of a yokel monologist goes back even further than radio, with roots deep in the American tradition. Most of the rural humorists of the nineteenth century supplemented their writing income with stage appearances and readings, but one of the first to develop strictly as an audio character was Uncle Josh.

Interestingly, Uncle Josh never made an appearance on broadcast radio—mainly because the actor who played him, Cal Stewart, died at just about the time the possibilities of commercial broadcasting were first being realized. Uncle Josh was strictly a product of records intended for home use, and as such falls somewhat outside the scope of this book. However, since this funny fogey in many ways provided the inspiration for most of the stand-up country comedians who would follow, he deserves at least a brief mention here.

Stewart developed his Uncle Josh characterization during his years on the vaudeville circuit in the late 1800s. Like many of the radio acts that would follow, Uncle Josh was supposed to be a typical New Englander, rooted in the fictional community of Punkin Center. In 1897, Thomas Edison got Stewart/Uncle Josh to make recordings of some of his vaudeville monologues, and the cylinders (predating flat records) became best sellers of their day, with such titles as *Uncle Josh and the Photographer*, *Uncle Josh's Arrival in New York*, *The County Fair at Punkin Center*, and *Uncle Josh on the Automobile*. Stewart died on December 7, 1919, at the age of sixty-three; had he lived for another decade or so, he would probably have found a whole new career as a radio comedian.

After radio got started, most of its monologue comedians (as opposed to those who played in comedy serials) came from the same vaudeville heritage as Stewart and his Uncle Josh persona. This was the background of Will Rogers, whose stage personality only barely fits the criteria for a rural comedian. With his chaps, ten-gallon hat, and rope tricks, the Oklahoma-born Rogers more closely fit the mold of a western character than a true rural one in the hillbilly or small-town sense. Rogers made many appearances on radio from the medium's inception until his death in a plane crash in August 1935, but by and large they consisted of Rogers giving his own mildly bemused commentaries on the current political scene and other topics of the day. His "rural" attributes, when they could be said to be present, mostly consisted of his accent and the fact that he preferred to look at the shenanigans of the political elite with a common man's practicality. Rogers's more direct connection to the rest of rural comedy would come from his movies more than his radio work, as we shall see in the next chapter.

Probably no rural comedian had a more sudden and rapid rise to the top of the heap than Bob Burns. It is also possible that no rural comedian in the years hence had to endure more loathing from his own hometown. Burns came from Van Buren, Arkansas, a fact that he mentioned often in his routines—precisely what seems to have made Van Buren hate him so.

Burns had knocked around in vaudeville for years without really hitting on any successful formula. His main claim to fame was his oddball musical instrument he called the bazooka. Long before the word became applied to a World War II weapon or a brand of bubble gum, Burns's bazooka was an odd conglomeration of two interlocking pieces of pipe and a whiskey funnel, played somewhat

Arkansas comedian Bob Burns joined the cast of Bing Crosby's *Kraft Music Hall* show in January 1936. His musical numbers on the bazooka and his tall tales about life in Van Buren, Arkansas, made him so popular that he and Crosby appeared together in the movie *Rhythm on the Range* that same year.

like a trombone. He used the bazooka as a part of his various vaudeville acts, but true fame eluded him until mid-1935, when he landed some successful appearances on Rudy Vallee's radio variety show. In those spots, Burns patterned his monologues after those of Will Rogers, with a country philosopher's view of politics and American life. After Rogers's sudden demise, Burns's career looked to be in as much jeopardy as that of satirist Vaughn Meader after the assassination of John F. Kennedy. Burns dropped his political commentary and started telling stories about Van Buren, which got him a regular role beginning in January 1936 on the *Kraft Music Hall* show hosted by Bing Crosby.

On each episode, Burns would amble to the microphone, drawl out, "I remember one time back in Van Buren, Arkansas," and proceed with some outrageous story about his fictitious relatives and townsfolk, including Uncle Fud, Aunt Peachy, Grandpa Snazzy, and others. Typical of his yarns was one he spun for a writer for *Better Homes and Gardens*: "There's a girl back in Van Buren they call Arbutus. They call her that 'cause she's always trailin' somebody. She was out with my Cousin Purnell on the beach. He's kinda poetic, ya know, an' he said, 'Roll on, O sea!' Then Arbutus took a look at th' ocean an' said, 'Purnell, yo're wonderful. Hit's a-doin' it!'"

He once described the toughness of the Arkansas razorback hog with a tale about how one of the family swine ate sixteen sticks of dynamite and was subsequently kicked by a mule. The resulting explosion killed the mule and blew all the windows out of the house, "an' we had a purty sick pig thar fer a couple o' days," Burns concluded. He also described the vast difference between his origins and the world of network radio: "Back home, they mash up a bunch o' corn and get corn likker. Out here, they mash up a bunch o' corn an' git a radio program."

Burns's popularity grew like that corn, and in 1941 he secured his own *Bob Burns Show*, which was partly monologue and partly situation comedy. Apparently the only folks who were not amused by his Van Buren stories were the people in Van Buren. It was not always that way; in the 1930s, the town's former King Opera House was converted to show movies and the name changed to the Bob Burns Theater. By the 1940s, however, people were beginning to grumble about the image his comedy was perpetuating. In real life, Burns proved that he was not the country jake he portrayed. He invested his income in San Fernando Valley real estate, and at the time of his death on February 2, 1956, he was considered one of the wealthiest actors in Hollywood. Even this sort of success stuck in the craw of his former neighbors, as illustrated by the remarks some of them made in a 1983 newspaper interview. Milton Willis, the director of

Bob Burns (*center*) and fellow Arkansans Chester "Lum" Lauck (*left*) and Norris "Abner" Goff appear to be enjoying each other's company in this backstage photo. Not everyone from Burns's home state was as happy with his style of humor, however.

the Van Buren Chamber of Commerce at the time, summed it up: "Bob Burns didn't really do anything for Van Buren, he just used us. . . . He didn't donate any libraries or anything, and he died a wealthy man. I was a fan, I used to listen to him, but I think he should have done something for Van Buren. He didn't do anything except make jokes about us." Another resident, attorney Clyman Izard, had similar feelings: "He pictured Arkansas as a bunch of people who were barefooted and ignorant. I thought he was funny, but a lot of people here didn't like that. He was just an old Van Buren boy who could tell a pretty good story."

Part of the erasing of Burns's name from Van Buren's history was the removal of the Bob Burns Theater sign and the conversion of the facility back into the King Opera House, as part of a $6 million renovation and restoration of the town. Today, Van Buren would rather not discuss Bob Burns at all. In the end, perhaps the main reason for all of this animosity was that Burns chose to use the town's real name instead of a fictitious creation such as Lum and

Abner's Pine Ridge was in the beginning. Or perhaps Burns always knew what was coming, because he told a reporter from the *New York Times*, "I'm supposed to be the 'Ozark sage.' To be a sage, I guess the formula is to stay a long way off from where you're born, or else you'll get found out."

Just to prove that not all hillbilly comics were male or came from Arkansas, we now take up the case of Judy Canova. Her origins were about as far removed from the mountains as possible while remaining in the southern states: born in Starke, Florida, Canova apparently decided early on that there was no burgeoning market for comedians who made jokes about beaches, palm trees, and flamingos, so she formed a hillbilly act with her sister, Annie, and brother, Zeke, and they set out to wow the city folks with their talents.

The Three Canovas, as they were billed, made an early radio appearance on one of Lum and Abner's "Friday Night Sociables" in the early 1930s and later racked up many credits on the variety shows of the era. A broadcast with bandleader Paul Whiteman in 1939 exemplifies their act:

> *Judy*: You know, none of us feel very good tonight. We jes' got a tellygram that our grandpappy died.
>
> *Whiteman*: Why, that's too bad. I'm awfully sorry. How old was he?
>
> *Judy*: 110.
>
> *Whiteman*: 110! Just think of that! What caused his death?
>
> *Judy*: Women and liquor.
>
> *Whiteman*: Women and liquor?
>
> *Judy*: Yep, he couldn't git either one, so he jes' laid down an' died.

As a solo act, Judy Canova appeared in a number of movies and Broadway revues until she finally landed her own radio series in 1943. It gave her ample opportunity to sing, in both her hillbilly and natural voices, and featured a solid supporting cast of radio's best actors, including Verna Felton, Mel Blanc, Sheldon Leonard, and Hans Conried. Throughout all of her appearances, Canova held on to her trademark catchphrase, "You're tellin' I!" *The Judy Canova Show* lasted until 1953.

Judy Canova started her career as one-third of a musical comedy trio with her sister, Annie, and brother, Zeke, but she became far better known as a solo performer, with a radio series that lasted from 1943 until 1953.

(Multiple Internet sources give the erroneous information that Judy Canova and Bob Burns were husband and wife for a period in the late 1930s. One even goes so far as to claim that she patterned her hillbilly persona after his—a difficult thing to do, considering that she was already a star before he ever attracted any national attention. In fact, Canova had a husband named Robert Burns, but he was an insurance salesman from New York, not the country feller from Van Buren.)

While all of these comics of a slightly different breed were taking over the airwaves in the late 1930s, reliable old Lum and Abner were continuing to mosey right along with their established, successful format even as their would-be imitators such as Si and Elmer dropped away and were forgotten. In early 1938, Lum and Abner switched sponsors from Horlick's Malted Milk to General Foods and its coffee substitute, Postum (with its cryptic slogan, "There's a reason"), but otherwise few changes occurred in the format. At the end of March 1940, Lum and Abner bid farewell to their listeners in a tearful episode in which the fictional Jot 'Em Down Store was locked up. The reason, as given in the story line and in real life, was that Lauck and Goff were about to begin production on their first motion picture, and they felt there simply would not be enough hours in the day to handle both radio and movies.

When that initial movie was completed, Lauck and Goff found that it was easier to go off the air than to get back on it. After more than a year of trying to interest potential sponsors in reviving their

Lum and Abner landed Miles Laboratories, makers of Alka-Seltzer, as a sponsor beginning in 1941. The company also sponsored the *National Barn Dance*.

show, in May 1941 they finally hitched up with Miles Laboratories, the makers of Alka-Seltzer, Miles Nervine, and One-a-Day vitamins. The Miles company was a real pro when it came to making sure its sponsored radio programs didn't fizz, but its first series of *Lum and Abner* episodes was heard on the West Coast only. Finally, in September 1941, the show returned to the national NBC network and regained its status as a nightly habit for millions of radio listeners.

Those listeners probably did not realize it, but some major changes were taking place behind the scenes. Lauck and Goff had written their own scripts for the ten years they had been on the air up to that point, but as Lauck acknowledged in one interview, "We had just about exhausted our imaginations." The solution was to hire a writer who could continue the Lum and Abner story lines without it being obvious to the audience that a new scribe was at the helm. Lauck and Goff finally chose Roswell "Roz" Rogers, who had been toiling anonymously on the staffs of several other radio series—none of them noted for being particularly rural. Nevertheless, it did not take long for Rogers to assimilate the necessary Pine Ridge culture, and for the rest of the program's run, he was responsible for the vast majority of the scripts.

Rural comedians of the stand-up rather than the situation comedy variety had two major outlets for their craft. WSM in Nashville had been broadcasting the *Grand Ole Opry* every Saturday night since 1925; WLS in Chicago had been running its *National Barn Dance* about a year longer. Both the Nashville and Chicago series concentrated primarily on "hillbilly music," but comedians were a vital part of their lineup as well.

It is difficult for even the most knowledgeable historians to determine just who would most deserve to be called the first comedian on either barn dance show. Most of the musical acts featured at least some comedy, even if it were limited to the leader making brief jokes about some member of the group by way of introducing the next number. Early *Grand Ole Opry* performers such as Uncle Dave Macon dressed in a comically old-fashioned manner, but of course this was more for the benefit of the live audience than the listeners at home, who could not tell whether a singer looked like a million dollars or two miles of bad road.

By the early 1930s, the *Opry* was beginning to develop acts that made comedy their main order of funny business. Jamup and Honey were blackface comedians in the *Sam 'n' Henry* and *Amos 'n' Andy* mold rather than being truly rural in the usual sense of the word. Possibly the earliest actual "rural" comedy team on the Nashville broadcast was Sarie and Sally. Unfortunately, very little information about these two gossips has survived, although their antics were well documented in WSM's publicity photos. Margaret Waters (Sally) died at age sixty-four in 1967, while Edna Wilson (Sarie) must have been proof positive that laughter is the best medicine, because she made it to age ninety-eight before her death in 1994.

The *National Barn Dance*, in at least one fashion, pulled ahead of the *Opry* in 1933, when a portion of the weekly WLS broadcast was picked up by the NBC network and beamed nationwide under the

Sarie and Sally (Edna Wilson and Margaret Waters) were among the first comedy acts to appear on Nashville's legendary *Grand Ole Opry* in the early 1930s.

sponsorship of Miles Laboratories. The *Opry* had to wait until 1939 to receive the same treatment from NBC, which began carrying a Saturday night half hour on behalf of Prince Albert tobacco. (This no doubt gave a big boost to that wheezy old crank telephone call, "Do you have Prince Albert in a can?") It was considered one of the greatest honors in country music to be chosen for the network portion of either show.

One comedian who made good on that honor was Pat Barrett, an ex-farmer who became known on the *Barn Dance* as Uncle Ezra. His yarns about life in Rosedale became so popular on the part of the show carried by NBC that in 1934, the network gave him his own weekly fifteen-minute spinoff series, *Uncle Ezra's Radio Station.* This format gave Barrett ample opportunity to spoof his own medium through the facilities of "Station E-Z-R-A, the powerful little five-watter," and he continued his low-key brand of homespun humor until 1941.

WLS discovered the youngster who would become the *National Barn Dance*'s principal comic after the Uncle Ezra era quite by accident. Eighteen-year-old Pat Buttram had journeyed to Chicago

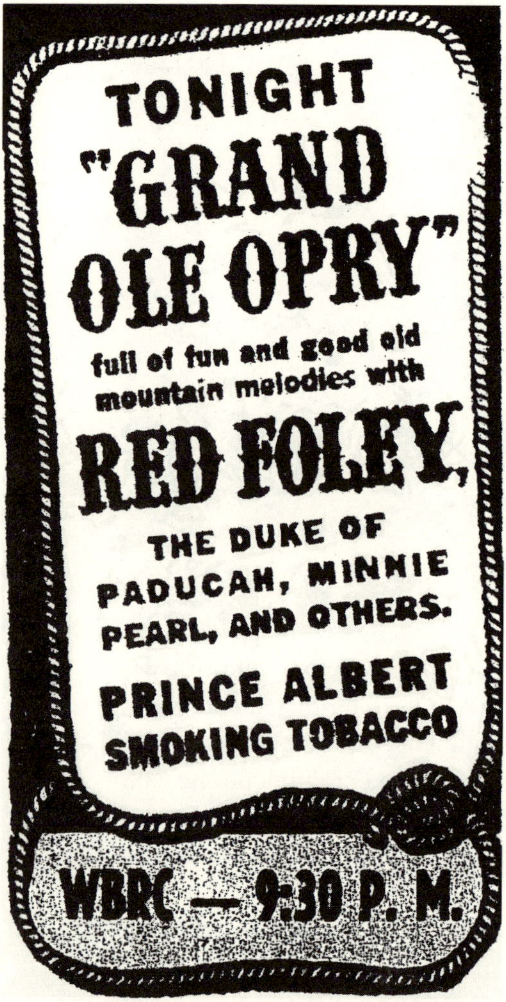

After comedy had been introduced to the *Opry*, it proved one of the show's most popular features. It was considered quite an honor for any act, especially a comedian, to be included in the half hour sponsored by Prince Albert tobacco and carried over the NBC network.

from his home in rural Winston County, Alabama, to see the 1933 World's Fair. For whatever reason, a WLS news team covering the fair picked Buttram out of the crowd for an interview, and his offbeat answers to their questions (delivered in a raspy twang) sent the audience into hysterics. At least that was the way his future publicity agents would tell the story. More realistically, Buttram had established himself with his comedic comments on radio stations WKBC and WBRC in Birmingham, Alabama, and it is more likely that his appearance on the WLS remote was more than mere happenchance. Regardless of what skullduggery was involved in getting him noticed in Chicago, Buttram was immediately signed for the *Barn Dance*, and he remained with the show until after World War II.

Although performers commonly got their start on either the *Barn Dance* or the *Opry* and then went on to national fame, as Buttram did, acts much less frequently crossed over from one series to the other. An exception to the rule was Whitey Ford, known as the Duke of Paducah, who dressed in an ill-fitting suit with pants that were at least six inches too short. (As with his predecessors, the effect of this outfit was lost on the radio audience at home.) Ford could deliver the corniest lines and make them sound fresh again. "I jes' got a wire from my sponsor," he would declare. "It wasn't the kind ya read, he brought it down to th' office and tried ta wrap it around my neck!" Or, another time, "Once I had the chance ta be married ta a pretty li'l doll at the same time as my big fat wife. But I never done it, 'cause that'd be bigamy, an' you all know th' penalty fer bigamy—TWO mother-in-laws!" Ford, alias the Duke, always closed his monologues with "I'm goin' back to th' wagon, now—these shoes are a-killin' me!"

For the first true comedy superstar the *Opry* would produce, probably no one would have picked out Sarah Ophelia Colley, a former dramatics instructor and graduate of Nashville's prestigious Ward-Belmont College. Since her childhood in Centerville, Tennessee, Colley had longed for a career as an actress, but the nearest she had come to that was traveling on behalf of a theatrical company and helping put on plays in innumerable small towns across the South. Colley later recalled that during one such stopover in the backwoods of the north Alabama hills, near the town of Cullman, she had encountered a happy-go-lucky mountain woman who seemed to her the perfect model for a character. Colley filed away some of the characteristics of the woman and her family in her mind, although becoming a comedian was not her main ambition—in fact, it was not one of her ambitions at all.

In the late 1930s, Colley began accepting bookings as an entertainer at various local conventions and business meetings. Looking for something to demonstrate her versatility, she decided to present to her audiences what she considered to be an "interpretation" of a typical hill country girl she named Minnie Pearl. For several years, Colley dragged Minnie out of storage whenever needed, but she considered the routine (she had only one set of jokes) simply another aspect of her intended acting career.

That changed unexpectedly when she performed Minnie at a bankers' convention where one of the attendees was sufficiently impressed to recommend her to the management at WSM. Colley was offered a guest spot near the end of an *Opry* broadcast; as she later related, WSM assumed that many of the regular listeners would have gone to bed by that time, and the network portion would have been long over, so even if she bombed it would not hurt the overall show. Colley said that one *Opry* executive was a bit concerned: "He said that he knew my background—that I had been raised in the country but had gone to an exclusive girls' school, and that I had traveled as a drama director for six years—and he was afraid the *Opry* audiences would find that out and suspect that I was a phony. He feared they would think I was putting down country people." (One wonders whether that WSM exec had gotten wind of what was being said about Bob Burns over in Van Buren.)

Minnie Pearl made her late-night *Opry* debut in November 1940. From what has been documented about that first appearance, it was quite different from the raucous style of comedy for which she would become so well known. "I went on in a sort of daze and told the gags in a gentle, soft country dialect," she wrote. "I don't really remember what sort of response I got—I had nothing to compare it to." At some point prior to her *Opry* performance, while she was still doing the convention circuit, Colley had come up with a stage costume for Minnie, but it too was as subdued as her dialect. "I dressed the way a young country girl would really dress to come to town for a day," she said. Only later would she add the touch of a hat with its price tag still dangling ostentatiously from the string, the image that became Minnie Pearl's trademark above all others.

Price tag or no, the listeners who were still up to hear Minnie's initial *Opry* spot thought she was worth something, because approximately three hundred of them wrote letters to her at the WSM address. By the Wednesday after her first show, WSM had invited her back for an appearance the following week—causing some problems, since she had only one set of jokes. However, she was not about to let that get in the way of progress, so over the next few days she and one of her sisters cooked up some new corn, and when she showed up for her second broadcast, she was informed that WSM wanted to make Minnie Pearl a regular weekly feature of the *Opry*.

Audiences could not get enough of Minnie's stories about life back home in Grinder's Switch—a real location, by the way, but hardly the same type of community she portrayed. The actual Grinder's Switch was not much more than a loading platform along the railroad leading to and from Nashville, but Minnie made it a town all her own. Listeners got to know all about her Uncle Nabob ("He jes' takes a drink ever now an' then to steady his nerves. He gits awful steady. Sometimes he don't move atall."); Aunt Ambrosia; Minnie's boyfriend, Hezzie; and her brother, named Brother ("Brother ain't a failure, he jes' started at the bottom an' he likes it there.").

Bolstered by material of this type, Minnie's popularity continued to grow throughout the 1940s, but she later said that if anything could have been said to be holding her back, it was that "even though I may not have been fully aware of it then, I was embarrassed about what I was doing. I was 29 years old, a mature young woman, and I just couldn't see my way clear to cut loose and act a fool. I had still not given up the other dream of being a dramatic actress." During the World War II years, when traveling troupes of *Opry* performers regularly visited military bases to entertain servicemen and -women, Colley/Minnie finally learned how to abandon all pretense of genteelness and go for all-out belly laughs.

The line she used to open her act offers a good example. When she first joined the *Opry*, Colley continued introducing herself as she had during her personal appearances at conventions, with a soft, "Howdy, I'm just so proud to be here." Once the character of Minnie was added to the network portion of the *Opry* in 1942, someone with the ad agency handling the Prince Albert account came up with a new gimmick. Now, when Minnie made her entrance, she would shriek "HOW-DEEEEEEEE!!!!!!" at the top of her voice, to which the audience would yell "HOW-DEEEEEE!!!" right back at her. That new, more bombastic greeting embodied the change in Minnie's character that would enable her to sustain a career for the next fifty years.

By the time the war ended, the *Opry* had added other comedians, but as before, most of them were members of one or another of the musical groups on the show. Jim Summey was Cousin Jody, a rubber-faced, toothless imbecile who played the steel guitar. Doctor Lew Childre dressed like a snake oil hustler and dispensed jokes while he tap-danced. Pete Kirby was "Bashful Brother Oswald," a

Four of the comedy acts that brought down the house on the *Grand Ole Opry* in the late 1940s were (*clockwise from top left*) Minnie Pearl, Cousin Jody, Lonzo and Oscar, and David "Stringbean" Akeman.

member of Roy Acuff's Smoky Mountain Boys. Banjo picker David Akeman was known as Stringbean because of his tall, lanky appearance—made even more ludicrous by his long shirt and pants with their waistband where most people had their knees. Grandpa Jones, having toured in personal appearances since his departure from *Lum and Abner*, joined the *Opry* in 1947. He was still wearing exaggerated old-man makeup inspired by his time with Lauck and Goff, and he usually introduced his banjo numbers with lines such as, "I wanna dedicate this next song to my ol' Aunt Minnie. She went to th' Boston Tea Party an' she wuz th' first ol' bag they threw overboard."

The biggest comic to emerge in the late 1940s was, like Minnie Pearl, an act all his own. Rod Brasfield was a veteran of the touring medicine-show circuit, and when he joined the *Opry* in 1947, he was as big a smash as Minnie had been a few years earlier. Whereas the Duke of Paducah wore a suit that hardly fit his frame, the diminutive Brasfield went in the opposite direction, donning baggy clothes that threatened to swallow him alive.

Someone finally got the brilliant idea of teaming Minnie with Brasfield, and the term she used for those routines was "double comedy." This simply meant that they took turns setting up the straight lines for each other's gags rather than having one of them get all the laughs. Brasfield had false teeth that fit him about as poorly as his suit, and he would use their clacking to punctuate his lines:

> *Rod*: By Ned, Minnie, I wanna walk you home tonight [clack, clack]. I've allus wanted to walk home with an experienced girl.
>
> *Minnie*: But Rodney, I'm not experienced.
>
> *Rod*: No, and you ain't home yit, neither [clack, clack].

Another type of comedy act that proved to be extremely popular on the "barn dance" radio shows was the type in which the music itself was humorous. The *National Barn Dance* exported this type of material with its resident wacky group, the Hoosier Hot Shots. This group had its genesis sometime during the mad days of the 1920s,

(*Left*) The Hoosier Hot Shots get a rise out of fellow *National Barn Dance* performer Uncle Ezra. (*Right*) Pat Barrett was rarely seen by fans without his Uncle Ezra makeup, but this photo from a radio fan magazine captured him as he looked in everyday life.

The Hoosier Hot Shots did not dress in hillbilly outfits, but the manufacturers of this toy drum set nevertheless appropriated the group's name. The characters depicted here appear to be close (and unauthorized) cousins of the *Li'l Abner* cast from Dogpatch.

when brothers Paul and Ken Trietsch began fooling around with getting music out of washboards, cowbells, and other such unusual instruments. When they began touring with a vaudeville act, Ezra Buzzington's Rube Band, Paul became known as Hezekiah and Ken took the stage name of Rudy Vaselino. After vaudeville was dead and buried, the Trietsch brethren added two more musicians to the group, Otto Ward (known as Gabe) and Frank Kettering, and became known as the Hoosier Hot Shots because all of them except

Kettering were native Indianans. Like many bands, comedy and otherwise, they had a trademark: their routines always began with Ken Treitsch shouting to his brother, "Are ya ready, Hezzie?!" The catchphrase caught on and stayed popular for decades afterward.

The Hot Shots joined the *Barn Dance* around 1933, but it seems the longer their act continued, the less truly rural they became. They specialized in giving the washboard-and-cowbell treatment to popular songs of the day—in a style that Spike Jones and his City Slickers would later expand on—and occasional novelty tunes of their own devising, including "I Like Bananas Because They Have No Bones." Apparently having gotten their fill of dressing like rubes during their days with Ezra Buzzington, the Hot Shots were typically costumed as something resembling college students, with snappy straw hats and sometimes sweaters with their names across the chests. They remained a fixture on WLS until 1946, when they made a hot shot for the West Coast and shifted their primary focus away from radio and toward movies, records, and personal appearances.

At about the same time the Hoosier Hot Shots were hotfooting it for sunny California, back in Nashville a different pair of musical maniacs was invading the *Grand Ole Opry*. The team of Lonzo and Oscar was somewhat unusual in that, over the course of the duo's long career, Oscar played with three different Lonzos. The cornerstone of the act was Rollin Sullivan, who played the electric mandolin as part of the band accompanying Eddy Arnold on his personal appearances and *Opry* gigs. When another musician, bass fiddle player Lloyd George, teamed up with Sullivan to perform comedy material as a sort of warm-up for Arnold's act, the pair became known as Lonzo and Oscar. Arnold used his influence to get his funnymen a contract with RCA Victor records, and their biggest hit came in 1948, "I'm My Own Grandpa." With convoluted lyrics that defy any attempt at explanation, the song reportedly sold some 4 million copies.

By that time, Lonzo and Oscar were also appearing regularly on the *Opry*, but in 1950 Lloyd George decided to try for a solo career under the name Ken Marvin. Into Lonzo's goofy garb stepped Rollin

Homer and Jethro (Henry Haynes and Kenneth Burns) gained fame with their hillbilly interpretations of other popular artists' hit songs.

Sullivan's brother, Johnny, who played the role until his death in an automobile accident in 1967. Undaunted, Rollin found a third Lonzo, David Hooten. In this incarnation, the seemingly indestructible team continued their corny jokes and music into the 1980s.

Yet another comedic musical duo was Homer and Jethro (Henry Haynes and Kenneth Burns), but with the exception of some time spent on the *Midwestern Hayride* show from WLW in Cincinnati and a later stint at WLS in the 1950s, most of their initial fame came from their records rather than broadcasting. They concocted a formula of writing hillbilly parodies of popular songs of the day; their biggest hit came in 1959 with "The Battle of Kookamonga," a spoof of Johnny Horton's "Battle of New Orleans." Homer and Jethro's primary broadcast work took place in the early 1960s, so we shall be looking in on that a few chapters from now.

With all of these comedians getting horselaughs on the *Opry* and the *Barn Dance*, rural characters began turning up as regulars on more citified comedy shows as well. One example was ventriloquist Edgar Bergen's bucktoothed friend, Mortimer Snerd, added to the cast of *The Charlie McCarthy Show* in 1939. Mortimer was conceived as the polar opposite of the suave, smart-alecky Charlie McCarthy, spending a lot of time talking about how bad things were back on the farm in his hometown, Snerdville:

Mortimer: We got sixteen new mouths ta feed.
Bergen: Are they pigs or chickens?

Mortimer: No, my Uncle Sorghum and Aunt Busillas an' their kids.

Bergen: Well, that must make things pretty crowded around your house.

Mortimer: Yuh, they're even wearin' my clothes . . . Cousin Jerkimer got up this mornin' and got right into my best suit.

Bergen: Well, now, that is annoying.

Mortimer: Yuh, what's more, he didn't even give me time ta git out of it first. I didn't realize how dirty the house was 'til the dog came in an' tried ta bury a bone in the livin' room. We got wall-to-wall dirt now.

Bergen: Well, how could they drag so much dirt into the house?

Mortimer: Well, when the little kids go ta sleep, they play "This little piggy went ta market."

Bergen: That's nice.

Mortimer: Yuh, with real pigs they play it.

Comedian Red Skelton had been toiling in obscurity for several years and had even starred in at least one undistinguished radio series when he suddenly hit on a winning formula and shot to the top of the ratings with his program sponsored by Raleigh cigarettes in October 1941. Skelton's success seems to have resulted from a seemingly endless parade of kooky characters featured in his skits, chiefly country bumpkin Clem Kadiddlehopper. Most of the Clem stories involved the happy hayseed getting into trouble while trying to adjust to life in the big city and surviving via a number of one-time-only jobs:

Clem: Well, I gotta git back ta work here . . . [hammering sounds] I dunno what I'm hammerin' on, but I gotta fix it . . . [hammering sounds]; Shore looks like it's in bad shape . . . [hammering sounds] Oh, now I recognize it . . . it's mah thumb.

Announcer: Hi, Clem.

Clem: Oh, howdy do . . . kin I be of any service to you, sir? An' if you're smart, you'll say no.

Announcer: Say, what sort of business is this?

"Allen's Alley" was the most well remembered segment of the *Fred Allen Show*. Its four residents were the loudmouthed Senator Claghorn; the taciturn rustic, Titus Moody; the Jewish housewife, Mrs. Nussbaum; and the quarrelsome Irishman, Ajax Cassidy.

Clem: Well, didn't yuh read th' sign on the door?
Announcer: Yes, I read it.
Clem: Well, would yuh read it ta me?

Other skits revolved around Clem's relationship with his equally rustic girlfriend, Daisy June (played by Harriet Nelson, later of *Ozzie and Harriet* fame). Clem and Daisy June engaged in demented dialogue:

Clem: Hey, Daisy June, kin I come inta your house?
Daisy: Nope, not 'till you wipe yore shoes off.
Clem: Well, I ain't goin' home to git 'em just fer that.

As most entertainment buffs know, Clem and his bumbling adventures continued through the rest of Skelton's radio career and well into his days on television. A character who did not make the transition from radio to video so readily was introduced on *The Fred Allen Show* in October 1945. Although he was new to the Allen show, his voice was certainly more than familiar to radio listeners.

Although Allen's and Skelton's styles of comedy were about as far apart as possible while still existing on the same planet, the two comedians shared one thing: both men tried varying program formats before arriving at the one that audiences seemed to like best. In Allen's case, he had already had a couple of successful series (*Town Hall Tonight* and *The Texaco Star Theater*) before the emergence of his own *Fred Allen Show*, with its recurring "Allen's Alley" routine.

On each week's show, Allen would visit the varied denizens of this mythical street, posing questions relating to a newsworthy topic of the day. Several different character actors and their roles came and went during the first couple of years of the "Allen's Alley" skits, but by October 1945, they had congealed into Kenny Delmar as the blowhard Senator Claghorn ("Ah'm from the SOUTH! The only cups Ah drink out of are Dixie cups!"), Minerva Pious as the Jewish housewife Mrs. Nussbaum ("You ver expecting maybe Emperor

Shapirohito?"), and Parker Fennelly—yes, our old friend of *Stebbins Boys* and *Uncle Abe and David* repute—as the taciturn New England farmer Titus Moody ("Moody by name, moody by nature," as he described himself).

Even though Fennelly had played many other roles in radio, Titus Moody truly made his voice familiar to millions. Allen admitted that Moody was his favorite character of the "Allen's Alley" cast—and since Allen himself wrote most of the comedy material, he seemed to take particular pleasure in crafting the Titus Moody dialogue. While it reads well on paper, its true genius was Fennelly's deadpan delivery of the most outrageous lines, never evidencing the slightest bit of emotion. Even his weekly greeting, a mumbled "Howdy, Bub," got laughs from the audience and frequently cracked Allen up as well. Their routines often ran longer than anticipated because virtually every line got a huge laugh:

Allen: Well, Mr. Moody, how do you think most people spend their vacations?

Moody: Why, it seems t'me that most people spend their summers drivin' around in automobiles. I run a roadside stand for motorists.

Allen: What do you sell?

Moody: My sign says, "Gen-u-wine farm eggs, strictly fresh."

Allen: How many chickens do you have?

Moody: Oh, I don't have none.

Allen: Well, with no chickens, how can you run an egg business?

Moody: Ever mornin' I buy a lot o' eggs at th' A & P supermarket. I set th' eggs out on my roadside stand in nests, then I dress up as a rube.

Allen: You dress up as a rube?

Moody: Yep, I put on a big straw hat, tie a red bandanna 'round my neck, stick a piece o' straw in my mouth, then I go down by the road an' lean on a long rake.

Allen: What happens when a motorist drives up?

Moody: Why, I start yellin' "Well I swan" an' "By heck" an' other rustic expressions. So the motorist, he thinks he's dealin' with a country

> jay, a pea-picker. He says, "How 'bout it, Zeke? Them eggs fresh?" An' with that, Miz Moody . . . she's under the counter . . . she starts cluckin'. I ain't missed a sale in twenty years.

We will be encountering Fennelly and further variations on Titus Moody again, but since Fred Allen never made a successful transition to television, that character would be relegated to living forever in radio's "Allen's Alley." Fennelly would have to find other ways to utilize his dry, New England humor in the visual media.

During the immediate postwar years, singing cowboy Gene Autry sent for his old WLS *National Barn Dance* colleague Pat Buttram to migrate from Chicago to Hollywood and join him as comedian on *Gene Autry's Melody Ranch,* sponsored by Wrigley's gum. Buttram fit right into the proceedings as one of the hired hands on the ranch, and each show featured his comedic exchanges with "Mr. Artery," as he mangled his boss's name. When Autry asked, "Patrick, did you saw that wood yet?" Buttram would reply, "Lissen, Mr. Artery, you might see me see it but you ain't never gonna see me saw it!" Their work together in radio led Buttram to join Autry as a sidekick in his movies, about which we shall say more later.

Before temporarily leaving this discussion of radio to address other topics, another aspect of the business should be mentioned at least briefly. Radio comedy shows of all types commonly used rural or hillbilly themes on single occasions, although such sketches usually turned out to be burlesques of the expected routines. For

Among the four residents of "Allen's Alley," Fred Allen's personal favorite was Parker Fennelly, star of some of the earliest rural radio comedies, as deadpan New England farmer Titus Moody.

example, a 1945 episode of *The Charlie McCarthy Show* was partly devoted to Charlie's own version of the hit play and movie *Tobacco Road,* which he had translated into *Cornsilk Alley.* In a typical bit of radio stunt casting, the female lead was essayed by Brazilian bombshell Carmen Miranda; hearing her deliver hillbilly dialogue with her south-of-the-equator accent was wildly funny in itself. Equally incongruous was Ray Noble, the series' British orchestra leader, as a revenue agent:

Carmen: Look, Clem, there's a stranger a-comin' up the road. Howdy, howdy!

Charlie: How you be, stranger?

Ray: Ah'm the revenooer, and I-un's come up here special for to speak to all of you-uns and all that hillbilly sort of rot, you know.

Charlie: [to audience] I guess you notice that the actor shortage has hit us particularly hard . . . Well, lemme tell ye, revenooer, that in these parts th' last feller that come around here died with a bullet in his head.

Ray: Well, I'm not surprised; that sort of thing is apt to be fatal, you know.

The whole skit winds down when "Happy Dan, the traveling man" arrives to sell the family a bathtub:

Carmen: Well, what will they think of next?

Dan: Say, you're an attractive little mountain blossom—you're so intriguing, exotic, and bewitching!

Carmen: Get the gun, he call me names.

Charlie: Well, Mister Travelin' Man, you've gone jes' about as fer as you kin go.

Dan: Oh no, I'm goin' to Natchez and Mobile!

Charlie: Oh, YEAH?

[*Sound*: Gunshot]

Dan: Uh oh, trip's off.

[*Sound*: Thud]

In a vastly different style from a completely different type of humor, an April 1950 episode of *Fibber McGee and Molly* found the couple minding the Wistful Vista general store after the regular storekeeper had become ill. Jim and Marian Jordan and their writers obviously could not ignore the possibility for an inside joke, so when the store's phone rang, Fibber absentmindedly answered, "Smackout, the store down on the crossroads of the air—Luke Gray speakin'. . . Hey, what am I sayin', that was twenty years ago!" The total lack of response from the studio audience would indicate that practically no one remembered the Jordans' long-ago venture into hayseed humor.

It seems a bit surprising that Jack Benny would have been one of the radio comedians who employed hick comedy so frequently, since his usual style was so urbane. In the late 1930s, screechy-voiced character actor Andy Devine was a regular on Benny's show, forever telling stories about life down on his farm:

> *Devine*: We've been purty busy—a lotta harvestin' ta do. But it worked out swell fer us; we got twelve purty college girls helpin' us pick termaters.
>
> *Benny*: Say, I'll bet that makes your pa happy.
>
> *Devine*: Oh, he loves it. I caught him out in th' field with all th' girls yesterday an' he had a sultan suit on!
>
> *Benny*: A sultan suit? You mean he was dressed like a sultan?
>
> *Devine*: Yep, a Turkish towel and a pair o' Maw's red bloomers!
>
> *Benny*: Well, isn't your ma jealous with him out in the field chasing all those pretty girls?
>
> *Devine*: Oh, he'll never ketch 'em—Maw's got a flatiron tied to his beard!

On at least one occasion, the role of Paw Devine was played by Norris "Abner" Goff in a rare radio appearance away from his usual Pine Ridge setting. But even aside from the routines with Devine, Benny seemed to have a particular fondness for introducing rural scenes into his shows whenever possible. In the late 1940s, character actor Sam Hearn had a recurring role as a farmer from Calabasas (a then-rural suburb of Los Angeles) whom Benny would encounter in various settings. Benny and his writers never gave this humorous figure a name: Jack would simply encounter him at the most unexpected moments. In one show, Benny ran into him at the hospital, where the farmer announced that his wife had just given birth to the latest in their long string of children, this one named Blue Cross. "You named your kid Blue Cross?" Jack asked in disbelief. "Yep, after havin' so many, we felt like we owed 'em somethin'," Hearn cracked.

We will be revisiting the Benny show later, in our discussion of television, where he made hillbilly skits a sort of running gag in the visual medium. Before getting to that, though, we must now press forward and see what was going on in the local movie houses while all of these comics were gagging it up on the radio. Grab your popcorn and have your ticket stubs ready!

Chapter Three

Hillbillies Go Hollywood

While rural comedians and musicians were first making their mark—even though a good number of them could actually write their names—in radio, the folks in the seedling movie industry also found country themes to be new ground. While radio could present rural dialects and hillbilly music without providing a visual image to go along with it, the first movies to feature such characters were silent and could not rely on the surefire gimmick of an exaggerated voice.

Two scholarly books have already attempted to address this topic as part of their broader scope. Both J. W. Williamson's *Hillbillyland: What the Movies Did to the Mountains and What the Mountains Did to the Movies* and Anthony Harkins's *Hillbilly: A Cultural History of an American Icon* primarily examine the evolution of the standard hillbilly image. Williamson and Harkins include noncomic portrayals alongside the comedic ones; their definition of a hillbilly type is sometimes stretched to include characters such as Davy Crockett and Daniel Boone. However, their massive research provides a starting point from which we can try to determine how rural comedy came to the motion picture world, keeping in mind that there are other forms of rural in addition to hillbilly.

That said, both authors agree that the word *hillbilly* first appeared in print in the *New York Journal* in 1900, where this singular figure was defined as "a free and untrammeled white citizen of Alabama, who lives in the hills, has no means to speak of, dresses as he can, talks as he pleases, drinks whiskey when he gets it, and fires off his revolver as fancy takes him." This definitive description meshed perfectly with the image of mountaineers as it was already being portrayed in literature and the often sensationalistic press of the time. There was a particular fascination with the previously unfamiliar practice of feuding between families in the southern mountains, as typified by the real-life escapades of the Hatfields and McCoys.

Williamson claims that the first time the word appeared in the title of a movie was 1915's *Billie the Hill Billy*, which was not a comedy but a serious drama about the violence presumed to be so common in the backwoods. Both Williamson and Harkins discuss several examples of straight portrayals of hillbilly types in silent films of the 1910s and 1920s, but both authors—perhaps drawing on the same research sources—claim that the first comedy film to include what would be considered a modern hillbilly was *Rainbow Riley* (1926), in which comedian Johnny Hines played a cub reporter who blunders his way through misadventures in feud country. In this instance at least, the comedian was the city feller and the mountaineers simply provided a setting for his antics. Williamson reports that much the same pattern was followed in *The Big Killing* (1928), with Wallace Beery and Raymond Hatton as a pair of city slickers who end up in the Ozarks and have to contend with a typical mountain feud.

Both Williamson and Harkins chose to ignore, probably because it fell outside the normal hillbilly definition, the fact that one long-running series occupied much of the time period between *Billie the Hill Billy* and the late 1920s efforts. This series came out of the world of early animated cartoons, and the star was the indefatigable Farmer Al Falfa.

Animator Paul Terry introduced this bewhiskered old custodian of the soil in 1916. Considering the primitive state of animation at the time, it was somewhat remarkable that the character caught on as well as he did. Farmer Al Falfa was not much of a comedian per se—most of the humor in his cartoons stemmed from his problems dealing with the ever-obstinate livestock on his farm. The animals generally delighted in making Farmer Al Falfa's life a living night-

Paul Terry's coverall-clad hayseed Farmer Al Falfa first appeared in silent animated cartoons in 1916 and continued his career off and on all the way into the mid-1950s television era.

mare by heaping abuse on his straw-hatted head, but somehow he managed to survive it all.

Every time Paul Terry began a new series—his productions became known by the brand name Terrytoons—he seems somehow to have found a way to work Farmer Al Falfa into the mix. After the character's first rush of success in 1916–17, he came back for more punishment in the early 1920s. After the sound era arrived, he was revived again for a series that ran sporadically between 1931 and 1937. The bald trouper starred in no subsequent cartoons but continued to turn up in roles supporting Terry's later, more famous characters, such as Heckle and Jeckle. No one ever claimed that

Terrytoons were masterpieces of art or wit (one theater owner was quoted as saying he included them in his programs because they ran the audience out of the building, making room for more paying customers to replace them), but at least they were durable, and Farmer Al Falfa was one of the hardiest of the lot.

When the CBS network bought the Terrytoons library in the mid-1950s, among the various ways the cartoons were packaged was in a half-hour *Farmer Al Falfa and His Friends* series sponsored by Tootsie Rolls. New animation of the seedy hayseed, still encountering all manner of difficulties in his fields, pastures, and farmhouse, was produced to serve as "bumpers" before and after the commercials. The TV series even gave the rube the honor of his own theme song:

I swan, here's a feller you all know well
Farmer Al Falfa, he's the farmer in the dell
Well, he's some slicker an' I do declare
You see him in the flicker-pitchers ev'rywhere.

This series, and the inclusion of his older cartoons in the other Terrytoons packages, kept Farmer Al Falfa visible in toys and other merchandise long after most other characters who originated in the silent era had been forgotten (the most notable exception being Felix the Cat).

During a brief period from the late 1920s to the mid-1930s, cartoon characters almost single-handedly carried on rural comedy in the nation's movie theaters. The barnyard was the setting for more cartoons than could possibly be counted; even the first Mickey Mouse adventure to be put into production, *Plane Crazy* (1928), had the future theme park host and entertainment icon using various fellow farm inhabitants to build his own ramshackle airplane. Most likely because of Walt Disney's fond childhood memories of Marceline, Missouri, it took several years and lot of animation before Mickey escaped the rural lifestyle for good. Even when making occasional forays outside this realm in the early days, the farm was never very far away: in Mickey's first appearance with sound (and the first of his cartoons to be released), *Steamboat Willie* (1928), the action takes place on something resembling the Mississippi River but affords Mickey the chance to play "Turkey in the Straw" on a variety of animal parts.

The Warner Bros. cartoon studio eventually produced more hillbilly-themed theatrical shorts than any other, but even that future titan of the animation world worked into the genre through barnyard humor, with *The Booze Hangs High* (1930). Lacking a plot, this musical cartoon simply provided an excuse to show various cows, horses, and ducks dancing merrily while a family of pigs gets drunk on a bottle of bootleg whiskey found in the feeding trough. After this undistinguished beginning, Warner's went on to produce what may be the first true hillbilly cartoon in history, *Moonlight for Two* (1932). As plotless as most other non-Disney cartoons of the period, the action centers on a hillbilly couple making their way to a neighborhood barn dance, where the musicians take time out between stanzas to spit their chaw of terbacky. One tall, skinny rustic downs the contents of a jug of moonshine, which incinerates his innards and reduces him to elf size. Prominently heard on the sound track is "She'll Be Comin' 'round the Mountain," which became such a cliché of rural comedies that it later evolved into a source of humor itself.

All of this, of course, was taking place during the same period when radio was first feeling its way through hillbilly music, and the early popularity of the genre inspired a hit song of the era, "I Like Mountain Music." In 1933, Warner Bros. used the melody as the title tune of yet another in its long series of cartoons in which characters came to life off book and magazine covers. The rest of the animated short was unrelated to rural humor, except for a cameo appearance by a gum-chewing Will Rogers caricature who emerges from the *Oklahoma Gazette* and carefully studies an October 1929 issue of *American Business*, then places a cash register's "no sale" tab in front of the magazine, declaring, "All I know is what I read in the papers." When the moment comes for the title song to be sung, even though the lyrics clearly state "I like mountain music, good ol' mountain music / Played by a real hillbilly band," the performers are a group of cowboys, not mountaineers.

Rogers's animated appearance would have been instantly recognizable to moviegoers of the time, because, according to preeminent film historian Leonard Maltin, in the early 1930s Will Rogers was the country's top box-office star. Amazingly for someone who was primarily a vaudeville monologist, Rogers's first movies were made during the silent era and depended on title cards to put across his humorous observations. Even at that, his on-screen characterizations were less unusual than his bon mots; at one point, Rogers griped, "All I do is run around barns and lose my pants."

He fared better and was able to get away from his usual trick-roping cowboy character when the movies began to talk. His first sound film, *They Had to See Paris* (1929), cast him as a small-town garage owner who strikes oil and moves into high society with his eccentric family. (As you might surmise, this was not the last time this plot device would be used in the rural comedy genre.) Subsequent films found him working a variety of rural jobs; in *Handy Andy* (1934), Rogers runs a small drugstore that becomes the target of a city slicker's attempt to buy it out and incorporate it into a chain. Rogers's observation that "chain stores are about as friendly as chain gangs" would ring true with many small-town business owners even more than seventy years later.

Of Rogers, Maltin wrote, "In many of his films, he plays an iconoclast, wiser than the so-called leaders in the town but too honest to be accepted by them." Maltin cites *Dr. Bull* (1933) and *Judge Priest* (1934) as two of the best examples of this plot. Rogers's death in the infamous August 1935 plane crash left his studio with two completed films that had to be released posthumously, *Steamboat 'round the Bend* and *In Old Kentucky*. It also put the kibosh on what would have been another animated cartoon appearance for him. The Disney studio was preparing a short, *Mickey's Polo Team*, in which the players were all celebrity caricatures. Rogers was to have been one of them, but he died early enough during its production to be removed from the final film. (Just the fact that Mickey Mouse's settings had moved from barnyards to the polo field says a lot about how much progress Disney had made in show business in just a few years.)

Just as the curtain was closing on Rogers's long career, a golden age of sorts was beginning for other funny things of a rural flavor. Besides the ongoing popularity of the music and shows such as *Lum and Abner* on the radio, hillbilly humor was now being perpetrated in newspapers and magazines as well. The year 1934 saw the debut of three print features that would become mainstays of rural comedy for decades.

In June of that year, the title character of the long-running *Barney Google* comic strip discovered that a distant relative had left him some property in the North Carolina mountains. Going to check on his inheritance, Google encountered the sawed-off moonshiner Snuffy Smith; Snuffy's gargantuan wife, Lowizie; and the other backwoods denizens of their home turf, Hootin' Holler. The preliminary research undertaken by the strip's creator, Billy DeBeck, has led comics historians to deduce that he had decided to permanently change the focus of his strip from Barney's world as a racehorse owner—that is, if his lethargic steed, Spark Plug, counts as a racehorse—to a more or less authentic mountain setting.

Less authentic but no less successful was a strip launched by young Al Capp in August 1934: *Li'l Abner.* Newspaper readers were soon hooked on the saga of life in remote Dogpatch, Kentucky, and the relationships among giant-muscled and pea-brained Abner Yokum, his parents, and the pathetic Daisy Mae Scragg (looking rather anorexic in her earliest appearances), who pursued him to no avail.

While Snuffy and the Yokums were mixing things up in the funny papers, over in the sophisticates' lair at *Esquire* magazine, Paul Webb introduced his monthly panel cartoon known as *The Mountain Boys.* Whereas the hillbilly characters in *Barney Google* and *Li'l Abner* were likable when readers got better acquainted with them, the Webb figures were by and large characterized exclusively as moral and legal degenerates, to be laughed at rather than with. (One of his most famous panels was among his earliest, with three of the bearded loafers hanging around the front porch of the cabin while one of them wonders "if Maw's had her baby yit—I'm gittin' hongry.") The Webb style of hillbilly—and, even more, the DeBeck and

The Columbia cartoon studio attempted the first translation of the *Barney Google and Snuffy Smith* newspaper comic strip into animated form in 1935–36, but the series expired after only four films.

Capp variety—would receive increased exposure in the broadcasting and motion picture media very shortly after their print debuts.

The Columbia cartoon studio, headed by Charles Mintz, licensed the *Barney Google* comic strip cast from King Features Syndicate for a short-lived series that began in late 1935 and expired in early 1936. As with the newspaper strip itself, the first episode in the new series, *Tetched in the Head,* featured the hillbillies of Snuffy's world more prominently than Barney himself. Within the first few minutes, we see Snuffy doing his usual lazy lounging while Lowizie slaves over a washtub; so devoted is she to the well-being of her "shif'less skonk" of a husband that she even uproots an entire tree and replants it where he is sleeping, just to give him a little shade. She is also interrupted from her laundry duty every time a fly lights on Snuffy's bulbous nose, as he whistles for her to come give the pesky insect a smack.

Barney Google arrives via Spark Plug and immediately runs afoul of his sometime friends by suggesting that Snuffy get up and go to work. Snuffy gets up, all right, but only to blast Google with his shotgun and cause him to fall into Lowizie's wash. Trying a different tactic, Google then becomes the victim of the Smith couple's young 'uns. As part of the comic strip story line in January 1935, Snuffy and Lowizie had outdone the Dionne quintuplets by producing *six* babies at once. The ornery little tots would somehow be forgotten as the strip continued over the years, but they make their screen debut in *Tetched in the Head,* resisting Google's attempts to teach them arithmetic by attacking him with rifles, slingshots, bows and arrows, and any other implements of warfare that might be handy. When Google catches one of them and puts the brat over his knee for a well-deserved spanking, Lowizie retaliates by putting Google over her knee and administering the same punishment. Google escapes by jumping atop Spark Plug and hightailing it for parts unknown as Snuffy goes back to sleep and Lowizie resumes her washing.

Each of the three succeeding Columbia/Google cartoons featured Snuffy and family in roles of diminishing importance. In *Patch Mah Britches,* the entire cast of DeBeck's comic universe descends on Google's house for Thanksgiving dinner, including the Smiths and what appears to be Snuffy's nephew, Jughaid, and his identical twin. *Spark Plug* returns the series to the comic strip's racetrack origins, with Snuffy visible in only a few shots as he sleeps off a drunk in the stands. The final episode, *Major Google*, is not an army epic, as the title might imply, but a spoof of the popular *Major Bowes' Original Amateur Hour* radio program. Snuffy, Lowizie, and the twin Jughaids appear as contestants on the show.

Over at Universal's cartoon division, Walter Lantz got into the backwoods sweepstakes by putting Oswald the Rabbit into a film called simply *The Hill Billy* (1935), but since the Lantz output of the 1930s is not generally available for public viewing, the title is all that is known about this lost epic. Not so with the Warner Bros. products, which really surged ahead of the other studios during 1935–36. Probably the most typical of the batch was *The Country Mouse*, released in August 1935. It opens with Elmer, the title hick, practicing his boxing lessons and singing a song that brags about his prowess ("I'm stronger than ol' Higgins's mule / There's no horse team I cain't out-pull," he boasts musically). His pugilistic fun is interrupted by his Granny, who smokes a corncob pipe and generally seems to be boss in the area. When Elmer's attempts at chopping wood don't seem to suit her, Granny rolls up her sleeves—revealing Popeye arms—and knocks a tree into kindling with her bare fists.

Against Granny's wishes, Elmer sneaks away to the big city to enter his first professional boxing match against the current champ, a tough-looking bulldog. Our hayseed hero soon learns how it feels to come second in a two-person fight. Granny is listening to the match over her cathedral radio at home and becomes so incensed that she jumps on her bicycle, pedals to the city (black smoke pouring from her pipe like a locomotive), leaps into the ring, and kayos the champ with a single punch. As the audience cheers her as the new champ, she then administers a sound thrashing to Elmer.

Granny shares most of the characteristics that would eventually become the hallmarks of Mammy Yokum in *Li'l Abner*. By the time this cartoon was released to theaters, Mammy was just beginning to develop her superhuman strength in the newspaper pages, so it is difficult to say just who might have been inspiring who or whether both Capp and Warner Bros. were simply going along with some other preestablished hillbilly type.

The three 1936 Warner releases vary in their approach to rural settings. *Page Miss Glory* is set at the hotel in Hicksville, where lanky Abner the bellhop cannot distinguish between automobile horns and the noises made by the livestock freely roaming the streets outside. *Let It Be Me* is a sordid tale centering on a Bing Crosby caricature rooster (Mr. Bingo) whose "buh-buh-buh-booing" singing style makes all the hens swoon. Out for a joyride far from the city lights, Mr. Bingo spots Emily the farm chick and her dopey boyfriend, Lem. With some smooth talking, Mr. Bingo lures Emily away to the city with him, leaving Lem to turn green with envy. Once away from the country, Bingo tries to get Emily drunk before he tosses her aside in favor of a French singer in a nightclub. Back on the farm, Lem finally decides to go searching for his fickle sweetie, first stopping by the radio station to beat the cookies out of Mr. Bingo. Lem and Emily are finally reunited, and one dissolve later, they are happily married with a house full of chicks. When they hear one of the peeps practicing "buh-buh-buh-booing" at the piano, they bean him with a heavy book.

Just to prove that the standard feud plot was not yet dead, the third of Warner Bros.'s 1936 rural cartoons, *When I Yoo Hoo*, introduces the mountain community of Hickory Holler, where the Weavers and the Matthewses are blood enemies. The sheriff posts a notice that the feud is to be settled by a cockfight, and the losing family must leave the county. At the fight, the Weaver rooster at first has the upper hand—er, beak—er, claw oh, forget it—but after the Matthews chicken gulps down some moonshine from a jug, he evens up the match by knocking all the Weaver poultry's feathers off. When the two pullet pugilists have beaten each other senseless, the sheriff declares the fight a draw, which don't hardly set well with the two feudin' families. As the story ends, all the Weavers and all the Matthewses are fighting it out in the ring while their two roosters cheer them on from the stands.

The year 1936 also saw Warner's begin promoting its new cartoon star, Porky Pig, who had been introduced in an incidental

Mountain Music (1937) was one of two feature films that teamed Bob Burns with large-mouthed comedian Martha Raye.

role the year before. Porky's films of the 1930s, including the 1936 episodes *Porky's Poppa, Milk and Money,* and *Porky the Rainmaker,* often involved farm life but really added nothing new to the rural comedy genre. For the next thirty years, through theatrical shorts and into the television era, Porky continued returning to farm and barnyard settings. Such is the price one pays for being born a pig, we suppose.

Outside the loony world of animated cartoons, you will remember from our last chapter that 1936 was the year Bob Burns first shot to stardom thanks to his weekly appearances on Bing Crosby's radio program. This quite naturally caused movie studios to think about utilizing his talents as well. Burns was teamed with Crosby for *Rhythm on the Range* (1936) and then appeared with Jack Benny and other radio stars in *The Big Broadcast of 1937*. In *Waikiki Wedding* (1937) and *Mountain Music* (1937), he was paired with loudmouth comic star Martha Raye.

Burns finally got his name at the top of the billing for *Radio City Revels* (1938). Like the *Big Broadcast* movies, this one was part of the trend of cramming as many radio stars as possible into a single movie. Burns plays Lester Robin, a showboat operator in (where else?) Van Buren, Arkansas—quite an accomplishment since Van Buren is on the opposite side of the state from the Mississippi River. Burns even gets to play a couple of short solos on his bazooka when the whole town turns out for a big hootenanny on the riverbank. (One can only imagine how the residents of the real Van Buren felt about the way their town was portrayed in this film.) One comical scene shows an elderly granny-type mountain woman herding her several dozen children to the shindig; emerging from her cabin, they range in diminishing size from young adults in their twenties to a crawling infant bringing up the rear.

The plot, such as it is, does not get started until Robin/Burns goes to New York City to try to break into the songwriting business. He is taken in (in more ways than one) by struggling songwriter Harry Miller (Jack Oakie) and Miller's accomplice (a young Milton Berle). This diabolical duo soon discovers that when their new friend sleeps, he subconsciously composes and performs magnificent songs, but he remembers nothing about them when he awakens. Before the story ends, Oakie and Berle have made millions off Burns's somnambulistic talents, and Burns has fallen hard for cuter-than-cute dancer Ann Miller. He tells her, "You're purtier'n a seed catalog tomato" but eventually ends up with her older sister instead. In the closing scene, Oakie has a rare surge of conscience and presents Burns with a sizable check for his latest composition. Burns replies, "Aw, that's all right—I'll half it with ya," and promptly tears the check in half.

Some hoopla was made about *The Arkansas Traveler* (1938) being Burns's first starring film. Even though he received top billing in *Radio City Revels,* he could not have been considered the true star of the vehicle, what with so many other broadcasting veterans (including *Jack Benny Program* alumni Kenny Baker and Don Wilson) taking turns in the spotlight. When *Time* saw fit to review *The Arkansas*

Traveler, the magazine made much of the fact that Burns seemed to be the heir apparent to that brand of rural humor formerly mastered by Will Rogers. The reviewer noted that the "principal cinema attribute of Rogers was to make it seem that Right not only triumphed on all occasions, but that it did so without working up a perspiration. Strict adherence to the Rogers formula gives *The Arkansas Traveler* much of the same amiable, folksy entertainment value."

It was easy to tell that Burns was becoming a familiar figure to moviegoers, as gags relating to him began turning up in the Warner Bros. cartoons. *Speaking of the Weather* (1937) was yet another of the "magazine covers coming to life" series, with Burns playing the bazooka on the cover of *Radio Stars*. In *The Major Lied 'Til Dawn* (1938), the titular old British major weaves an outlandish Baron Munchausen–like tale about his exploits hunting big game in Africa; at one point, he stops in the jungle long enough to consult his road map, which turns out to be labeled "Map of Van Buren, Ark.," with "Uncle Fud's house" designated by a dot. Even years later, the "coming to life" theme was still going, and in *Book Revue* (1946), a grotesquely caricatured Burns (in overalls and with bare feet) briefly honks his bazooka on a copy of *The Arkansas Traveler*.

The real-life Burns followed his initial screen triumphs with *I'm from Missouri* (1939), *Our Leading Citizen* (1939), and *Alias the Deacon* (1940, which gave him a rare opportunity to be a villain), but his second release of 1940 torpedoed the rest of his movie career. Paramount's *Comin' 'round the Mountain* was not the only movie in history to go by that title, but it distinguished itself by stuffing its running time with practically every rural comedian then appearing on radio, with the notable exception of Lum and Abner, who were occupied making their own film debut at another studio. Chief among the cast members were Pat Barrett as Uncle Ezra, his character from the *National Barn Dance* and *Uncle Ezra's Radio Station*; Bill Thompson as the Old-Timer from *Fibber McGee and Molly*; Cliff Arquette, rapidly becoming well known for his portrayal of old men (and sometimes old ladies!); and a lady billed only as "Mirandy," who was part of a Los Angeles–based country music group known as the Beverly Hill Billies. This gaggle of radio actors was rounded out by a few who were not of the rural type: Jack Benny's announcer, Don Wilson; Jerry Colonna from Bob Hope's cast; and Harold Peary as the Great Gildersleeve.

By the time Bob Burns appeared in *Comin' 'round the Mountain* (1940), the people in his native Arkansas were beginning to let it be known loud and clear that they were tired to death of his jokes at their expense.

Somewhere among all these talents was a plot, once again dragging out the feuding families gag. This time it was the Beagles and the Blowers, and Jed Blower (Bob Burns) returns to his home in Monotony, Tennessee ("So far back in the country, some of 'em ain't never seen Miz Roosevelt," he explains), just as things are heating up. He gets to play a brief piece on the bazooka before the story proper begins, with the entire Blower family hillbilly band getting to be a big hit on Uncle Ezra's radio station and turning Monotony into a destination for tourists. This particularly benefits the general store run by the Smoot brothers (the film's substitutes for Lum and Abner), played by Thompson and Richard Carle. In one scene, a lady tourist from the city bargains with Thompson's Old-Timer character over a squirrel-tail cap:

> *Customer*: Are you sure this squirrel was shot by a real hillbilly?
>
> *Old Timer*: Daughter, not only was that squirrel shot by a hillbilly, but the hillbilly was shot by ANOTHER hillbilly!
>
> *Customer*: There ought to be a law against that.
>
> *Old Timer*: There is—ya cain't shoot squirrels no more. Come back tomorrow, I might have a hillbilly that was shot by a squirrel.

Among all the other high jinks (and some low jinks as well), Burns has ample opportunity to tell stories about his family, such as his sister, who didn't get her first pair of shoes until she was twenty-

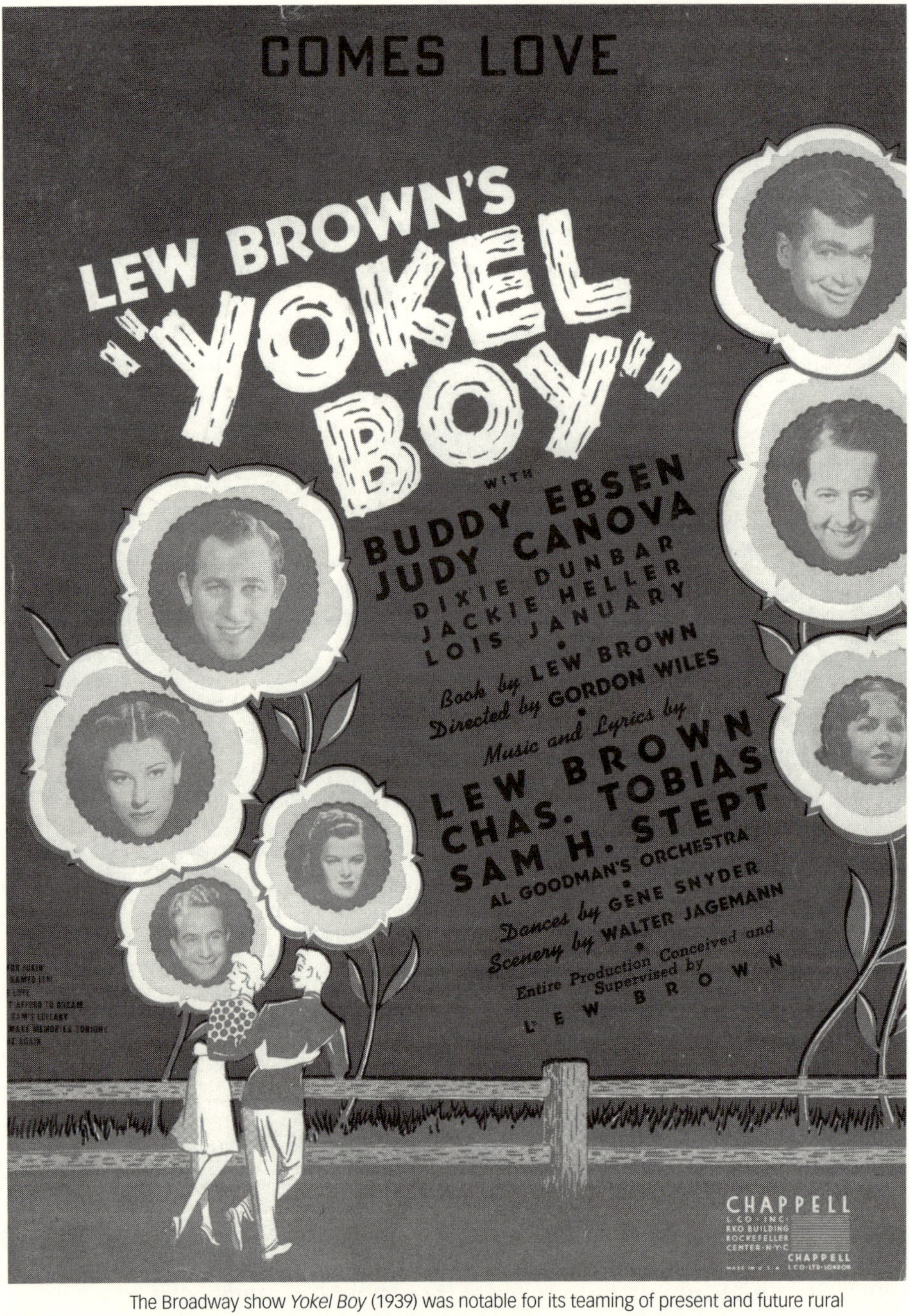

The Broadway show *Yokel Boy* (1939) was notable for its teaming of present and future rural comedy superstars Judy Canova and Buddy Ebsen.

eight years old: "By then, her feet was so tough and rugged, she wore her first three pairs o' shoes out from th' inside." He also describes his Aunt Pruney's dancing abilities: "She'd bend over backwards an' pick up a handkerchief with her teeth—then, fer an encore, she'd pick up her teeth."

Ironically, even though *Comin' 'round the Mountain* was specifically set in the Tennessee hills, its release caused the good folks back in Burns's beloved Arkansas to become quite vocal about their resentment of this type of humor. In 1942, *Time* magazine reported that "the state declared war on denigrating native son Burns, forcing him to return to a Little Rock mass meeting and explain." Burns apparently was contrite in his appearance before his fellow Arkansans, and part of his penance consisted of withdrawing from the next movie Paramount had planned for him. The title was to have been *The Wizard of Arkansas,* but something about the script made Burns realize that making the film would have been suicide once it hit the screens back home.

As it turned out, withdrawing from a film that was already in the preproduction stages was career suicide of a different type for Burns. *Time* explained, "When Paramount sued, all Arkansas rose in Burns's defense." While his radio work continued for most of the rest of the decade, Burns's pooh-poohing of Paramount put an end to his film career as soundly as a bullet in a revenooer.

Considering that many radio historians mention Judy Canova in the next breath after Bob Burns, it is somewhat surprising that her film career did not follow nearly the same path as his. This might have something to do with the fact that Canova (and her brother and sister) achieved her initial fame on Broadway simultaneously with radio, and it was well known that she could sing and act seriously as well as comedically, so perhaps the movie studios felt she deserved more flexibility in her roles. In such Warner Bros. films as *In Caliente* (1935), *Broadway Gondolier* (1935), and *Going Highbrow* (1935), Canova was consistently cast as the diamond in the rough, but that outline could take the form of a waitress or the heroine's best friend without necessarily being a billie from the hills. Moving to Paramount, she faced similar treatment in *Artists and*

Models (1937, a Jack Benny vehicle) and *Thrill of a Lifetime* (1937). Finally, realizing that she was seemingly going to be forever cast in supporting roles, she left Paramount's mountain peak for the wide-open spaces of Republic Pictures, the studio that was best known for churning out B Westerns starring Roy Rogers, Gene Autry, and their cowpoke companions.

Republic seemed to get a grip on Canova's character and presented her in her first actual starring film, *Scatterbrain* (1940). The story takes full advantage of her radio-honed hillbilly personality. It involves a fictitious studio, Perfection Pictures, that is planning an equally fictitious hillbilly drama, *Thunder over the Ozarks.* The studio's publicity man conceives of a great stunt, planting a professional actress—who also happens to be his fiancée—on a farm in the hills, where she will be "accidentally" discovered by the film's director, with all the resulting hype the publicity department can muster. Of course, the farm chosen for this momentous event turns out to be Canova's, and when the director "happens by" on his trip, he sees the strapping young girl and mistakenly assumes she is the planted actress hamming up the yokel bit.

The director learns of his mistake when he gets Canova to Hollywood and the publicity man informs him that her hillbilly persona is not an act. (The farm where Canova is discovered is supposedly within driving range of Los Angeles, thereby making her one of the few hillbillies of the nonsouthern variety.) However, as one might expect, her singing and dancing talents in her screen test overwhelm everyone, and she becomes a star in spite of everything.

Whereas performers such as Burns and Canova built their reputations on their rural personas, other comedians dipped their big toes into the pool of hillbilly humor for occasional onetime events. Stan Laurel and Oliver Hardy encountered practically every sort of fine mess during their long careers, but their only real attempt at the rural theme was in *Them Thar Hills* (1934). Even then, the hillbilly antics were kept to a minimum, with the main story involving the thin and fat duo attempting a trip to the mountains to steady Hardy's nerves. Some moonshiners have dumped the evidence of their business into a well, and soon the boys and a stranded motoring husband and wife are feeling quite high in their fruit jars.

The manic trio known as the Ritz Brothers (Tom, Harry, and Al) followed the trend in Twentieth Century Fox's *Kentucky Moonshine* (1938). Like *Radio City Revels*, the plot unfolds against the background of New York's radio industry. Singer Tony Martin's ratings are dropping because his program is offering nothing new; the sponsor decides to try hillbilly music for a change but insists that it has to be authentic. He uses the example of Bob Burns, who is a radio superstar because he truly comes from that background. Martin and an assistant will head for Kentucky to search for a hillbilly band that they can feature on their show.

Word of these plans is intercepted by the Ritz Brothers and their equally out-of-work girl singer chum, played by Marjorie Weaver. The four of them plot to get to the mountain community of Coma, Kentucky, ahead of Martin and hole up in a ramshackle cabin, where they will pose as three brothers and their sister. Much of the comedy involves the Brooklyn natives attempting to pass themselves off as genuine mountaineers, especially when confronted with the feud between the Hatfields and the Slacks. (Wouldn't you know they'd be borrowing the old Slack cabin?) Martin features the whole "family" in a special shortwave broadcast from a local barn, where the townsfolk are baffled by the APPLAUSE sign the radio show's announcer holds up at strategic points. "Whut's that sign say?" asks one illiterate pappy, to which his young offspring responds, "I dunno, sompin' 'bout applesauce." After their ruse is discovered, the final third of the film forgets about hillbilly humor and becomes the brothers' showcase for their typically zany humor, including an extended parody of Walt Disney's *Snow White and the Seven Dwarfs*, as they become big comedy stars on Martin's radio show.

Before the 1930s ended, Warner Bros. had two more cartoons in which to get its love for feud funny business out of the way. In *A Feud There Was* (1938), it's the Weavers and the McCoys who are at it, and they don't even need the faintest hint of a plot for the gags to start flying along with the bullets. One bearded old geezer gets half of his whiskers shot off, causing him to crack, "The old gray hair ain't what it used ta be!" After an embarrassing silence, he apologizes, "Well, hit sounded funny in rehearsal." Another rube has at least a dozen triggers on a single gun, remarking, "In these here new cartoon pitchers, a feller kin git away with most anything." *Naughty Neighbors* (1939) opens with the announcement, "Our story unfolds in the quiet old hills of old Kaintucky where, in contrast to the troubled outside world, the hill folk live in peace and harmony," cueing a shot of acres full of hillbilly critters in a royal free-for-all. The headlines of the *Ozark Bazooka* newspaper (we wonder how many of the cartoonists had been out looking for the Ozarks in Kentucky) blares that the leaders of the two families, Porky Pig McCoy and Petunia Hatfield, are to patch up the feud by being married. An uncomfortable truce is reached, wherein their families (portrayed as chickens, ducks, geese, and practically anything else except pigs) pretend to be buddies while secretly plotting ways to murder each other. Finally the feud erupts again in all its glory, and Porky is forced to pull out his heavy ammunition: a heart-decorated hand grenade labeled "Feud Pacifier." When the smoke clears, the formerly feuding fowl are playing marbles, embracing each other, and dancing around a maypole. Somewhat oddly, after so many years of one hillbilly reference after another, Warner Bros. did not revisit the theme until after the end of World War II.

That did not mean that other cartoon studios could not carry on the tradition. Columbia, which had put the Barney Google/ Snuffy Smith series to rest three years earlier, revisited the setting in *Mountain Ears* (1938). This time the hillbillies were all of the generic variety, presented as the subjects of a newsreel narrated by an impersonation of Jack Benny's voice (reportedly supplied by actor Jack Lescoulie). He makes sarcastic comments about the daily doins of mountain life and seems to take particular pleasure in irritating a young Jughaid-type boy wearing a coonskin cap. When the young 'un emerges from the underbrush with his trusty rifle and dog, narrator Benny begins spouting his version of a hillbilly dialect: "Wall, howdy thar, Dan'l Boone, have you-all been out huntin' b'ar in them thar hills with that thar shootin' iron?" To which the young brat cracks to his hound, "Listen, a furriner!" He returns to bedevil

Benny throughout the rest of the film, finally beaning him with a rock from his slingshot.

The Fleischer studio, based in New York City rather than the West Coast, had somehow managed to avoid hillbilly stories throughout the years, instead becoming better known for its portrayals of the grimy streets of the big city. The studio moved its operations to sunny Miami, Florida, in the late 1930s, and perhaps the atmosphere of the Southland rubbed off on its story department, because both *Be Up to Date* (1938) and *Musical Mountaineers* (1939) placed the sexy Betty Boop right smack in the middle of the hills. In the first of the two films, Betty arrives with a trailer that converts into a department store full of modern conveniences for the benefit of the backwoods residents. They turn most of her objects into musical instruments, stealing a generous amount of thunder from the Hoosier Hot Shots. As she departs, Betty sings one last verse of the cartoon's theme song:

I came around the mountain
Yes, I came around the mountain
And brought you hillbillies up to date!

A year later, in *Musical Mountaineers*, Betty has been redesigned to give her more realistic proportions and has given up her portable department store in favor of a snazzy sports car that runs out of gas on the outskirts of a mountain town. Toting her gas can, she finds a nearby cabin and comments, "It looks like the people who moved out don't live here anymore." Having mistaken her auto's backfires for gunshots, the inbred inhabitants are lying in wait for her, but once they find out she is a performer, they all take part in a foot-stompin' hoedown. At the end, they pour a jug of corn squeezins into her car's gas tank and give the vehicle some real go power.

Some live performers who looked like they stepped straight out of a cartoon were the Weaver Brothers and Elviry, yet another vaudeville act that found a whole new life in movies. Frank and Leon Weaver were the real McCoy (oops, that's probably the wrong thing to call them with so many feuds going on), from the town of Ozark,

The vaudeville act of the Weaver Brothers and Elviry resembled a sort of hybrid of the Marx Brothers and the Three Stooges. Abner was the straight man, Cicero was the silent one who communicated through whistles and funny faces, and Elviry was the battleaxe who kept the two menfolk in line.

Missouri. The third member of the trio was Frank's wife, June; oddly, however, she was always cast as Leon's wife. (During their vaudeville days, June *was* married to Leon. They divorced, she married Frank, and apparently this caused no dysfunction in the family unit.) For their act, they took on names that were more in keeping with their rube characterizations: Frank became Cicero, Leon became Abner, and June became Elviry.

Their routines, at least to judge from their existing film work, make them seem like a sort of hybrid of the Marx Brothers and the Three Stooges. Leon/Abner might have been the group's straight man, the solid foundation for the others' antics. Frank/Cicero was the Harpo-style mute, communicating only through whistles and some incredibly rubbery facial expressions. And speaking of faces, June/Elviry had one that looked like it could give a hatchet some serious competition, with a cackling voice to match. She provided the brains—and frequently the brawn—of the outfit, ready to use physical violence if necessary to protect her loved ones.

After years on the stage, the Weavers three made their motion picture bow in, of all things, a Humphrey Bogart film, *Swing Your Lady* (1938). Bogart reportedly much preferred that this effort on his part be kept under wraps, as he was not particularly fond of his attempt at hillbilly humor. They next played second guitar string to Roy Rogers in *Jeepers Creepers* (1939) and were reunited with the crooning cowpoke for *Arkansas Judge* (1941). Between those two oaters, the Weavers appeared in *Friendly Neighbors* (1940), *In Old Missouri* (1940), and a film that occupies a special place in the annals of rural comedies, Republic Pictures's *Grand Ole Opry* (1940).

The Weaver Brothers and Elviry made their movie debut in *Swing Your Lady* (1938), which Humphrey Bogart considered his absolute worst film.

Yes, while many different radio series attempted to make the transition to movies—much as they would try to adapt themselves for television a decade later—somehow WSM's Tennessee hootenanny does not seem like the most logical one to make that step. However, faced with its undeniable national popularity, Republic licensed the title from WSM and imported several of the regulars from Nashville to play major roles in the story. Even though the Weavers were not a part of the regular *Opry* proceedings, all of the performers managed to blend their unique talents together in a film that turned out to be better than it had any right to be.

In the town of Hopeville (no state specified—and for good reason, as we shall soon see), Abner Weaver is the mayor, Cicero Weaver the police chief, and Elviry Weaver the schoolmarm. Other townsfolk include George D. Hay, the Solemn Ole Judge; Uncle Dave Macon; and farmer Roy Acuff. In a courtroom scene, Judge Hay is hearing the case of a city slicker who claims Acuff fired rock salt at him. "He wuz headin' north an' I hit him south of the border," explains Acuff.

For a movie that runs only approximately an hour (depending on which severely edited version one can locate), an amazing number of elements are crowded into what might laughably be called the plot. The reason for the ambiguity as to the locale becomes obvious when the story involves all manner of crooked politicians: the governor of the unnamed state is assassinated, the weasel of a lieutenant governor takes over but is under the control of the skunk who serves as editor of the state's biggest newspaper. Not exactly the sort of thing that would make anyone want to think it is Tennessee or Arkansas or anywhere else, huh? Mayor Abner lands in the headlines when his town jails the new governor for speeding and thus enables the voters to pass a certain farm bill that the old governor supported but that the new one (and his confederates) firmly oppose because it harms "big business." Following this, are you? When the punk politician attempts to make a speech against the farm bill directly from his cell at the Hopeville courthouse, the townsfolk drown him out with good ol' hillbilly music, courtesy of Acuff's Smoky Mountain Boys.

Before long, Abner is talked into running for governor. Some of the jealous professional politicians attempt to sabotage his campaign by booking a lady opera singer on his first radio broadcast. Listeners turn off their radios and half the studio audience starts to leave until Elviry takes gun in hand and runs the highfalutin' singer and her minions away. Acuff then takes over with "Wabash Cannonball," after which Judge Hay announces that their music may not be grand opera, but the Grand Ole Opry is going to be the official music of the Weaver for Governor campaign.

By the time all is said and done, Abner is indeed elected and Acuff has had plenty of opportunities to sing "Great Speckled Bird" and for the whole cast to join in on "Down in Union County" (the only hint that this could possibly be Tennessee after all). Taken in the spirit in which it was made, *Grand Ole Opry* might not be Academy Award material, but it certainly did a commendable job of presenting the WSM cast for their longtime listeners to see for the first time.

As we have already seen and will see again, basing movies on radio programs could be a hit-and-miss proposition, with more misses than box office hits. A similar problem plagued occasional

Republic Pictures turned the *Grand Ole Opry* into a feature film in 1940. In addition to radio stars Roy Acuff, Uncle Dave Macon, and George D. Hay, the Weaver Brothers and Elviry added to the humor. Here Elviry uses her particular musical talents to squelch a speech by the state's crooked governor.

attempts to turn newspaper comic strips into live-action movies, presenting an even greater set of difficulties than trying to make the transfer from funny papers to animated cartoons. In the late 1930s, the most successful of these were Columbia's series of *Blondie* films, based on the comic strip by Chic Young. Their only connection to rural comedy was their casting of Irving Bacon as the postman who is flattened daily by Dagwood's mad dash out the front door on his way to the office; Bacon would turn up in either a major or minor role in nearly every hick comedy of the period. The success of the *Blondie* series in particular and hillbilly comedy in general may have prompted RKO Radio Pictures to agree to a feature based on Al Capp's much-beloved *Li'l Abner.*

This 1940 movie was not the first attempt to dramatize Capp's groundbreaking strip. In 1939, a *Li'l Abner* radio serial had aired briefly; its influence on the medium was minimal, notable mainly for the fact that Pappy Yokum was played by Clarence Hartzell, en

Abner (Granville Owen, *right*) and his friend, Hannibal Hoops (Doodles Weaver), contemplate the reward for capturing outlaw Earthquake McGoon in the first film adaptation of Al Capp's comic strip, *Li'l Abner* (1940).

route to greater radio fame as part of the casts on the serials *Vic and Sade* and *Lum and Abner*. The voice of Abner was John Hodiak, who did not build his future movie career on country bumpkin roles. The radio program apparently did not provide the inspiration for RKO's production, which instead reached back into the newspaper morgue and cobbled together plot elements from six years of *Li'l Abner* strips. A thorough chemical analysis of the resulting concoction is a fitting way to end the decade—and, not incidentally, this chapter.

First, the story. The filmmakers resisted any temptation to try to explain the characters' origins or their motivations; they simply spring from printed page to movie screen full-blown, on the assumption that anyone who saw the film would already be familiar with the strip. From the opening scene, the beautiful blonde Daisy Mae is pining for her lifelong love, Li'l Abner, who is equally determined to remain a bachelor. The first threat to this shaky relationship comes in the form—and *what* a (gulp!) form—of Daisy Mae's sophisticated Cousin Delightful, on a visit from the neighboring town of Pineapple Junction. Delightful does some powerful wooing of Abner under the pretext of showing Daisy her "technique." Abner is saved from Delightful's clutch by Daisy's judicious application of a giant stick to his skull.

After all the excitement, Abner prepares himself a sandwich that would make Dagwood Bumstead's stomach growl; by the time he is finished, it contains most of the edible and inedible contents of the cabin, topped off with mustard (even though Mammy Yokum warns him, "Yo' know yo' has been allergic to mustard ever since yo' ate that mustard plaster when yo' was a young 'un!"). By the time he wolfs down the ptomaine sandwich, he has "a powerful misery in mah stummick." Remembering from a newspaper clipping that a renowned doctor named Barbour is due to pass through on the noon train, Abner and his half-witted friend, Hannibal Hoops, go down to find the good doctor for treatment. Instead, Abner encounters the train's barber, who thinks the whole thing is vastly amusing. He diagnoses Abner as having "scrombosis" and tells him, "You're dead now from the neck up." Pressed for more details, the barber tells Abner that the rest of him will be dead in twenty-four hours.

With this news to give him courage, Abner first tells Daisy Mae that he will marry her at noon tomorrow (by which time, he figures, he will certainly be gone). He then determines to leave Mammy and Pappy with untold riches by collecting the twenty-five-dollar reward for the capture of villain Earthquake McGoon. Abner beards the bearded giant in his lair in Skonk Hollow, and with Mammy's help he subdues the monster and sets out for home through the swamps. However, he becomes lost and encounters Wendy Wilecat, McGoon's intended, who offers to show him the way back home to Dogpatch if he will agree to marry her tomorrow at noon. Figuring he will be too dead to marry one girl, let alone two, Abner agrees.

When he awakens miserably alive the next morning, Abner finds that he has two problems on his hands—or, more correctly, a beautiful girl in skimpy clothes on each of his hands. With the annual Sadie Hawkins Day race fast approaching, Mayor Gurgle designates Abner as off-limits to any of the Dogpatch gals except

During the Sadie Hawkins dance in *Li'l Abner* (1940), Abner Yokum (Granville Owen) finds himself entrapped by two beautiful mountain gals, Wendy Wilecat (Kay Sutton) and Daisy Mae (Martha O'Driscoll). He gets no help from Lonesome Polecat (Buster Keaton) and Hairless Joe (Bud Jamison), seen here helping themselves to the refreshments.

Daisy and Wendy. They make the most of this limitation during that evening's dance, where the females stomp the livin' daylights out of the menfolks' feet so they will be too crippled to run tomorrow.

The Sadie Hawkins race, as one might expect, is a slapstick affair with cartoony sight gags aplenty. While both Daisy and Wendy pursue Abner and town loafers Hairless Joe and Lonesome Polecat try just as hard to get caught, Earthquake McGoon escapes from jail and sets out after Abner to settle their score (and Abner's hash). Just after the sheriff and his men corner McGoon and use dynamite to temporarily incapacitate him, Wendy and Daisy trap Abner in the middle of a bridge, with no hope for him to escape. And there the story ends—or, does it?

Capp historians have long debated what happened to the supposed ending of the film. Daisy reaches Abner just ahead of Wendy, embracing him and declaring, "Oh, Li'l Abner, yo' is mine at last!"

The 1940 *Li'l Abner* film combined characters who looked relatively normal, as with Abner and Daisy Mae here, with others who wore exaggerated makeup to resemble their comic strip counterparts, as evidenced by Mammy and Pappy Yokum.

However, the next shot is of Abner racing away over a hill, with Daisy Mae in hot pursuit, as the picture fades out and the "The End" title appears. What happened? No one seems to know for sure. It has been speculated that Al Capp saw the finished film and objected to letting Abner and Daisy get married, as he had no intention of changing the focus of his strip. Whether that is true or not, it remains one of the strangest nonendings in movie history.

But then, there are a lot of strange things about this movie. One of them, which the preceding description somewhat hinted at, involves the actors' dialogue. Rather than having everyone use what Hollywood would consider a backwoods or southern accent, the characters speak just as Capp spelled their dialect in his strips. Therefore, *you* is pronounced *yo,* and sentence structure is sometimes at odds with any known way of speaking in the hills or anywhere else (for example, at one point Abner chuckles to himself and Daisy indignantly snaps, "What air so hoomorus?"). There is no doubt that the filmmakers felt they were being totally accurate in transferring this aspect of Capp's creation from strip to screen.

Likewise, the way many of the characters look exactly like their cartoon counterparts is terrific from the point of accuracy but makes them look rather creepy alongside the characters who look like ordinary people (such as Abner and Daisy). Mammy and Pappy Yokum are probably the spookiest, with their bulbous noses and Mammy's protruding chin. Hairless Joe might also be a sight for sore eyes, except that he does not have any—or, if he does, they are buried beneath his layers of facial hair, with only his golf-ball-shaped proboscis to show that there really is a "hoomin" in there somewhere.

With all the work that went into turning the newspaper strip into a live-action cartoon, even mentioning the casting seems like an afterthought. The film's creators obviously felt that the characters and the strip's reputation alone would bring in viewers. That said, the amazingly large cast generally comprised actors taking their first steps up the movie ladder (Granville Owen as Abner, former child actress Martha O'Driscoll as Daisy Mae) or comedians who were relics of the silent movie era and needed work (the incomparable Buster Keaton as the inept Native American, Lonesome Polecat, or Chester Conklin as Mayor Gurgle). Abner's best friend, Hannibal Hoops, was played by Doodles Weaver, the comedian who would find greater fame as part of Spike Jones's madcap musical mess later in the decade. In addition to the principals, the movie Dogpatch was populated with dozens of minor characters from the strip, most of whom have only a single scene in which to shine: Cornelius Cornpone (Edgar Kennedy), Abijah Gooch (Frank Wilder), Cicero Grunts (Mickey Daniels), Barney Bargrease (Eddie Gribbon), and so on.

One of these bit players deserves special mention because we will be hearing from him again. In the strip, Marryin' Sam was a fairly major character, Dogpatch's answer to *Lum and Abner*'s Squire Skimp and *Amos 'n' Andy*'s Kingfish, a con man with an eye for a fast buck. Sam hardly appears at all in the 1940 *Li'l Abner,* but in his couple of routines—mainly beginning a long-winded speech and being squelched by the mayor—he is played by portly actor Dick Elliott. Remember that name, because Mr. Elliott will reappear in some unexpected places as we move along, ranging from Pine Ridge to Mayberry and beyond.

Whether anyone realized it, movies such as *Li'l Abner* and most of the others discussed in this chapter represented the end of a genre as it had always been known. When the 1930s rolled over in bed and emerged as the 1940s, world events waiting outside transformed the nation and its style of humor almost overnight. The cornpone comedies of the depression era would suddenly look even more outdated than they had when first made, and most of them (along with their more laid-back stars) were soon forgotten in the hectic days to come.

Chapter Four

Feudin', Fussin', and A-Fightin'

Some historians—but by no means all of them—believe that, in many ways, decades cannot always be defined in ten-year increments, such as 1930–39, 1950–59, and so on. Instead, they feel, decades can be more accurately measured by dividing them according to historical events or even pop culture. This line of thinking designates the 1930s as beginning with the stock market crash of 1929 and ending with U.S. involvement in World War II in 1941. That event would mark the beginning of the 1940s, which would end culturally at the conclusion of the war in 1945—or, possibly, the 1948 presidential election, in which Dewey did not defeat Truman. The 1950s would stretch until the Kennedy assassination in 1963, and the 1960s would extend until the Watergate era of 1973–74. Confusing, isn't it?

At any rate, movies released in 1940 somehow seem to belong to the previous decade. We have already examined the live-action *Li'l Abner* film and others that were released that year because they and their subject matter were products of the 1930s, but before diving headfirst into a global conflict, we need to get another couple of matters out of the way.

You will recall that way back when, we mentioned that *Lum and Abner* had temporarily left the air in March 1940 so Chester "Lum" Lauck and Norris "Abner" Goff could make their first movie. That film was finally released by RKO as *Dreaming Out Loud* in August

Lum and Abner's first movie, *Dreaming Out Loud* (1940), had less comedy and more drama than their future films.

1940. Appropriately, it had what the press lauded as an "all-Arkansas premiere," with celebrations taking place in Little Rock, Hot Springs, Fort Smith, and Lauck and Goff's hometown of Mena all within a few days' time.

Dreaming Out Loud differs markedly from subsequent Lum and Abner films. Although audiences undoubtedly went to see it because of the pair's radio comedy reputation, what unreeled on the screen turned out to be a fairly serious story with the two Pine Ridge storekeepers adding some comedy scenes to keep things moving. The main plot deals with the town's need for a mobile medical unit, as the old local doctor (played by Frank Craven) suffers a stroke as a result of overwork and can no longer perform his duties. Adding to Lum and Abner's problems is the fact that Effie Lou, daughter of town drunk Wes Daniels (the ubiquitous Irving Bacon), is killed by a hit-and-run driver—and if the town had had the proper medical facilities, she might have lived. Wealthy old Jessica Spence (Clara Blandick, best known as Aunt Em in *The Wizard of Oz*) has the needed moolah to make this dream a reality, but because the old doc jilted her affections years ago, she has become bitter and refuses to do anything that would help him. Her beautiful niece, Alice (Frances Langford, who sings the title song), and Alice's young brother, Jimmy (child star Bobs Watson), are caught in the middle, especially since Jimmy saw the hit-and-run and knows that the "death car" belonged to his Aunt Jessie. Is all of this sufficiently tear-jerking?

Amid it all, Lum and Abner have not only comedy scenes but genuinely touching ones as well, as they demonstrate the same humanity as portrayed on their radio programs (which were not always yuk-it-up fun and games either). They demonstrate their true acting ability in moments such as when they comfort the grief-stricken alcoholic Wes Daniels after his daughter's murder; Wes gives up drinking on the spot and becomes a deputy constable, with his main thought being to track down Effie Lou's killer. In one of the more lighthearted moments, Lum and Abner's never-ending checker game is interrupted by a phone call, and while Lum takes down an order, Abner continues playing, controlling both sides of the checkerboard. He gets into such a loud argument with himself over whether he is cheating that Lum cannot hear the customer on the phone.

Dreaming Out Loud differs from all the future Lum and Abner movies not only because of its dramatic plot but also because none of the other characters from the radio show are part of it. There are brief references to Grandpappy Spears, Squire Skimp, Cedric Weehunt, and others, but they are never seen. It is also somewhat strange that during this period, when animated cartoons were constantly using radio catchphrases and caricaturing celebrities such as Bob Burns, none of these works seems to have contained any direct references to *Lum and Abner.*

The nearest instance occurred in a 1940 release from MGM's cartoon studio, *Tom Turkey and His Harmonica Humdingers.* While nearly every character in the film—which features an all-poultry cast, by the way—has some parallel in the *Lum and Abner* world, the resemblance may well have been unintentional. The cartoon almost totally lacks dialogue, relying instead on the incredible harmonica harmonies of a vaudeville and movie group known as Borrah Minevitch and His Harmonica Rascals (hence, no doubt, the title of the short). The few lines spoken are delivered by cartoon voice maestro Mel Blanc, in the days before he signed an exclusive contract with Warner Bros.

Tom Turkey is first seen strolling down the wooden sidewalks of a Pine Ridge lookalike town, playing (what else?) "Turkey in the Straw" on his harmonica. Arriving at the general store, he soon has all the local loafers joining in. (We see a couple of old buzzards who have been sitting at the checkerboard for so long that they have cobwebs growing on them.) The harmonica hoodlums get so carried away that they soon wreck most of the merchandise displays in the store, after which Tom picks up a ladle and uses it as a microphone, announcing, "Hello, Maw! Hello, Paw! Our next number will be entitled 'Mother, You've Worked fer Me All Your Life—Now Go Out an' Work fer Yerself.'"

A running gag is a shrimpy little bird wearing a Confederate uniform who insists on playing "Dixie" on his fife in counterpoint to whatever melody the harmonicas are carrying. Every time he gets started, Tom angrily snatches the flute away, only to have the octogenarian magically produce another. This plot device shows up in many different cartoons over the years, most notably in Disney's *The Band Concert* (1935), in which Mickey Mouse and Donald Duck battle it out for musical supremacy. Tom Turkey finally gets so carried away dancing with a mannequin in the store's window (to the tune of "Darktown Strutters' Ball") that the local ladies' auxiliary comes to the rescue, running their no-count spouses back home with brooms, rolling pins, and other weapons of marital destruction.

Back in chapter 2, you will recall, we discussed the fact that when the *Lum and Abner* radio serial finally returned to the airwaves after its hiatus while *Dreaming Out Loud* was being filmed, Lauck and Goff soon enlisted the help of Roswell "Roz" Rogers to serve as head writer. It is difficult to say just how the program might have evolved if not for Rogers's input, because the bombing of Pearl Harbor on December 7, 1941, launched all of radio into an orbit it

After the United States entered World War II in December 1941, the *Lum and Abner* scripts often included references to rationing and other wartime sacrifices.

had never seen before. The movies would eventually follow suit, but since radio was the more immediate medium of the two, it was charged with getting the most urgent messages out to the public.

Top broadcasting stars were expected to do their part to help spread the government's wartime pleas, so it seemed that Pine Ridge and the citizens who lived there were suddenly forced to become much more aware of what was going on in the world around them. True to form, the dictums to conserve rubber and gasoline and not to buy meat on the black market were always presented humorously and within the context of the ongoing story line. On the phone, trying to placate an irritated customer who did not understand the concept of sugar rationing, Abner loses his patience and barks, "Don't blame me fer this war we're in! Blame that crazy paper hanger, that Adolf Schickelgroober or whatever his name is!"

On a few memorable occasions, as in *Dreaming Out Loud*, the show would depart from its customary humor for an all-too-realistic look at how a small town dealt with tragedy. During one continuity, the two old storekeepers decide to open up a sideline of designing and printing greeting cards. Remembering that local young serviceman Robert Blevins has an upcoming birthday, Lum phones "Miz Blevins" to find out just when that occasion will be. However, when a neighbor answers the phone instead of Miz Blevins, it turns out to be the type of news that is becoming far too common:

Abner: Lum, ya fergot to ast when Robert's birthday is.

Lum: Abner . . . Robert ain't gonna have no more birthdays.

Abner: HUH? Y-you mean . . . oh, my goodness . . .

Lum: That's right, Abner. But he done jist what you'd 'spect him ta do, he went down fightin' . . . an' fightin' agin some purty heavy odds, too. Hit taken five airplanes ta git him.

Using the old reliable party line to address their listeners, Lum turns the grim news into something positive:

Lum: I dunno how many o' you fokes know about Robert Blevins yit, but Bob's a hero now. He's been doin' some good work with his airplane over ther in th' Pacific, but he fought his last battle th' other day, an' he fought it fer us. It warn't one airplane that got him, er two er three . . . hit taken five of 'em ta do it. An' right ther is wher th' enemy made its biggest mistake! Robert Blevins is a Pine Ridge boy, an' Pine Ridge ain't gonna take this settin' down. We're gonna git ever one o' them five airplanes! An' here's how we're gonna do it . . . All o' you fokes is pledged ta give 10 percent o' yer earnin's fer War Bonds an' Stamps. Well, that ain't enough now. Ever citizen o' Pine Ridge has got ta give more'n that . . . not only this week, but ever week. We gotta keep it up 'til we git things evened up fer Bob! So, start buyin' them War Bonds an' Stamps right away, fokes. 'Cause yer buyin' these fer Robert Blevins, an' boys like him.

Other than the injection of such wartime necessities, one of the only noticeable changes in *Lum and Abner* during the 1940s was that more and more of radio's top supporting actors were brought in to play various characters to supplement the regulars voiced by Lauck and Goff. Some of these extra characters appeared in only one or two episodes, while others stuck around for months. Chief among this secondary cast were Elmore Vincent as Abner's half-senile Civil War veteran father, Phinus Peabody; busy cartoon voice actor Frank Graham as Diogenes Smith, who ostensibly came to Pine Ridge looking for an "honest man" but instead turned out to be a counterfeiter; Dink Trout as Zed Whitzit, the ornery and cantankerous owner of a small gas station outside town; Jerry Hausner as numerous characters, both friend and foe; former silent movie idol Francis X. Bushman as assorted millionaires, government officials, and other stuffed shirts; Howard McNear as various eccentric visitors, including the half-mad Dr. Roller the Pest Controller (he would later be best known as the equally pixilated Floyd the Barber of *The Andy Griffith Show*); and Lurene Tuttle as virtually every female character who passed through the Jot 'Em Down Store, from ditzy Mabel Melrose, a would-be surrealist painter, to tough-as-hardtack Sergeant Viola Hartford, late of the Women's Army Corps.

With Roswell Rogers on hand to take on the radio scriptwriting, Lauck and Goff were able to get back to their movies. Their second feature, *The Bashful Bachelor*, was released in April 1942. Unlike *Dreaming Out Loud*, there was nothing serious about this one—it was an out-and-out comedy, probably resembling the radio show more than any other film they would make. This was for good reason, as much of the plot came from story lines they had done on the radio in 1936–37. Lum is determined to make a hero of himself so he can win the hand of Miss Geraldine (ZaSu Pitts), but somehow most of his schemes involve more physical danger to Abner than to Lum. This time, more of the radio characters were added to the plot, except of course Lauck and Goff could not play them on the screen, as they traditionally did on radio. Cedric Weehunt was portrayed by Grady Sutton, a character actor most famed for his several films with W. C. Fields. Since the radio Cedric was supposed to be a lovable oaf in his late teens or early twenties and Sutton was in his mid-thirties at the time, the movie Cedric came across as something like a case of arrested development. Squire Skimp was played by Oscar O'Shea, who looked perfect for the role physically but had a thick Irish accent that in no way resembled Goff's Squire voice. Others in the cast included Constance Purdy as Widder Abnernathy, Danny Duncan as Uncle Henry Lunsford, and the beautiful Louise Currie as Squire's niece, who takes sides with her favorite "old dears," Lum and Abner. Irving Bacon was back, not as town deputy Wes Daniels but as the sheriff of the entire county.

In *The Bashful Bachelor* (1942), Lum is caught between Pine Ridge spinster Miss Geraldine (ZaSu Pitts, *left*) and Widder Abnernathy (Constance Purdy, *center*) and her multitude of children. All Abner can do is look on helplessly.

The Bashful Bachelor was followed a year later by *Two Weeks to Live* (1943), which recycled yet another plot device that had been used by comedians before and would turn up again later: through an honest mistake in the doctor's office, Abner is led to believe that he will be dead in fourteen days, and Lum forces him to take on a number of life-threatening jobs to pay back a debt they owe. Irving Bacon makes his third appearance in a row, this time as an eccentric poet, Mr. Gimple, who spouts doggerel that would leave Dr. Seuss scratching his head. None of the Lum and Abner movies to date had directly addressed the war issue, but that would change with *So This Is Washington*, released in September 1943.

The war provided the axis for the entire plot. Abner hears over the radio that Mr. Marshall, a Washington politico (played by stuffy

Alan Mowbray), is putting out a call to all common citizens of the country to invent something that will help win the war. Through sheer dumb luck, Lum and Abner think they have developed a formula for synthetic rubber, and they set out to deliver their invention to the government. Once in the capital city, they have trouble getting through the hordes of crackpot inventors in Marshall's waiting room, but they take a respite on a park bench and soon find themselves helping senators and congressmen solve their problems with good old-fashioned rural common sense. (They are kept from starving to death by their old Pine Ridge friend Robert Blevins, now a newspaper writer in Washington—apparently the radio show rumors of his death a year earlier must have been inaccurate.)

Just as Abner is about to demonstrate the formula for the synthetic rubber before a crowd of reporters, a heavy statue in Marshall's office falls on Abner's head and gives him amnesia. He takes to calling himself Buster V. Davenport, based on the three initials he found in his underwear, and his friends haul him back to Pine Ridge in the hope that the familiar sights around the Jot 'Em Down Store will restore his memory. He gets it back just in time to learn that the substance he has fabricated is not synthetic rubber but a new instant-hardening type of asphalt for building airplane landing strips. Along with all the other goings-on in this plot, Grandpappy Spears makes his screen debut as played by Danny Duncan, a semiregular on the radio series at the time.

To one extent or another, the war affected the other radio comedians who were involved with movies during that trying period. An exception, of course, was Bob Burns, who had allowed his movie career to self-destruct in five seconds rather than endure any more kibitzing from his home state of Arkansas. When *Time* magazine caught up with Burns in 1942 to report on his changed outlook, Burns shot them one of his new-style Arkansas gags: "Now take my Uncle Doug. He used to walk barefoot on a barbed-wire fence with a wildcat under each arm. You know Doug—Douglas MacArthur."

Judy Canova also brought the war into her motion picture output, but not much. Of her three movies released during 1942, only one, *Joan of Ozark*, had a plot in which the war was the central factor.

Judy Canova mows the kitchen floor in a scene from *Puddin' Head* (1941).

In her traditional mountain setting, Judy shoots down a bird that turns out to be a Nazi carrier pigeon. This soon causes her to be of great interest to both the Germans and the U.S. government, with each determined to get its hands on her first. Since she is quickly spirited away to a New York nightclub to be alternately wooed and threatened by both sides, her hillbilly origins soon become rather moot as far as the story is concerned. As one of her biographers summarized it, "She stumbles into the real spy nest at the club, and after much confusion and bungling on her part, she is responsible for the roundup of the enemy and the destruction of a Japanese submarine in American waters."

The global conflict served only as background for Canova's *True to the Army*, another of her 1942 films. After witnessing a murder, Canova has to hide out at the Fort Bragg army camp. An idea of how seriously the situation is treated can be gauged by the fact that

In the *Scattergood Baines* films released by RKO in 1941–43, Guy Kibbee (*left*) brought to life the kindly old storekeeper and philosopher of Coldriver. His comical companion was Dink Trout as Pliny Pickett.

Canova's boyfriend, who happens to be stationed at the camp, is played by Bob Hope's zany pop-eyed, walrus-mustached radio sidekick, Jerry Colonna. In the end, Canova's marksmanship helps bring the killers to bay. Canova's third release that year, *Sleepytime Gal*, was not a wartime story, but by setting its plot in Miami it at least got her back to her genuine native state—a fact that the public had no doubt forgotten after her many roles as a resident of the hills or the Wild West.

Another rural radio series that made its way into the movies during the war years was *Scattergood Baines*, based on a series of short stories by Clarence Budington Kelland. Now, it is somewhat difficult to say whether this property rightfully belongs in our discussion here—neither the radio program nor the movies were expressly comedic, although they did feature some amusing supporting characters and the humorous cracker-barrel philosophies of Scattergood Baines himself. The setting was the small New England town of Coldriver, where Scattergood ran his general store and stuck his nose into the personal lives of his fellow citizens. His sidekick was vinegary old town busybody Pliny Pickett, played to perfection by Dink Trout, later such a vital member of the *Lum and Abner* cast. Trout's high-pitched voice was enough by itself to produce chuckles from an audience, and he was largely responsible for whatever low-key comedy there was in any version of the series.

All of the Scattergood movies were released by RKO during a two-year period: *Scattergood Baines* (1941), *Scattergood Pulls the Strings* (1941), *Scattergood Meets Broadway* (1941), *Scattergood Rides High* (1942), *Scattergood Survives a Murder* (1942), and *Cinderella Swings It* (1943, reportedly originally titled *Scattergood Swings It* but changed because the series was not faring so well at the box office). These movies were filmed on the same exterior set that was concurrently posing as Pine Ridge in the Lum and Abner movies, and the Jot 'Em Down Store doubled as Scattergood's mercantile establishment.

The Scattergood radio program originally ran as a daily fifteen-minute serial on CBS from 1937 through 1942, ending just before the movie series did. The radio show would return on the Mutual network in 1949 as a weekly half-hour program; with Dink Trout unavailable, the new character of Hannibal Gibbey was introduced as the principal comic. He was played by that veteran of rural New England sitcoms, Parker Fennelly. Today, few people remember the Scattergood Baines movies or radio shows or even the short stories from which they were taken, but at least for a while the citizens of Coldriver made certain that not all rural comedies were set in the South.

While Coldriver was portrayed as a perfect, picturesque New England hamlet, in many ways the world inhabited by the Weaver Brothers and Elviry was even more of a fantasyland, largely as a result of the trio's eccentric personalities. Even at that, it did not remain untouched by the war. *The Old Homestead* (1942) almost totally revolved around a wartime theme, involving gangsters turning the Weavers' titular homestead into a den of sin, attracting (and then bilking) the servicemen from a nearby army camp. In the denouement, Abner and Elviry manage to capture the baddies by uncovering their hoarding of sugar—a precious commodity in those ration-ravaged times—and of course everyone lives happily ever after. The Weavers made only a couple of additional films during the war—*Shepherd of the Ozarks* (1942) and *Mountain Rhythm* (1943)—before retiring from show business. Leon/Abner died in 1950, so the act never had a chance to move into the television era, even if the actors had been so inclined. Frank/Cicero, the "silent" one, survived until 1967, with his widow, June/Elviry, hanging in there until November 1977.

As cartoonish as the Weavers might have seemed, they looked positively normal when put up against the next attempt to bring the rustic antics of the *Barney Google and Snuffy Smith* comic strip to

Private Snuffy Smith (1942) attempted to re-create the newspaper strip with live actors. Bud Duncan starred as Snuffy, with Sarah Padden as his gargantuan wife, Lowizie, and Edgar Kennedy as the former revenooer turned sergeant who has to put up with Snuffy in his army camp.

life in the movies. Probably few people even remembered the handful of Barney/Snuffy animated cartoons Columbia had released in 1935, so when Monogram Pictures—notorious for grinding out low-budget quickie flicks—decided to turn the strip into a live-action feature, the idea must have seemed like something new. The first entry in what was apparently intended to be a series was *Private Snuffy Smith* (1942).

First, a word or several about the casting of this film. The role of Snuffy Smith himself called for a performer with, um, rather unique physical characteristics—and Monogram found one in the personage of fifty-nine-year-old Bud Duncan. A veteran of more than 150 silent films, Duncan stood less than five feet tall, proving once again the old adage about there being no small parts, only small actors. He had enjoyed quite a measure of success as the bottom half of a silent movie comedy team, Ham and Bud, and in the late 1920s had even tackled the role of another comic strip character, the latter part of the duo *Toots and Casper,* based on the newspaper feature by Jimmy Murphy. Prior to donning a tennis-ball-sized false nose for the role of Snuffy Smith, Duncan's voice was most familiar to radio listeners as the Irish-accented title character in the much-beloved children's Christmas serial, *The Cinnamon Bear* (1937).

Others in the cast came with show business pedigrees of one type or another. Lowizie was played by Sarah Padden, a moon-faced actress who endured several layers of padding to give her the necessary girth to duplicate Snuffy's blimplike spouse. A black kerchief tied around her head made her a dead-on duplicate of cartoonist Billy DeBeck's drawings. Padden had made a career out of playing farm women and small-town characters; she was the original choice for Aunt Em in *The Wizard of Oz,* losing out to Clara Blandick at the last moment. As we have already seen, Blandick ended up working in the first of Lum and Abner's movies in 1940; Padden would follow her lead, appearing as Aunt Charity Spears in Lum and Abner's *So This Is Washington* the year after her role as Lowizie Smith. Edgar Kennedy, long famed for his "slow burn" takes in which the viewer could fairly see his temper rising to the boiling point, had a major role as the revenooer trying to capture Snuffy and break up his still. Mixed into the plot is Jimmie Dodd as a young soldier from Snuffy's neck of the woods; of course, Dodd would find his greatest fame in television thirteen years later as one of the two adult hosts of Walt Disney's immortal *Mickey Mouse Club.*

The plot of *Private Snuffy Smith,* in its most basic form, follows a story line that had appeared in the newspaper strip over a period from late 1940 into early 1941—long before the United States had entered the world war. In that story, as in the film, Snuffy decides to enlist in the army when he learns that soldiers receive "free food, a place ta sleep, gold buttons, cacky britches, an' thutty dollars a month." At first the military finds too many things wrong with him to allow him to serve—his size being paramount among these flaws—but after he saves the life of a general by pushing him out of the path of an oncoming jeep, the general pulls some strings and Snuffy is in the army. This all takes place around the same time the soldiers are preparing for important maneuvers (giving away the fact that this story was originally written in peacetime). The general wants to hold the war games in the Ozarks, but Snuffy talks him into changing the location to his own home turf: Hootin' Holler, Great Smoky Mountains. (Unlike *Li'l Abner* and a host of other rural comedy fixtures, there was no hesitation about specifically identifying where Snuffy and his friends and enemies supposedly lived.)

The hill folk do not know what to make of the sudden influx of planes, tanks, and soldiers, although the general consensus holds that the plethora of "cacky britches" are revenooers, come to take over by sheer numbers. (When the original version of this story ran in newspapers, it had the distinction of being the first *Barney Google and Snuffy Smith* continuity to be entirely written and drawn by Billy DeBeck's assistant, Fred Lasswell; after DeBeck's death, Lasswell inherited the entire strip and continued it for the rest of his life.)

The movie fleshes out this thread of a plot with several detours. It even manages to throw in a couple of comical songs, "Time's A-Wastin'" and "Snuffy Smith, the Yard Bird," warbled by Jimmie Dodd. An important subplot involves Dodd's invention of a new, improved range finder that falls into the hands of a pair of unscrupulous fifth columnists before Lowizie manages to capture them (and it). We should not forget the built-in complications when Ed Cooper the revenooer (Edgar Kennedy) becomes an army sergeant and has to contend with private Snuffy just as he did when they were both civilians. (Snuffy is equally outraged: "Balls o' fire! Takin' orders from a revenooer!") At one point, Snuffy hides from his nemesis inside a corn shock, but only Cooper's assistant sees the tepee-shaped pile of plants start to move away. "I know the liquor up here is potent," Cooper reprimands him, "but don't tell me the corn itself is strong enough to walk!" There is also some discussion of Snuffy's trusty shootin' iron, Ol' Tombstone. One moonshiner remarks, "That thar's th' only gun I ever seen that kills 'em an' buries 'em all at th' same time!"

Audiences apparently reacted favorably enough to *Private Snuffy Smith* for Monogram to forge ahead with its plans for a series. The second—and ultimately final—installment was *Hillbilly Blitzkrieg*, released later in 1942. Duncan and Kennedy returned in the two leading roles, and Dodd was back too, only this time he had no songs to perform and little else to do with the plot. Strangely, even though Kennedy was playing the same revenooer turned sergeant as in the first film, his name was changed from Ed Cooper to Homer Gatling. (We assume this was intended to remind people of the Gatling gun, not the Smokies resort town of Gatlinburg.)

Once again the story involves the army's need for a new secret weapon, this time a remote-controlled rocket developed by a typical absentminded professor and his beautiful daughter. For secrecy, they are holed up in a barn at Saddleback Lodge, deep in the Great Smokies, and Sergeant Gatling, Snuffy Smith, and other soldiers from the nearby camp are sent to guard the rocket and see that its planned demonstration for the War Department comes off without a hitch. Snuffy arrives first and discovers that the manager of Saddleback Lodge is none other than his cousin, Barney Google, played by Cliff Nazarro. This comedian's name is all but forgotten today, but in the 1930s and 1940s his voice was everywhere, as he had raised the concept of double-talk to a new art form. Nazarro had the unique ability to ramble on and on, with 80 percent of

The live-action Snuffy Smith movies ended suddenly after *Hillbilly Blitzkrieg* (1942). This time, Bud Duncan and Edgar Kennedy were joined by famed double-talk comedian Cliff Nazarro as Barney Google.

his speech being garbled nonsense words, generally confounding his friends and foes alike. Nazarro uses this routine in a couple of scenes as Google, but otherwise he remains fairly close to the comic strip version of the character: a hustler always on the lookout for a way to make a fast buck.

It seems that Google has invested a healthy sum of money in the professor's rocket, which needs only five hundred dollars more to be ready for the demonstration. Google's only remaining asset is his broken-down horse, Spark Plug, and he puts his nag up against a speedy army mule, P-40, with the stakes being the five hundred smackers and half ownership in the rocket. Unknown to Barney, Snuffy and the rest, Saddleback Lodge has been infiltrated by enemy agents (including the requisite femme fatale) out to get their clutches on the rocket, and they conspire to help the mule win and thus keep Barney from getting the needed funds. Their plan backfires, and the sleeping powders meant for Spark Plug end up in Sergeant Gatling's digestive system instead.

Things get desperate when the sarge hides Snuffy inside the rocket to guard it, just before the spies, having failed to hook it by crook, arrive to steal the device. In the ensuing battle (enemy agents versus Gatling, Google, and the professor), the rocket is launched into the stratosphere—a fact of which Snuffy is unaware until he climbs out of the hatch and finds himself soaring over the countryside at several thousand miles per hour. He rides the rocket as if it were a horse, repeatedly bellowing "LOWIZIEEEEEEEEE!!!!!!" to no avail (since Sarah Padden isn't in this picture). The War Department representatives are sufficiently impressed to purchase the plans for the rocket from Google and the professor, and all ends well.

Although we can all probably see the ending gag coming from a mile away, it is still funny. The professor's daughter wants a souvenir photo of Snuffy and Sergeant Gatling sitting astride the grounded rocket, and wouldn't you know that inside the barn, her father chooses that moment to accidentally hit the detonator again? The rocket again zooms into space with its two unwilling passengers holding on for dear life. Looking down, Snuffy comments, "Thar's

Pearl Harbor!" The sarge responds, "Yeah! Next stop, Tokyo!" as they disappear into the endless sky.

Hillbilly Blitzkrieg apparently generated a reaction far short of what Monogram was expecting, and plans for any further live-action Snuffy Smith movies (with or without Barney Google) were quickly scrapped. The Hootin' Holler gang would return to the printed page to await their next adaptation into the film medium, while Bud Duncan retired from the movies altogether. He died in 1960 at the age of seventy-seven.

While the war was still raging, Lum and Abner made one more film that had no direct connection with the conflict. *Goin' to Town* was released in 1944, and its publicity made much too much of a brief sequence in which the Pine Ridge storekeepers visit a posh nightclub and get roped into the floor show with a line of beautiful chorus girls. Seemingly every poster or ad for *Goin' to Town* emphasized this cheesecake aspect of the film, which was not unpleasant to watch but had little to do with the overall story. Perhaps the movie had more to do with the war than met the eye, and the girls were actually put in to boost the morale of the battle-weary servicemen.

From the standpoint of rural comedy history, the main feature of *Goin' to Town* is that it introduces a new actor in the role of Pine Ridge's canny con man, Squire Skimp, replacing O'Shea (who had been Squire in *The Bashful Bachelor* and in a single brief scene in *Two Weeks to Live*). The new Squire is our old friend from Dogpatch, Dick "Marryin' Sam" Elliott. Younger and more spry than O'Shea, who leaned heavily on a cane and walked with a noticeable limp, Elliott obviously tackled the character of Squire with much enthusiasm, and he continued playing variations on the role for the rest of his film and television career. This will not be the last time we encounter him in this book. After an absence of two films, Grady Sutton returned as Cedric Weehunt.

One type of movie that was hardly affected at all by wartime conditions was the Western. Now, what does that have to do with our subject of rural humor, you ask? The two approaches were at least somewhat related in that Westerns were certainly closer to being rural than urban. However, Western film historian David Rothel

Lum and Abner irritate town crook Squire Skimp (Dick Elliott) in *Goin' to Town* (1944). In the rear stands Cedric Weehunt (Grady Sutton); if this were Mayberry, he would probably be saying, "GAWWW-LEEE!"

had a real point when he summed up the key differences: "There was a vast difference in attitude in the minds of a lot of the audience toward Western and hillbilly. 'Western' translated into cowboy, with all the adventure of horses, ranches, cattle, wide open spaces and outlaws that was associated with cowboys. 'Hillbilly,' on the other hand, translated into rube country boys, stills in the hills, half-moon outhouses and the hills of the southeastern United States. Most kids (and adults, for that matter) wanted to be cowboys; few wanted to be hillbillies."

The many different types of comic sidekicks who bumbled their way through the Westerns of the 1940s included a few who crossed over that nearly invisible line between cowboy and hillbilly humor. Chief among these, for his name if for no other reason, was Arkansas Slim Andrews. He was probably the most "pure hillbilly" sidekick ever seen in Westerns, although others would come close. Andrews really did come from northwestern Arkansas, and in his youth he toured with traveling tent shows as a musician and comedian. A chance 1939 encounter with singer Tex Ritter led to Andrews's move to Hollywood and entry into Western films. In a shapeless felt hillbilly hat, Andrews rode through his scenes on a mule named Josephine. As he explained to Rothel, "My humor was mostly verbal; a lot of the comics developed expressions that they used in pictures. Gabby Hayes had his 'Yer durned tootin',' for example. I had 'Great gobs o' goose grease!' And when I would jump on Josephine, I'd say 'Hi ho, Josephine,' and whistle." Andrews sidekicked for Ritter in ten films released in 1940 and 1941, then served the same function for cowboys Tom Keene and Don "Red" Barry in 1941 and 1942. He continued making personal appearances with Ritter until 1950, when he decided to stay home nights and for a while hosted a local children's show in Los Angeles.

Among all the grizzled old prospector types who usually filled the sidekick role in Westerns, Andrews's nearest hillbilly approximation was Dub Taylor, who (in Rothel's words) "kept falling into horse troughs, stumbling into mudholes, having pails of water drop on his head, and generally cavorting in an imbecilic manner throughout a long list of screen credits." Die-hard Western fans such as Rothel rarely found anything to like about the more hillbilly sidekicks. He frankly admitted, "Dub's hillbilly accent was also overdone (at least for this writer's taste). His thick-as-molasses southern accent and occasionally mangled words were to his Western films what Leo Gorcey's Brooklyn accent and fractured English were to the Bowery Boys films. It is possible that they both could have cut back by half on their verbal abuses and still have come close to the border of excess." The naysayers notwithstanding, Dub Taylor and his sidekick shenanigans helped him make a living through ten years of Westerns between 1939 and 1949, in the company of such lantern-jawed, steely eyed heroes as Wild Bill Elliott, Russell Hayden, Charles Starrett, and Jimmy Wakely. Unlike Arkansas Slim Andrews, whose post-Western career mostly centered on local television, Taylor remained at the forefront in television rural comedies, where we shall next encounter him.

A number of Western sidekicks later modified their characterizations but slightly and became integral parts of the more accurately rural comedy tradition. Rufe Davis specialized in imitating barnyard animals and did so in fourteen films in Republic Pictures's Three Mesquiteers series between 1940 and 1942. Former song-and-dance man Buddy Ebsen served as a down-home sidekick for Rex Allen in 1950–51. Of course, we cannot forget that after his days with the *National Barn Dance*, Pat Buttram had do-si-doe'd out the door and hooked up with fellow WLS alumnus Gene Autry for a long string of movies and television shows. Other future rural comedy stars who got at least part of their training as Western sidekicks were Andy Clyde, Andy Devine, Horace Murphy, Slim Pickens, and Chill Wills. And then there was the king of all the sidekicks, Smiley Burnette, who later teamed with Rufe Davis and rode a certain train called the Cannonball into a remote TV outpost known as *Petticoat Junction*—but that was all far in the future.

Dub "Cannonball" Taylor was one of the Western movie sidekicks who went after more of a hillbilly or countrified image than a cowboy one. He parlayed his film roles into a highly successful string of personal appearances.

Former *National Barn Dance* comedian Pat Buttram (*left*) joined up with fellow WLS alumnus Gene Autry for a series of movies and eventually television shows beginning in 1948.

In addition to the sidekicks who received star billing along with the heroes, during the late 1930s Republic Pictures tried to cram another hick comic duo down the audience's collective throat. Billed in movie after movie as Oscar and Elmer, the pair was painfully unfunny to watch, but Republic apparently was determined to keep using them until someone—anyone!—laughed. Ed Platt was Oscar, whose dumb-as-a-dead-mule expression and monotone voice gave him little to work with in the comedy department. He still had it better than Lou (Elmer) Fulton, whose main business was to talk rapidly with a stutter that rendered half of his dialogue unintelligible. The unlikely imbeciles were brought in for brief scenes in such Republic productions as *The Old Corral* (1936, with Autry and Burnette) and the serial based on the comic strip *Dick Tracy* (1937). They made their final joint appearances in 1938, but Fulton managed to survive unscathed to appear in bit parts throughout the war years. Fortunately for the reputation of rural comedy, they are mostly forgotten today.

As the war began to wind down, the Columbia cartoon studio decided that it would give hillbilly humor one more chance. You will recall that this was the same studio that had birthed the first round of *Barney Google and Snuffy Smith* cartoons in 1935–36, but since Monogram had already tried and failed with the two-episode series of live-action Snuffy films, Columbia was not anxious to revisit that territory. They might as well have, though, because ultimately they chose to base their new series on *Li'l Abner*, and the resulting films made the 1940 live-action *Abner* production look like a masterpiece.

Columbia did not seem to know how to get in sync with the fertile brain of Al Capp, as just about everything in its *Li'l Abner* cartoons strayed as far as possible from the type of humor and satire that made the newspaper strip so popular. The deformed-looking character designs were not helped at all by the fact that the *Li'l Abner* cartoons featured, frankly, some of the worst voice work in the history of the medium. None of the voice actors were credited, and their identification has escaped even the most diligent animation researchers. It seems fairly apparent by listening to the sound tracks that Daisy Mae and Mammy Yokum were voiced by the same actress, but Li'l Abner's high-pitched, nasal whine sounds like a bad imitation of Pat Buttram. Occasional minor roles seem to have been played by Frank Graham, who was toiling away in Columbia's much more successful *Fox and Crow* cartoons of the period (as well as playing a multitude of incidental characters on *Lum and Abner*).

Perhaps Columbia's contract with Capp was valid only for a specific period of time, because all five films in the *Li'l Abner* series were ground out during a period between March 1944 and the end of the year. The first, *Amoozin' but Confoozin'*, may have been the weakest and most disjointed of the batch, certainly not a prime way to launch a new series. Abner complains that he is "sick an' tarred" of life in Dogpatch and hops a train to the big city to get some culture. He returns with a new invention that he is certain will lead to a better way of life for his fellow citizens: a bathtub. In one of the film's few funny moments, an undershirt-clad, fly-infested Dogpatcher

Columbia had high hopes for its series of *Li'l Abner* cartoons in 1944, but they completely failed to capture the flavor of the newspaper strip. Al Capp was reportedly horrified when he saw them.

roars indignantly, "Air you-all sayin' we is DIRTY?" Abner's fellow citizens soon have become a lynch mob, and he escapes with life and limb intact only through the superhuman efforts of Mammy Yokum. (The animators evidently decided to pattern Mammy's screen role after Popeye—she even "toot toots" her corncob pipe before springing into action.) To her credit, the animated Daisy Mae is even more alluring than Martha O'Driscoll in the live-action role; the artists obviously spent many hours working on the details of her anatomy. In future films, Daisy's design would be simplified to eliminate such tedious labor—probably much to the animators' dismay.

Sadie Hawkins Day was the second release, and it plays like an extended version of the race sequence from the 1940 film. It even repeats the same gag of Hairless Joe and Lonesome Polecat attempting in vain to get caught. Marryin' Sam makes his only animated appearance, sounding not like Squire Skimp or Dick Elliott but like the Lucky Strike tobacco auctioneer on Jack Benny's radio show. Mammy Yokum uses all of her powers to help her darlin' boy stay out of Daisy Mae's grasp, although in future stories she became determined to see Abner settle down and get married. The third installment, *A Pee-Koo-Lyar Sitch-ee-Ashun,* adds little that is new or unique but at least gives Daisy Mae a chance to shine as she attempts to make Abner jealous by romancing Disgustin' Jones (an appropriate moniker if there ever was one).

In *Porkuliar Piggy,* the Yokum family swine, Salomey, wanders too far from the cabin and falls prey to a bizarrely designed butcher whose truck blatantly advertises his specialty, pork sausage. Of course, Abner comes to the rescue, but Mammy has to rescue both the rescuer and the oinking rescuee. The villainous butcher ends up hanging on a meat hook, pummeled by one of his own sides of beef. In a sure sign that the series had already run out of steam, Abner and Daisy Mae were featured only briefly in the final installment, *Kickapoo Juice.* Most of the footage is devoted to an extended chase in which Mammy tries to confiscate Hairless Joe's and Lonesome Polecat's gargantuan tub of Kickapoo Joy Juice. The potent stuff finally falls to earth and turns Dogpatch into the Grand Canyon.

And thus endeth Li'l Abner's latest film career, but never fear—the Dogpatch denizens would be back at the end of the 1950s, and this time someone would finally get it right.

The explosion of rural comedies in the immediate postwar years, in all media, would at least rival that caused by the mishandling of Kickapoo Joy Juice. In our next chapter we shall take a look at what happened when peacetime returned and how it gave them thar hillbillies a chance to go back to blastin' each other instead of worrying about a war in some fer-off furrin country, by cracky.

Chapter Five

Peace in the Valley

After the war ended in August 1945, the entertainment industry had to retool itself to resume peacetime production. The returning soldiers immediately set to work producing a bumper crop of children, which would lead to the well-known baby boom that lasted until the early 1960s. The former soldiers had been exposed to much less restrictive forms of entertainment while overseas—both foreign productions and American ones that operated under a more relaxed form of censorship—and some postwar movies, even cartoons, consequently became sexier and slightly less uptight than had previously been the case.

With most of the former rural movie stars, including Bob Burns and the Weaver Brothers and Elviry, having gone back to the hills during the war, live-action features took a while to rediscover hillbillies as a source of humor. Animated cartoons still thrived on such caricatures, though, and they soon prepared for the brave new world.

Back in the late 1930s, we saw a pair of Betty Boop cartoons produced by Max and Dave Fleischer and released through Paramount. During the early war years, Paramount had elected to evict the Fleischers and reorganize its animation department as a new entity, Famous Studios. Many of the animators, story staff, and other personnel remained the same. In 1946, Famous Studios made yet another in the string of attempts to drag *Barney Google and Snuffy Smith* kicking and screaming from the newspaper page to the movie screen, and the result was a single cartoon short, *Spree for All.* This film has become legendary among animation historians if for no other reason than the fact that no one has ever seen it. Somehow, while most other Famous Studios cartoons of the era are available in one form or another, *Spree for All* has seemingly disappeared entirely; the only thing known about its plot is that it involved Snuffy's return to Hootin' Holler after his wartime service. That's it. Cartoon fans would have to wait until the television era to enjoy a more visible series of Snuffy Smith cartoons.

When the Fleischers departed their own studio, most of the characters they had created (such as Betty Boop) were consigned to the film cans as well. However, the Fleischers' biggest hit series was not one that that they had created. They had been producing *Popeye the Sailor* cartoons since 1933, licensed from King Features Syndicate and probably the most successful animated cartoons ever to be based on a newspaper strip (to the point that many people today know Popeye only from his cartoons, not from the original print source). Famous Studios was not about to let such a profitable franchise get away, continuing the Popeye series well into the late 1950s. In 1949, studio officials decided to combine the usual Popeye/Olive Oyl/Bluto cast with hillbilly images: the result was *Silly Hillbilly*.

The basic idea was more than a little reminiscent of Betty Boop's *Be Up to Date* (1939). Traveling salesman Popeye arrives deep in the Ozarks (or the Ouachitas or the Great Smokies or somewhar like that) with his "rolling department store." His first customer is a hillbilly version of Bluto, who manages to destroy or misinterpret every piece of "modern" merchandise he sees: he uses a radiator as an accordion, gives himself a shave with an egg beater, stretches out a corset to use as a hammock, and uses the cuckoo clock display as a shooting gallery. Popeye is just about to give him what fer when the hillbilly Olive arrives, looking for all the world like Daisy Mae without the microshorts (they probably wouldn't have looked good on her, anyway). Olive is looking for the department store's "beautyfyin' saloon," and Popeye soon gives her the works, converting her from dowdy to hillbilly slick chick.

Bluto is naturally enraged by all this attention to his girl and takes the direct approach, grabbing a huge mallet and flattening

Popeye into a bull's-eye, which he hangs on a nearby tree before shouting to his sleeping mountaineer cronies, "Hey, yo' critturs! Target practice!" While a dozen or so rustics fire at the target, Bluto resumes chasing Olive through the store, as she refers to him as "yo' backwoods baboon!" The target formerly known as Popeye gets to his spinach and quickly resumes his 3-D appearance. He returns the hillbillies to their eternal sleep and dashes to rescue Olive. He finds Bluto going after her with a vacuum cleaner. Popeye wallops the bucolic boob into a washing machine, where he can be pulverized by the agitators for the rest of his borned days.

While studios such as Famous were thriving in the late 1940s, the kingpin of them all, Walt Disney, was struggling. The war had rendered impractical the expensive animated features that had brought Disney fame in the late 1930s, and the whole studio seemed enveloped in a general malaise. One solution, just to get something out there before the public, was to produce features that were in reality just collections of short subjects, stitched together like an animated Frankenstein's monster. The first film to follow this format was *Make Mine Music,* released in April 1946. It featured ten unrelated sections featuring the musical and acting talents of such luminaries as Benny Goodman, Dinah Shore, Nelson Eddy, and Jerry Colonna, among others. The first of the ten segments, "The Martins and the Coys," was based on a 1936 song by Ted Werems and Al Cameron and looks much like what would have resulted had Disney rather than Columbia animated *Li'l Abner.*

"The Martins and the Coys" is performed by the King's Men, a quartet then best known for appearing weekly on *Fibber McGee and Molly.* As they describe in the opening lyrics, "The Martins an' the Coys, they wuz reckless mountain boys / An' they took up family feudin' when they'd meet (ever' durn time)." The animation bears this out, as the bearded hillbillies spend every waking hour either drinking moonshine or blasting away at their rivals. Finally, all the combatants on both sides are dead and sitting around on clouds in the heavens, with only a sole survivor on each side. These lone strangers are Grace Martin (a dead ringer for Daisy Mae) and Henry Coy, of whom Disney historian John Grant has said, "He looks like

The Walt Disney Studios' *Make Mine Music* (1946) featured, among its nine other segments, an animated rendition of the popular hillbilly tune "The Martins and the Coys."

he might have difficulty finding two brain cells to rub together"—and that's putting it generously. As one might expect, the two of them fall in love, much to the outrage of their deceased ancestors watching from above.

But never fear—the dearly departed have the last laugh. Grace and Henry marry, and the final scene shows their tiny love nest in the hills fairly exploding as they give each other a whuppin,' Henry finding out that Grace's good right arm is a formidable foe. The King's Men explain in their song that Henry and Grace "carried on the feud jes' like before," and so the segment ends. In recent years, when the Disney company has released *Make Mine Music* on both video and DVD, many fans have commented on the fact that the "Martins and the Coys" segment is mysteriously missing. Some speculate that the company is afraid of offending real hillbillies (who, in any case, frequently do not have DVD players in their mountain shacks), but a more realistic assumption is that all the gunplay and, yes, human deaths just do not go along with the image Disney wishes to present in these changed times. As far as we know, Grace and Henry are still beating each other to a pulp—you just can't see them doing it on the screen any more.

The Warner Bros. cartoons, after having hillbillied themselves nearly to death during the 1930s, did not return to the trend during the late 1940s. They did so during the next decade, but during the immediate postwar years their biggest contribution to the rural film library was the series starring the loudmouth rooster Foghorn Leghorn.

As people at the time would have realized, but it is almost unknown today, both Foghorn's name and his voice (one of Mel Blanc's funniest) were based on Kenny Delmar's characterization of Senator Claghorn on Fred Allen's radio show, which we visited briefly back in chapter 2. Claghorn was a quintessentially southern figure ("When Ah'm in New York, Ah never go through the Lincoln Tunnel!") but not necessarily a rural one. Likewise, Foghorn Leghorn's only claim to rural humor was that most of his episodes were set in the barnyard, hearkening back to *Farmer Al Falfa* and the early Disney output. Beginning with *Walky Talky Hawky* in 1946,

Singin' in the Corn (1946) was Judy Canova's only movie released between the end of World War II and the early 1950s.

the Foghorn series continued for the next fourteen years. As if to point up the difference between Foghorn's personality and that of truly "rural" stereotypes, in one late entry, *The Dixie Fryer* (1960), the Kentucky fried chicken goes south for the winter—leaving to speculation about what part of the country he normally lives in—and becomes the intended target of a pair of hillbilly chicken hawks.

The only prewar rural comics who were still making movies in the last half of the decade were Judy Canova and Lum and Abner. Canova barely counts, because between the war's end and the early 1950s, she concentrated almost totally on her radio work and turned out only one film, *Singin' in the Corn* (1946). It pointed the way toward the direction her movies would take in the future, because even though she retained the same look and mannerisms that had become familiar over the past decade, the setting for her adventures had shifted from the true hill country to the West. *Singin' in the Corn* involves mobsters who plan to turn Canova's ancestral

In *Partners in Time* (1946), Chester Lauck (*right*) and Norris Goff appeared without their old-age makeup to portray the young Lum and Abner of 1904. Pamela Blake played Abner's fiancée, Lizzabeth.

hometown—which she has just inherited—into the new Las Vegas or Reno, indicating that the locale is supposed to be Nevada. In the next chapter we will see how this odd blending of the southern hills and the western frontier resulted in some even odder films for Canova and her trademark pigtails.

Lum and Abner had one more film to make under their contract with RKO, and *Partners in Time* was released in the spring of 1946. It was by far the most "serious" story they had done since *Dreaming Out Loud* (1940), having the two old codgers relate the story of how they started their Jot 'Em Down Store. While Lauck and Goff appeared in their usual makeup for the framing sequences, in which Lum and Abner try to foil Squire (Dick Elliott) Skimp's latest scheme while simultaneously patching up a lovers' spat between a local couple (Teala Loring and John James), the true novelty came in the extensive flashbacks, in which they played the young Lum and Abner of 1904 by simply appearing as they looked in everyday life and speaking in their natural voices. The result was a truly heartwarming story, but it did beg the question as to what happened to Abner's grasp of the English language as the years wore on. As a young man, he states, "Yes, Elizabeth and I are to be married next week," but in the present day he cackles, "Yep, me an' Lizzabeth's bin married fer forty years!" (The young Elizabeth of 1904 is played by beautiful Pamela Blake, but no attempt is made to age her with makeup for the 1946 scenes, so, just as in the radio program, she is talked about but not seen.) Grady Sutton makes his final screen appearance as Cedric; for the 1904 sequences, he appears with oversized waxed mustache as Cedric's father, who is just as simple-minded as his progeny.

Although *Partners in Time* would be Lum and Abner's final movie for almost a decade—and when we get to their final final one, it's quite a different story—their radio show was still going strong. The most important addition to the cast in the immediate postwar years was Clarence Hartzell, who had gained tremendous popularity on the daytime comedy serial *Vic and Sade* as the eccentric Uncle Fletcher. (As we have seen, he was also Pappy Yokum in the 1939 radio version of *Li'l Abner* as well as a regular on *Uncle Ezra's Radio Station.*) *Vic and Sade* ended in 1944. In 1946, Hartzell moved from Chicago to the West Coast with the cast of another radio sitcom, *Those Websters*, and when Lauck and Goff found out that he was available, they immediately arranged to have him written into the show. Hartzell played a variation of Uncle Fletcher known this time as Ben Withers. Introduced in November 1946 as the new Pine Ridge veterinarian, Withers continued the Uncle Fletcher tradition by never listening to what anyone was saying, constantly responding with either "Fine" or "Yes," whether appropriate or not. He also interrupted whatever action was taking place to narrate long, drawn-out anecdotes about his old cronies over in Mount Idy. (Like most place-names used on *Lum and Abner*, Mount Ida was a real town. It was located about eighteen miles east of the real Pine Ridge and served as the county seat of Montgomery County.)

Ben: I recall attending an Easter egg roll on the Zinkafoose lawn in Mt. Idy one year . . . It was quite a traditional thing with the Zinkafoose family. I recall this one particularly well. There were the two Zinkafoose boys, Herbert and Kenneth, all dressed up in their sailor suits and straw hats . . .

Lum: Ben, I wonder if you'd 'scuse us, me an' Abner's got a awful lot o' work ta do . . .

Ben: Fine. Well, the egg roll started off in the traditional fashion, with Kenneth rollin' the egg to Herbert and then Herbert rollin' it back to Kenneth.

Abner: Well, sounds like fun.

Ben: Then th' old man, Mr. Zinkafoose, joined the festivities. He caught up the egg an' rolled it first to Kenneth and then once to Herbert . . .

Lum: What'd they do, jist have one egg?

Ben: Fine. Then their mother, Miz Zinkafoose, gaily rushed out onto the lawn to catch up the egg, but she stepped on a croquet ball and broke her hip and had to be carried out of the fun.

Abner: Oh, hit's a shame she had ta miss out on all that fun.

Ben: Well, the nice part of it was, the Zinkafooses put on this same traditional ceremony every year at Easter.

Abner: Ever' year?! Musta been hard on Miz Zinkafoose.

Ben: Fine.

While writer Roswell Rogers was busy thinking up new old friends for Ben Withers and how to incorporate them into *Lum and Abner* story lines, he somehow found the time to write scripts for yet another sitcom starring a rural comic, *The Opie Cates Show*. A native of microscopic Clinton, Arkansas (a prophetic name for a town if there ever was one), Opie Cates was a virtuoso clarinet player who had been part of a number of groups during the big band era and had eventually gone out on his own as a bandleader. He had served for a time on Judy Canova's radio show, but as a rule he only provided the orchestra music and did not actually speak on the air. One night, for some now-forgotten series, Cates introduced a few

Clarence Hartzell (*center*), formerly Uncle Fletcher of *Vic and Sade* and Pappy Yokum of the *Li'l Abner* radio show, joined the cast of *Lum and Abner* in November 1946. Here he amuses Lauck and Goff with one of his endless stories about the strange residents of Mount Idy.

of his band's numbers. The studio audience found his soft-spoken Arkansas drawl extremely funny, laughing uproariously at his otherwise-unfunny introductions, and some network executive got the idea that perhaps they had a budding Bob Burns on their hands.

The Opie Cates Show debuted as a sustaining series (that is, with no sponsor) on CBS in October 1947. Most of the cast and behind-the-scenes personnel were *Lum and Abner* veterans, including Roswell Rogers. Cates played himself, a naive and not-terribly-bright recent arrival in the big city, and his sweetheart (at least as far as he was concerned), Katherine Brown, was played by busy radio actress Barbara Fuller, who was better known for drama than comedy. (She enjoyed a long run with the epic serial *One Man's Family*; in one continuity during that show's history, she played opposite Clarence Hartzell as the family's visiting Cousin Jediah.) Katherine's father and Opie's boss, insurance company executive Mr. Brown, was expertly played by Francis X. Bushman, whose many appearances on *Lum and Abner*

Orchestra leader Opie Cates of Clinton, Arkansas, starred in his own radio sitcom in 1947. Featured in the cast was busy actress Barbara Fuller as Cates's unrequited love interest, Katherine Brown.

had demonstrated a flair for comic timing not previously evident in his career as a matinee idol of the silent movie era.

At the opening of each show, Cates delivered his trademark catchphrase, "The doggonedest thing happened to me th' other day," and the rest of the episode would set out to prove him correct. Perhaps it was just too late in radio's history for a new rural sitcom to make any sort of impression on the audience, because the series was certainly funny enough and impeccable in its cast members and their delivery of the dialogue, but for whatever reason *The Opie Cates Show* left the air after thirteen weeks. Undaunted, Cates would be heard from again within just a few months.

While the radio comedians were still holding down the ether, at least for as long as they could, in 1947 the movies suddenly brought forth what would become that medium's greatest rural comedy success. It actually had its beginning a couple of years earlier, with the 1945 publication of *The Egg and I,* author Betty MacDonald's wryly humorous account of her life as the wife of an amateur chicken farmer in the Olympic Mountains of Washington. The book was such a runaway best seller that it was a natural to be adapted for the movies, and Universal released the film version in 1947. It starred Fred MacMurray and Claudette Colbert as Bob and Betty, the city slickers turned farmers, and had a number of plot elements that did not appear in the book (which was more like a diary than a true novel). The flawless performances of the stars aside, however, much of the audience's attention seemed to be focused on a pair of supporting characters, Ma and Pa Kettle.

The Kettles, as they appeared in the original book, were a composite of families MacDonald had known during her years on the chicken ranch. In fact, several of those families reportedly recognized their characteristics and tried to sue MacDonald for libel after her book became such a hit. Be that as it may, the printed-page Kettles were relatively minor characters and were far more coarse than they would be portrayed on film. As MacDonald described Ma, for example,

> Mrs. Kettle had pretty light brown hair, only faintly streaked with gray and skinned back into a tight knot, clear blue eyes, a creamy skin which flushed exquisitely with the heat, a straight delicate nose, fine even white teeth, and a small rounded chin. From this dainty pretty head cascaded a series of busts and stomachs which made her look like a cooky jar shaped like a woman. Her whole front was dirty and spotted and she wiped her hands continually on one or the other of her stomachs. She had also a disconcerting habit of reaching up under her dress and adjusting something in the vicinity of her navel and of reaching down the front of her dress and adjusting her large breasts. These adjustments were not, I learned later, confined to either the privacy of the house or a female gathering.

MacDonald wrote that Pa Kettle was "a lazy, lisping sonofabitch," and his role in her book was, if anything, even more minor than his wife's. He had "a thick patch of stiff gray hair quite obviously cut at home with a bowl, perched on top of which he wore a black derby hat. He had a tremendous flowing mustache generously dotted with crumbs, a neckline featuring several layers of dirty underwear and sweaters, and bib overalls tucked into his black rubber hip boots." According to MacDonald, the Kettles had fifteen children, of which seven still lived at home in varying stages of imbecility, drunkenness, or both. One of their married daughters was unpretentiously known as Tits. The Kettles obviously would need to clean up their act to get past the movie censors of the late 1940s.

As they were portrayed in the final version of the film, Ma and Pa Kettle and their numerous children—so numerous that Ma keeps calling various ones by the wrong names—come off as a sort of mirror image of the maverick MacDonalds. Their main sources of humor are their slovenly wreck of a farm (complete with sign on the gate, "Beware of Childrun") and Pa's penchant for "borrowing" things from his neighbors. To prove that not everything about the film was goofy comedy, both of these gags later provide some genuinely touching moments; in one scene, Ma explains to Betty how she used to keep her house as neat as a pin until she married Pa and had all those kids, after which cleanliness just didn't seem as important any more. Later, after Betty and Bob lose most of their farm in a raging fire (started by the explosion of Pa Kettle's still, igniting his barn and the surrounding countryside), the entire community shows up with supplies to help them rebuild. The Kettles arrive with their wagon full of young 'uns, bearing not only everything Pa has borrowed but more besides.

The Kettles managed to be more than one-joke characters because of the casting of the roles. Ma was played by Marjorie Main, a large, gravel-voiced actress who had been kicking around Hollywood for a long time and who was equally well known for her dramatic roles as for comedy. Pa was Percy Kilbride, whose career had followed a different path. As a Broadway character actor, he had carved out his first niche in the play *George Washington Slept Here,* yet another plot involving a city couple trying to adjust to life in the rural countryside. Kilbride played Mr. Kimble, the caretaker of the couple's newly purchased property, which had supposedly served as a staging area during the Revolutionary War. When Warner Bros. decided to cast Jack Benny in the lead role for the movie version, Benny traveled to New York to watch the play and was overwhelmed by Kilbride's underplayed performance. Benny insisted that Kilbride be brought to Hollywood to play Kimble in the film, and many takes reportedly were ruined because Benny could not stop laughing at Kilbride's dry New Englander delivery of his lines. (Kilbride also made a handful of appearances on Benny's radio show during the first half of 1942, apparently while the movie was being filmed.)

Universal's 1947 feature film version of Betty MacDonald's best seller *The Egg and I* introduced the moviegoing public to the characters of Ma and Pa Kettle.

Universal knew it had something special with Main and Kilbride, prominently giving the team solo screen credit immediately following that for stars Colbert and MacMurray. Two years after *The Egg and I* was released, the studio decided that the Kettle family was good enough for its own starring vehicle, which was released in 1949 as simply *Ma and Pa Kettle.* As the story opens, some of the citizens of Cape Flattery, Washington, are demanding that the city condemn the Kettle property because it is such an eyesore. Chief among these is Birdie Hicks, the town busybody, who was introduced in a few brief scenes in *The Egg and I.* Just as it looks like the whole Kettle clan is going to be evicted, word comes out that Pa has won a contest sponsored by the King Henry tobacco company. Pa sent in a rhyming jingle to the company's slogan competition because each entrant was promised a brand-new tobacco pouch. Not only does Pa get the pouch, but the whole family is awarded a brand-new, modern "house of the future" with state-of-the-art technology. To celebrate, the elderly Kettles reenact a memo-

After making their screen debut as Ma and Pa Kettle in *The Egg and I*, Marjorie Main and Percy Kilbride went on to play their Olympic Mountain characters in films throughout the 1950s.

rable moment from their honeymoon: Ma carries Pa over the threshold.

Of course, much comedy ensues as the Kettles try to adjust to their new way of living. Pa gets his face sunburned by the sun lamps in the bathroom, and the kids accidentally lock him in the clothes dryer, where the suit he is wearing shrinks to minuscule size. Insanely jealous of all the attention her rivals are getting, Birdie Hicks thinks she has uncovered evidence that Pa copied his winning tobacco slogan from a nearly identical one on a local salesman's giveaway calendars. Just as the sheriff arrives to evict the family (and Ma and the kids prepare for war), it turns out that the salesman copied the slogan from Pa's winning entry, and the family gets to remain in the new home. A subplot involves the Kettles' oldest son, Tom, the first member of the family to go to college. He has an on-again, off-again romance with Kim Parker, a cute magazine writer who plans to document the Kettle family's rise from poverty to prosperity. In the final scene, it appears the romance is on again permanently, as Tom and Kim get married—a plot device that will figure in future installments.

One truly unique thing about the Ma and Pa Kettle movies is that they were presented as a sort of continuing serial in feature-length form. During the wedding scene at the end of *Ma and Pa Kettle*, Pa receives another telegram. Now it seems that he has won another jingle contest, this time sponsored by a soft drink company, and the whole family will be taking a trip to New York. The film ends on this note of promise, which will be fulfilled in the next movie—and in our next chapter.

Meanwhile, though, in those days when radio was getting ready to give way to television—only it didn't know that just yet—half-hour situation comedies had become the norm. *Lum and Abner* was one of the few comedies still being heard in daily fifteen-minute installments, especially after *Amos 'n' Andy* had been retooled into a weekly half-hour sitcom in 1943. In September 1948, *Lum and Abner* carried one final continued story line that involved the two storekeepers plus Grandpappy Spears, Cedric Weehunt, and Ben Withers bumbling their way through a visit to Las Vegas. At the end of that continuity, the long-running pair announced to listeners that the show would become a Sunday night half hour on CBS.

The new weekly *Lum and Abner* show, sponsored by Frigidaire, premiered on October 3, 1948 (after a "preview" episode the week before, in which Lum and Abner themselves made only a brief appearance at the end). It was immediately apparent that the carefully crafted world of Pine Ridge had to be sacrificed in favor of verbal gags that would get a reaction from the live studio audience, a feature with which the show had not contended since the early 1930s days of the "Friday Night Sociables." Roswell Rogers remained in charge of writing the scripts, although by now he had taken on a writing partner, Betty Boyle. Her function in the creation of the show remains somewhat hazy, but it is a fact that Boyle was one of the very few female comedy writers working in radio at the time. The new *Lum and Abner* scripts were funny, but not in the same homespun vein that had served the show so well. The Pine Ridge pair frequently came across as bucolic Bob Hopes, spewing out smart-aleck remarks based on current news events:

Lum: You know, by rights we orten't to be playin' checkers durin' store hours.

Abner: Ah-ah-ah, you cain't move that man ther, that's cheatin'.

Lum: I am not, I'm playin' jes' like you do.

Abner: Oh ho, so ya admit it, huh? Now, watch me . . . ther! Right inta yore king row! I doggies, it took me a long time but I finally got mysef a king.

Lum: Yeah, now you know how Princess Elizabeth feels.

In the early half-hour episodes, some of the Lauck and Goff supporting characters, mainly Cedric and Squire Skimp, from the past continued to appear. Clarence Hartzell also continued as Ben Withers, although he was usually no longer a vital part of the story; he was typically brought into each show for a scene in which he could slow down the action with another of his endless Mount Idy stories. The supporting cast included some of the best character actors in radio, with veterans such as Herbert Rawlinson, Gloria Blondell, Joseph Kearns, and Ken Christy appearing over and over again. Former Western movie sidekick Horace Murphy, who had occasionally appeared during the fifteen-minute days, played Ezra Seestrunk. Isabel Randolph, best known as snooty Mrs. Uppington on *Fibber McGee and Molly*, was Ezra's cousin, Rowena, on whom Lum had one of his many romantic crushes. In a truly odd bit of crossover in the world of rural comedy, town spinster and busybody Sister Simpson was played by Vivian Lasswell, whose nephew, Fred Lasswell, was gainfully occupied writing and drawing the *Barney Google and Snuffy Smith* comic strip at the time.

Only a few months into the new series' run, it became obvious that quite a large portion of its staff was not happy with it. Norris Goff later went on record as frankly admitting he hated every minute of the new show. Chet Lauck took a more benign view but also had to acknowledge that the new format was "Lum and Abner in name only." Clarence Hartzell had never liked the idea of performing before a live audience, and as a result, Ben Withers unexpectedly left the cast in March 1949. Brought in to fill the gap left by his absence was Opie Cates, no doubt at Roswell Rogers's recommendation. Cates took on the position of laconic storyteller, although his routines involved his real-life hometown of Clinton rather than Mount Idy.

At about the same time Hartzell left Pine Ridge as Cates moved into town, the show also debuted Andy Devine, a friend of Lauck's and Goff's since their move to Hollywood in 1937, in the role of town barber Mose Moots. This was yet another of the characters who had often been talked about but never heard in the fifteen-minute shows. Devine certainly changed that, with his rasp of a voice that

Abner described in one show as sounding like "a bulldozer with stripped gears tryin' to climb its way outa a gravel pit." Veteran screen comic ZaSu Pitts, who had previously appeared alongside Lum and Abner in *The Bashful Bachelor* (1942), was introduced as "Miss Pitts of the County Home Economics Bureau," constantly dropping not-so-subtle hints regarding her desires for Lum. *Scattergood Baines* comic relief Dink Trout was also added to the weekly cast in early 1949 as Luke Spears, the owner of the local restaurant, every bit as ornery as the characters he had played during the fifteen-minute series.

By the end of the first season in June 1949, the show was in trouble. The ratings were sinking, and even steadfastly loyal Roswell Rogers decided he could no longer go on turning out this bastardized version of *Lum and Abner*. When the show returned in the fall for its second and final half-hour season, Betty Boyle remained on the writing staff but had a new partner, Jay Sommers.

Frigidaire opted not to continue its sponsorship for the second season, so *Lum and Abner* joined the ranks of sustaining shows. The leaner budget was immediately apparent, as the large casts of supporting actors virtually vanished. Most episodes involved only Lauck, Goff, and their core cast of Devine, Trout, Cates, and Pitts. One major unexplained change was that in this second season, Devine still played the town barber but was no longer referred to as Mose Moots; he simply used his own name instead.

On the November 30, 1949, broadcast, the show had one of its few guest stars for that period, up-and-coming singer/actor Tennessee Ernie Ford. Outside of his hit recording of the song "Mule Train," which figured heavily into the plot of the show, Ford was known primarily in the southern California area, where he served as the disk jockey for a show on station KXLA. There the Bristol, Tennessee, native developed the twangy hillbilly voice characterization that would serve him so well in the future. Alongside this exaggerated dialect, Lum and Abner's voices sounded almost normal. One piece of dialogue from their joint appearance shows just how far the writers' concept of the characters had slipped:

Lum: Now look here, Tennessee, or Ernie, or whatever yore name is . . .

Ernie: Hit's Tennessee Ernie. They call me that 'cause I was borned in Georgy.

Lum: Well, why don't they call you Georgia Ernie, then?

Ernie: That'd be silly.

Lum: Well, tonight yo're gonna be singin' grand opera.

Ernie: I kin sing ennything.

Lum: Well, hit ain't so much the way you sing, hit's the way you talk. You sound so country. Grannies, ther ain't hardly time, but I'm gonna give you some lessons. You need some elocution. You know what elocution is?

Ernie: I ort to, I lost my daddy an' two brothers that way!

Lum: No, I mean try sayin' this . . . A, E, I, O, U.

Ernie: A, E, I, O, y'all.

Lum: "You all?"

Ernie: I told ye I wuz borned in Georgy!

Any time Lum and Abner were unfamiliar with southern terminology, it must be time to quit—and it was. Although the Ford Motor Company picked up sponsorship of a few half-hour *Lum and Abner* shows in the spring of 1950, the season ended early, with the final broadcast on April 26, 1950, nineteen years to the day since Lauck and Goff had introduced their rustic characters on KTHS in Hot Springs. During the final month of the series' tortured run, a new cast member was brought into the mix. It didn't help save the show, but it would certainly have far-reaching effects in the world of rural comedy.

Cliff Arquette had been knocking around radio since the 1930s, specializing in playing old men. He had been on *Fibber McGee and Molly* as the Old-Timer (a role later popularized by Bill Thompson) and was featured prominently on *Point Sublime* and *Glamor Manor*, among many other series. (On *Glamor Manor*, he added to his elderly repertoire by playing hypochondriac Mrs. Wilson, another character he revived from time to time over the years.) He had also been among the many rural radio comedians featured in Bob Burns's 1940 film *Comin' 'round the Mountain.* When he hooked up with *Lum and Abner* in April 1950, he continued using his "old man" voice, but like Devine and Pitts, he was simply called by his own name. In one show, he described the shenanigans at a recent party at the old folks' home:

> *Cliff*: Well sir, I don't like to brag, but did Louella Attlebury make a play fer me. First she winked at me, and I winked back . . . she winked at me again, I winked back . . . She winked, I winked . . .
>
> *Abner*: Yeah? Then what happened?
>
> *Cliff*: Nothin', we was both tuckered out from winkin'.

As we shall learn once we enter the television portion of this book, Arquette took some valuable information away from his brief period in Pine Ridge, most importantly the name Mount Idy. We'll see if we can get a letter from him a few chapters from now and see what's going on.

Cliff Arquette had been playing old men (and sometimes old ladies) on various radio shows since the 1930s. In 1950, he spent a brief time on *Lum and Abner*, where he first encountered the town of Mount Idy.

After the demise of the half-hour version of *Lum and Abner*, Lauck and Goff had plenty of leisure time, but their ex-staffers could not afford to take such luxuries. Writer Jay Sommers got down to brass typewriters and created a new rural-themed series to run as a thirteen-week summer replacement on CBS. His new brainchild was *Granby's Green Acres*, the saga of a city slicker who fulfills his lifelong dream of buying a farm in the country and attempts to reconcile his rose-colored ideas of rural living with its harsher realities. (Observers have speculated that Sommers was likely influenced by both *The Egg and I* and a 1942 book, *Acres and Pains*, by S. J. Perelman.) Gale Gordon, radio's master of the slow burn, starred as John Granby, with the extraordinary Bea Benaderet as his long-suffering wife. Louise Erickson played their daughter, and Parley Baer was their middle-aged hired man, Eb. Much of the humor came from Eb's skeptical attempts to help Granby learn the intricacies of farm life:

> *Eb*: Need some help with the milkin', Mr. Granby?
>
> *Granby*: No thanks, I've been milking this cow for three months and I think I can manage . . . Now let's see, where do I start . . .
>
> *Eb*: The best place is somewheres between the tail and the head.
>
> *Granby*: Very funny. Oh yes, here it is . . . hmm, there seems to be a problem . . . she's not giving anything.
>
> *Eb*: Mind if I make a suggestion? Use both hands.
>
> *Granby*: I AM using both hands!
>
> *Eb*: Yeah, but not on the same faucet.

Music for *Granby's Green Acres* was composed and conducted by Opie Cates, who did not appear on the show in a speaking role. Much of the rest of the supporting cast was drawn from *Lum and Abner*'s list. In the premiere episode, the role of hilariously absent-minded storekeeper Mr. Kimball was played by Howard McNear; for some reason, in the episodes that followed, the part was essayed by Horace Murphy. *Granby's Green Acres* ran for its allotted thirteen weeks during the summer of 1950 and then vanished from the CBS schedule. It was quickly forgotten by the public, but not by Jay Sommers, who eventually found a reason to dust off his concept and try it again. That would be fifteen years down the country road, though.

Rural sitcoms had all but disappeared from the radio airwaves by the early 1950s. Of course, many other genres were dropping like horseflies as well, as it became increasingly obvious that the listening public was rapidly becoming a viewing public. The rise of television was meteoric, and the radio stars who could not transfer their formats into the new medium were fated to disappear from the schedules. Lauck and Goff made one final attempt to revive *Lum and Abner* in its traditional daily fifteen-minute format. From February through May 1953, the show returned on the ABC network with scripts once more written by Roswell Rogers. Unable to attract any sponsors, the program left the air again, only to return late that year in an unusual format wherein ABC broadcast the show but sponsorship was picked up by local companies in the various cities where the network's affiliates were airing the program. Even more unusually, Lum and Abner themselves recorded introductory plugs for each sponsor, to be inserted at the proper point in each episode's opening. Many of the scripts were modified and shortened versions of earlier story lines, but at least some new material continued to be created right up until the show's permanent end in May 1954. When the longest running of rural radio comedies could no longer make a go of it, the entertainment world obviously had changed beyond all recognition.

Chapter Six

What It Was, Was the Fifties

When the time inevitably came that the radio audience defected to television, some tough decisions had to be made. Television was not certain just where its future lay, so with radio as the only prior comparable medium, much of TV's early programming was patterned after what had gone before. Ironically, the remnants of radio would not be television's biggest successes, but it would take a while before anyone figured that out.

With so many radio shows and stars already established, a smooth transition to television seemed natural, but actual events sometimes proved more difficult. As only one example, Fred Allen found television to be stifling to his satirical imagination. Faring the worst were the shows that depended so heavily on listeners building a mental image of the setting and characters.

Probably the earliest attempts at a rural comedy television series were three tries to adapt *Lum and Abner* for the new medium. With six feature films in its cracker barrel, the show would seem to have had plenty of trial runs, but somehow translating the Jot 'Em Down Store and the Pine Ridge setting to the small screen was a daunting task. The first *Lum and Abner* TV pilot was filmed for CBS in 1948 and tried to emulate the daily fifteen-minute format of the radio show. No characters other than Lum and Abner themselves appeared. CBS president William S. Paley supposedly liked it but felt that the market for fifteen-minute television programs was rapidly going to disappear. He commissioned a second pilot, which was filmed during the summer of 1949.

This version used the weekly half-hour version of *Lum and Abner* as its model. The script was based on a radio episode from May of that year, in which Abner pretends to be deathly ill so that he can sneak away from the store to go fishing. Lum, however, has found the fishing tackle Abner has hidden around the store and catches on to his partner's scheme. He insists on Abner going home to bed, where the formidable Widder Abernathy watches over him to make sure he doesn't try to get away. Radio cast regulars Andy Devine, Opie Cates, and ZaSu Pitts appear in their usual characterizations, although Dink Trout does not join them.

For whatever reason, the pilot was not considered a success, and the idea of a *Lum and Abner* series was temporarily dropped. The participants continued telling stories about the difficulties involved with filming the show for decades afterward; writer Roswell Rogers recalled an incident that occurred at the New York hotel where the cast and crew were staying during the production. For lack of anything better to define his ill-defined character, Opie Cates wore what looked like a tattered house painter's outfit. While he was relaxing in the lobby of the swank hotel, the management called security and nearly gave him the bum's rush before he could convince them that he was not a vagrant. Rogers also insisted that the film of this pilot, available through several video nostalgia sources over the years, is actually a kinescope of the dress rehearsal, as CBS lost its nerve and canceled the whole project even before the final pilot could be shot.

A third *Lum and Abner* pilot actually made it onto CBS's airwaves in February 1951. Again written by Rogers, much of this version was taken up by a routine Lauck and Goff had devised when they were making personal appearances during the 1930s. Abner needs a new suit—in this program he and "Lizzabeth" are celebrating their fortieth wedding anniversary—and Lum tries to measure him for it by standing him against the vertical boards that comprise the walls of their store. As one might imagine, this method of determining the length of his sleeves and the size of his waist (Lum measures how many boards Abner's middle section covers, then doubles it for the waist of the pants) produces a garment that is not exactly Hart, Schaffner, and Marx quality. Although the pilot received favorable reviews after its airing, it still did not lead to a series.

The most likely candidate for the first successful rural-themed series was also based on an established source, but tellingly, it was not radio. During the 1951–52 television season, CBS aired a daily fifteen-minute serial based on *The Egg and I* (both the book and movie versions, with some characters that originated in neither). This time, Bob Craven and Pat Kirkland starred as the would-be chicken champs, with Grady Sutton—long removed from his stint as Cedric in the Lum and Abner movies—as handyman Jed Simmons. Even Ma and Pa Kettle were on hand, but since Marjorie Main and Percy Kilbride were still occupied with their successful movies, for television the parts were recast with Frank Tweddell as Pa and Doris Rich as Ma. (Rich's greatest claim to cinema fame of some sort would come more than a decade later, when she was assigned the role of Mrs. Claus in that masterpiece of holiday cinema schlock, *Santa Claus Conquers the Martians.*)

The TV version of *The Egg and I* did not seem to hurt the ongoing Ma and Pa Kettle films, which continued without a pause throughout the first half of the decade. The third episode, *Ma and Pa Kettle Go to Town* (1950), picks up the thread of the story just a few days after the ending of the previous film. The Kettles are still living in their "house of the future" and having trouble with some of the modern devices while preparing for their trip to New York, which Pa won by submitting a testimonial letter to the Bubble-Ola soft drink concern. (Pa can't stand to drink the stuff but admits, "They don't give prizes fer NOT likin' it.") Just as the couple is despairing of finding anyone with the intestinal fortitude—or sheer lunacy—to take care of their brood of children while the parents are away, into their lives comes a notorious bank robber on the lam who takes refuge in their former (now-abandoned) farmhouse. The crook passes himself off as a poet ("I thought maybe you was a travelin' salesman," says Pa, "I hear they're always stoppin' at farms.") and, unaware

In *Ma and Pa Kettle Back on the Farm* (1951), the country couple find their property misappropriated by two con men, Peter Leeds (*center*) and Jerry Hausner.

of what he is getting himself into, agrees to house-sit for the kids if the Kettles will deliver a black leather bag to his brother in New York. Of course, the bag contains the heist money and the miscreant's "brother" is the head gangster.

Once in New York, Ma and Pa are reunited with Tom and Kim, their son and daughter-in-law, and set out to see the sights. They visit such landmarks as Rockefeller Center and the Central Park Zoo, all the time unaware that they are being stalked by gangsters who are in turn being stalked by police detectives. The cops finally put the country couple wise during a big society party, which Pa turns into a square dance, cleverly shouting instructions to Ma as part of his calling. The gangsters are apprehended, and the Kettles return home to Cape Flattery to find their house still in one piece, no thanks to the kids' escapades.

The saga continues in *Ma and Pa Kettle Back on the Farm* (1951), which concerns itself with the birth of Tom and Kim's first baby. Pa initially misunderstands and thinks he has fathered a sixteenth kid, but he finally comprehends what has happened. With Kim's highfalutin parents from Boston trying to help and bringing in a nurse to care for the baby, things are so crowded in the house that Ma and Pa move back to their original decrepit farm. They get there just as two shady characters (played by busy radio actors Peter Leeds and Jerry Hausner) think they have discovered uranium on the property, but it turns out that the only radioactive material is on Pa's grungy navy surplus coveralls, which apparently went through some atomic bomb tests. By the end of the film, Kim's parents have learned to like the Kettles' laid-back lifestyle, and her mother is talking like Ma.

Universal's success with the Kettle series apparently prompted the studio to put its other major comedy team, Bud Abbott and Lou Costello, into the same genre. The result was *Comin' 'round the Mountain* (1951), but the title was its only resemblance to the 1940 Bob Burns epic of the same name. The slim plot involves tubby Costello discovering that he is the long-lost heir to a treasure in the Kentucky mountain country, courtesy of his distant ancestor, Squeeze Box McCoy. He and his agent (Abbott) head fer the hills, where they have to contend with the ongoing feud between the McCoys and the Winfields. After the balance of power has shifted seismically several times, the pair accidentally discovers that the "treasure" is actually an underground vault that is part of Fort Knox.

Most Abbott and Costello fans do not hold *Comin' 'round the Mountain* in high esteem, but as an example of hillbilly humor in the early 1950s it is quite interesting. The leading lady is singer Dorothy Shay, who was well known at the time as the Park Avenue Hillbillie. Shay's career had taken off like a rifle bullet in 1947 when she had a hit song with "Feudin', Fussin' and A-Fightin'," with lyrics that celebrated the not-so-peaceful side of mountain living:

Water, the well water
The doggone stuff don't taste like it oughter
Look here, city slicker
That's why we all drink corn likker (hit's better with yer shoes off).

Shay's entire career was built on the contrast between her glamorous appearance and the clodhopper imagery of her songs. In *Comin' 'round the Mountain* she got to sing five of them, including the not-a-hit "You'll Be Jes' Another Notch on Father's Shotgun Iffin' You Don't Marry Me."

Shay was making her motion picture debut in this film, but other rural character actors were already familiar faces and would be seen again as well. The pivotal role of Granny McCoy—who fit firmly into the Mammy Yokum mold as well as prefiguring another Granny who would make it big in television—was played by Ida Moore, who had a running role as a harmless escapee from the

Bud Abbott and Lou Costello tried their hand at hillbilly humor in *Comin' Round the Mountain* (1951). They shared billing (and screen time) with singer Dorothy Shay, known as the Park Avenue Hillbillie.

funny farm in both *The Egg and I* and *Ma and Pa Kettle.* The most simpleminded of the McCoy clan was Luke, in the person of Robert Easton. Although he later became one of Hollywood's most respected dialect coaches, Easton's early career consisted almost entirely of playing dimwitted bumpkins; in *Comin' 'round the Mountain,* he explains that he can't get married because he was once kicked in the head by a mule. "Ah may be tetched, but Ah ain't that crazy!" he confides in Costello. The hulking head of the Winfield family, Devil Dan, was Glenn Strange, who had previously been seen with the skinny and fat duo as the title monster in *Abbott and Costello Meet Frankenstein* (1948). Strange would go on to a long television career as Sam the bartender on *Gunsmoke.*

Then, there was about the last person one would expect to find in a hillbilly comedy, although from a casting standpoint it would have been difficult to find anyone more suited to the role. Since Costello supposedly cannot inherit the fabled McCoy treasure unless he gets married, Granny directs him to the local magic worker, Aunt Huddy the witch. Abbott and Costello visit her creepy cabin and find that Aunt Huddy is played by the most famous movie witch of all time, Margaret Hamilton of *Wizard of Oz* renown. For providing Costello with a love potion, Aunt Huddy sticks him for ten bucks—literally, as she quickly fabricates a voodoo doll resembling Costello and repeatedly jabs it with a pin. He retaliates by making an Aunt Huddy voodoo doll and giving her a dose of her own magic. Naturally, even more confusion reigns when the bottle of love potion accidentally gets passed around during a party and the most unlikely characters start falling in love with each other.

Abbott and Costello might have seemed like an odd choice for hillbilly high jinks, but they looked positively at home when compared with the team known as the Bowery Boys. In 1952, they too threw their hillbilly hats into the rural ring with *Feudin' Fools.* The simple plot was already getting stale by that time: one of the gang, Satch (Huntz Hall) inherits some mountain property from a deceased relative, and the whole bunch of them journey from the canyons of New York to the high country to check it out. Naturally enough, they learn that Satch's family is not too well thought of in the neighborhood. A funny gag comes when one of the displaced Noo Yawkers has had it past here with the constant playing of "Comin' 'round the Mountain" by a string band on the radio: "Dey're ALWAYS comin' around da mountain!" he shouts hysterically. "Why can't dey come around somptin' else for a change? Couldn't dey come outa a STORE?!" Mixed into this familiar plot was the even more familiar face and voice of Robert Easton, sporting a long hillbilly beard this time instead of his normal clean-shaven appearance.

Animated cartoons were rediscovering the joys of rural roars in the early 1950s, perhaps prodded along by successes such as the Ma and Pa Kettle yarns. Warner Bros., after having expended so much effort on its hillbilly cartoons in the 1930s before ignoring them completely during the 1940s, came speeding back to life in 1950 with what would be the studio's definitive word on the subject: Bugs Bunny's classic *Hillbilly Hare.*

This cartoon's debt to the ones that had preceded it is evident from the first title frame, where the theme music is the "Arkansas Traveler," played on a close approximation of Bob Burns's bazooka. Deep in the Ozarks, Bugs is enjoying his vacation by strolling through the woods and singing "I Like Mountain Music" when he is suddenly accosted by the two bearded Martin brothers, each toting a rifle longer than he is tall. "Be y'all a Martin er be y'all a Coy rabbit?" they demand. Bugs, seeking to defuse the situation with a bit of humor, cracks, "My friends say I'm VERY coy!" Bugs apparently never saw *Make Mine Music*, or he would have known about the feud between the Martins and the Coys, but, be that as it may, he is soon having to outwit the pair of halfwits just to save his rabbit skin.

Finally, Bugs dresses in a skimpy Daisy Mae outfit that fools the Martin brothers into ignoring his long ears (tied into a ponytail) and fur. Female impersonator Bugs drops a coin into a convenient jukebox, which contains an entire mechanized hillbilly band. The Audio-Animatronic leader begins calling a square dance, in which Bugs and the brothers enthusiastically join according to the directions. The Martins are so caught up in the dance that they never notice Bugs shedding his mountain gal duds and picking up a fiddle. Disconnecting the jukebox from the electrical outlet, Bugs takes up the song and improvises lyrics that soon have the Martin brothers doing his dirty work for him:

Grab a fencepost, hold it tight
Whomp yer partner with all yer might
Hit 'im in the shin, hit 'im in the head
Hit 'im agin, the critter ain't dead!

The two yokels have soon converted each other into unconscious piles, freeing Bugs to continue his vacation and ending the film.

In 1951, Judy Canova decided to revive her film career, which had been dormant since her single post–World War II feature in 1946. She returned to Republic Pictures, where she had labored successfully in the early 1940s, but things were different. The coming of television had cost Republic its two biggest stars, Roy Rogers and Gene Autry, and since their brand was the main type of film Republic knew how to make and market, Canova's new series would somewhat incongruously bill her as "Queen of the Cowgirls." Er, uh—Huh? Yes, Canova's usual hillbilly persona was subtly changed to a Western setting in films such as *Honeychile* (1951), *Oklahoma Annie* (1952), *Lay That Rifle Down* (1955), and *Carolina Cannonball* (1955), which featured veteran comic sidekick Andy Clyde as her grandfather.

Of particular interest is *The WAC from Walla Walla* (1955), as it prefigures several future "rube joins the military" productions. In that film, Canova's short-tempered sergeant is played by petite Irene Ryan, who was to become intimately familiar with hick comedy herself within the next few years. One scene in particular proves that Canova's ability to handle a questionnaire had not evolved far from that of Sam 'n' Henry or Lum and Abner a generation or two earlier. She blunders into a Women's Army Corps (WAC) recruiting office in the mistaken belief that she is buying a new dress (which happens to be one of the WAC uniforms). The female officer in charge tells her she will have to answer a few questions:

Officer: Now, can you identify yourself?
Judy: [looks at her pigtails and her clothes] Yep, that's me.
Officer: I mean, what's your name?
Judy: Canova.
Officer: Given name?
Judy: Huh?
Officer: What do your parents call you?
Judy: "Loudmouth." 'Course, sometimes they call me Judy, too. You kin put that down if you want to.
Officer: Next question . . . Born?
Judy: You think I was hatched?
Officer: I'm trying to determine the place of birth, Miss Canova. Where were you born?
Judy: In th' front bedroom.
Officer: When?
Judy: 'Bout seven o'clock at night.

As more and more local television stations came on the air, especially after 1953, the tradition of the hosted children's show became ever more firmly established. Stations from coast to coast discovered the joys of filling time between cartoons with hosts dressed as grizzled sea captains, clean-cut cowboys, crazy clowns, and other such fun figures. A handful of stations—though not nearly as many as utilized these types—even stuck their hands into the rural comedy

Two of the many local children's television shows that featured rural characters as their hosts were (*top*) *Uncle Jed* (Kansas City, Missouri) and *Uncle Elihu* (Waco, Texas).

cracker barrel and pulled out hosts who could use their down-home appeal to sell nearly anything to their young audiences.

Some of these local shows stuck with the tried-and-true general store setting that had served so well in radio. *Hold 'Er Newt* (Chicago, Illinois), *Friendly Junction* (Columbus, Ohio), and *Mr. Cartoon* (Huntington, West Virginia) all presented kids with a store setting that would have been increasingly unfamiliar in the postwar age of the suburban supermarket. The store setting occasionally was combined with the affability of the grandfatherly host, as with *Uncle Albert's General Store* (Bowling Green, Kentucky), *The Hap Richards Show* (Hartford, Connecticut), *Uncle Woody's General Store* (Kirksville, Missouri), and *Gramps* (Waterloo, Iowa). Even when not running a store, the bucolic hayseed still manned the host's chair in *Grandpa's Place* (Washington, D.C.), *Grandpa Happy* (Rock Island, Illinois), *Uncle Elihu* (Waco, Texas), and *Uncle Jed* (Kansas City, Missouri).

Some shows had female hosts of the grinning Minnie Pearl variety. *Cousin Tuny* (Jackson, Tennessee) starred Doris Richards, who was a close friend of Sarah (Minnie) Colley, so the resemblance there was largely intentional. *Sunshine Sally* (Lubbock, Texas) took the same approach with the addition of some clown makeup. Then there was the ever-popular farm setting, as evidenced by *Fun Farm* (with acreage in both Toledo and Cleveland, Ohio), *Barn Party* (Washington, D.C.), and *Funny Farm* (Milwaukee, Wisconsin). The kingpin of Cincinnati kids' TV, Uncle Al Lewis, changed settings often, but his *Uncle Al's Farm* was one of them. (For more in-depth information about all of these shows and the phenomenon that was local children's programming in general, consult *Hi There, Boys and Girls! America's Local Children's Television Programs*)

And yes, the Ma and Pa Kettle adventures continued during this period as well. (Probably one thing that helped ensure that audiences would not get burned out on the pair's comedic situations was that the films were carefully released one per year, often enough to keep anticipation high but far enough apart to avoid monotony.) In *Ma and Pa Kettle at the Fair* (1952), son Tom and daughter-in-law Kim are nowhere to be seen, and Ma and Pa's daughter, Rosie, is the oldest child still at home. The plot involves the family's attempts to raise enough funds to send her to college; in the middle of all of this, Rosie falls in love with handsome Marvin Johnson (James Best, who would turn up in Hazzard County, Georgia, nearly twenty years later, helping give southern law enforcement officers a bad name). *Ma and Pa Kettle on Vacation* (1953) ignored the kids almost completely and packed the couple off to Paris on a joint trip with Kim's parents, Mr. and Mrs. Parker (last seen in *Ma and Pa Kettle Back on the Farm*).

With the Kettle movies proving to be consistent audience pleasers, Universal's cartoon department decided to jump on the hay wagon. With Walter Lantz still in charge, the studio's main output by the 1950s consisted of Woody Woodpecker cartoons, with occasional forays into other series of less renown. One of the least renowned was its parody of the Kettles, which began with a cartoon titled simply *Maw and Paw* (1953). Moviegoers would have instantly recognized the source material, as Maw and Paw live on a run-down farm swarming with their seemingly dozens of kids (putting even the live-action Kettle clan to shame). Paw's derby hat comes directly from Kilbride, but the character design for Maw goes in the opposite direction. Instead of being large and domineering, as with Ma Kettle, the cartoon Maw barely comes up to Paw's waist, although she packs a wallop that belies her minuscule size.

The initial cartoon briefly introduces all of the characters, including family pig Milford, identified in the opening titles as "the smart one." When Milford correctly oinks the answer to a radio host's telephoned question, the family wins a sleek new car that gives them as much trouble as the Kettles' modern house. With Milford at the wheel, the car careens around the property and repeatedly lands Maw in the hog wallow. (*Paw*: "Yer shore goin' to be purty, takin' all them mud baths, Maw.") The car finally slams headlong into a tree and transforms itself into a sedate Model T, which Paw and the kids can handle more easily.

All of the voices were provided by Lantz's two most durable actors, Dal McKennon (as Paw, Milford, and most of the kids) and Grace Stafford (aka Mrs. Lantz, also the voice of Woody Woodpecker) as Maw. While McKennon was clearly patterning his tones after

Percy Kilbride, Stafford simply gave Maw a hick accent that did not greatly resemble Marjorie Main. In other cartoons for other studios, voice specialists June Foray and Nancy Wible perfected their Main impersonations and got good use out of them. The Maw and Paw cartoons continued sporadically throughout 1954, with such titles as *Plywood Panic* and *Pig in a Picnic*, before finally wheezing to a stop with *Paw's Night Out* (1955). By that time, the resemblance to the Kettles had become less prominent, especially in McKennon's evolved Paw voice. Universal continued its Kettle features for several more years, but no one seemed to miss their cartoon counterparts after they returned to the ink bottle.

In the last chapter, we first encountered Tennessee Ernie Ford when he took a break from his Los Angeles radio show to make a guest appearance on *Lum and Abner*. In the years since, Ford had continued making records, but his comical hillbilly character had remained mostly confined to the southern California area. One of the main forces that propelled him out of that rut was his pair of May 1954 guest shots on the enormously popular *I Love Lucy* series.

As the story line would have it, Ernie is coming to New York on a visit from his hometown of Bent Fork, Tennessee. Through some misunderstanding engineered by Lucy Ricardo's ditzy mother, Ernie believes they are related and decides to hole up with "Cousin Lucy" and "Cousin Ricky," plus honorary kin "Cousin Fred" and "Cousin Ethel." The foursome does everything to get rid of their homespun houseguest, and when Lucy hears that Ernie's mama instructed him to stay away from "wicked city wimmen," she decides to become just that. Donning a slinky gown, a wig, and enough mascara to make Theda Bara look like Rebecca of

Yes, it is difficult, if not impossible, to imagine him looking like this, but this is the first attempt at a hillbilly characterization by Tennessee Ernie Ford, during his days as a disk jockey on a southern California radio station.

Sunnybrook Farm, Lucy gives Ernie the come-hithers in a desperate attempt to scare him back to the hills. However, Ernie is so happy to find out what he has been missing that he decides to stick around.

Originally, this episode was to have stood alone, but Ernie's bumpkin manner was such a hit with the audience that the writers decided to turn the situation into a two-parter, a rare event for the Lucy series. In the second episode, Ernie enters himself and his four bogus cousins in a television talent show, *Millikan's Chicken Mash Hour*, where they masquerade as Ernie Ford and His Four Hot Chicken Pickers. (Considering that the *Grand Ole Opry* started out with groups called the Gully Jumpers and the Fruit Jar Drinkers, the name was not as far-fetched as it might seem.) After a rousing rendition of "Y'all Come," the group wins the two-hundred-dollar first prize, Ernie lights out for home, and the Ricardos and the Mertzes assume they have seen the last of him.

But wait! During the next season, the show took on its longest continuing story line when the two couples made their epic cross-country trip to Hollywood. This plot, which would eventually occupy January through November 1955, is just getting under way when the Ricardos' car is stopped for speeding in a microscopic burg somewhere in the Tennessee mountains. (According to the sheriff, they were "goin' lickety-split at forty miles per hour.") When they find out that the town is Bent Fork, they call on "Cousin Ernie" to help spring them from jail. This is not as easy as it seems, since Ernie and the sheriff are not such good buddies, but Ernie finally tells them the lawman will let them go if they promise to take his twin daughters to Hollywood and get them into the movies. The girls turn out to be the inaptly named Teensy and Weensy, who between them might weigh a bit over a ton. "They're just as alike as two peas in a pod," observes Ernie. "Or two watermelons in a patch." When Ricky explains that he does not have any show business connections who could help the portly pair, the sheriff refuses to let the tourists go on their way. Finally, Ernie leads everyone in a square dance that allows the Ricardos and Mertzes to hogtie the sheriff and his pudgy progeny long enough to escape. That really was the last time the

New Yorkers would encounter Cousin Ernie, but never fear—he and Lucy will be reunited in our next chapter.

Since Ma and Pa Kettle had been found goin' to town, back on the farm, at the fair, and on vacation, it is no wonder that their 1954 episode was called *Ma and Pa Kettle at Home.* Another of the kids, son Elwin, is eligible for a college scholarship thanks to the essay he has written about growing up on the farm. Unfortunately, most of what he writes is based on how he wishes things were, which complicates matters when two of the contest judges arrive in Cape Flattery to check out the Kettle farm for themselves. The whole family moves from the "house of the future" back to their shack, attempting to re-create Elwin's vision of a pastoral paradise. (Pa borrows furniture and up-to-date farm equipment from the neighbors and patches up the decrepit buildings with cardboard facades—until it rains.) The final scene takes place during a Christmas Eve party at the Kettle home, where Elwin gets his scholarship and Pa plays Santa Claus in his red long underwear. Lum and Abner movie alumni Alan Mowbray and Irving Bacon take important roles in this plot.

The series really started stretching its premise with *Ma and Pa Kettle at Waikiki* (1955). According to the writers, Pa's cousin, Rodney Kettle, is a pineapple processing plant tycoon in Hawaii, and when the doctor orders him to take a rest, he sends for Cousin Pa to handle the company in his absence. (This could not have had anything to do with the letters Pa had been sending to Rodney, making it sound as if Pa had business interests aplenty and owned "half the state of Washington," as Rodney tells his board of directors.) Once Ma and Pa arrive in Hawaii, Pa quite unknowingly implements changes that vastly improve the output of the pineapple plant.

In an ill-developed plot point, gangsters working on behalf of a rival cannery kidnap Pa and take him to a remote island, in a scheme to get control of the Kettle empire. In the film's funniest concept, we meet natives Mama and Papa Lotus and their twelve children, who parallel the lazy Pa and domineering Ma and their brood. With the help of the Lotus clan, Pa is saved from the kidnappers and they all live happily ever after (except the kidnappers, of

Lum and Abner Abroad (1955) was actually three half-hour television programs filmed in Yugoslavia and then stitched together into a feature film. Many people, including Lum and Abner themselves, felt it should never have been released.

course). We also learn that Ma and Pa's names are Phoebe and Frank, although this information seems to be coming a bit too late in the series to do anyone much good.

Ma and Pa (or Phoebe and Frank) were not the only rural comedians to be doing a bit of traveling during this period. In 1954, soon after the end of their final series of radio programs, Lum and Abner had gotten an offer to film a television series in Europe. After reading the scripts, which detailed the adventures of the Pine Ridge duo as they visited such exotic locales as Paris and Monte Carlo while on a goodwill tour, Lauck and Goff decided to take on the project. They would live to regret that decision.

One of the first red flags to be raised was when they discovered that all of the footage, regardless of where it was supposed to be taking place, would be filmed behind the Iron Curtain, in communist Yugoslavia. The production company, Nassour Studios, had money tied up in Yugoslavia that could only be spent on making movies there, and who could be more appropriate to feature than Lum and Abner? Yeah, right. Three half-hour television episodes were produced during the latter months of 1954 and early 1955, but they would not see the incandescent glow of a TV screen. Instead, the three half hours were spliced together into a makeshift feature and released as *Lum and Abner Abroad.* (Some evidence indicates that the three individual segments may also have been made available to theaters individually, possibly as two-reel short subjects.)

In an appearance at a nostalgia convention in 1972, Norris Goff was asked whether *Lum and Abner Abroad* was their last movie. Typically quick with an ad-lib, Goff replied, "That would have been *anyone's* last movie!" He was right in that it is difficult to sit through *Lum and Abner Abroad* without experiencing some sort of ill effects. Since the three television episodes were to have no continuity between them except for the idea of Lum and Abner touring Europe, the resulting feature has no story. To make matters worse, some of the same actors appeared in different roles in the three shows, which would not have been so noticeable if they were seen a week apart but required some tedious (and inane) explanations in the final film. Over the course of ninety minutes, Lum and Abner help reunite a ballerina with her American sweetheart (the ballerina's family lives on a farm in a community designated as Pinevec Ridgeka), become the target of smugglers who try to use them to transport valuable jewelry, spend the night in a spooky castle where there roams a deformed monster known as Frankenshplen, and break the bank at Monte Carlo. The movie simply ends, with no resolution, and it also ended the official partnership of Lauck and Goff. They later related how, while miserably awaiting their next scene in the cold and clammy Yugoslavian castle, seemingly a million miles out of their element, they shook hands and decided that this was the end of Lum and Abner. They officially dissolved their business partnership on April 26, 1956, twenty-five years to the day after their debut on KTHS in Hot Springs.

Norris Goff had had enough of show business to last the rest of his life, but Chet Lauck still craved public attention, so he took a position with the Continental Oil Company of Houston, Texas. In that capacity, he toured the country as an after-dinner speaker, but he also had the opportunity to get his alter ego on television more regularly than was ever the case while teamed with Abner. In commercials for Conoco service stations, Lum was seen running the Jot 'Em Down Store alone (Abner was always away on some pretext or another) and dispensing homely wisdom along with the company's gasoline. In later commercials, the general store disappeared and was replaced by a modern Conoco station, with Lum still manning the pumps. In the most creative of these spots, through the magic of trick photography and careful editing, Lum is seen giving Chet Lauck's car a going-over. "You know, Lum," says Chet, "some people think we look alike." "Aw, I don't think so," replies Lum. "I'm a LOT younger than you air."

Just as veteran rural performers such as Lum and Abner were getting out of the business, new faces were coming in to replace them. In the mid-1950s, the most promising of the newcomers was a native of Mount Airy, North Carolina, with a cornpone accent and wide grin. His name was Andy Griffith, and while Mount Airy would not qualify as nowhere, that is seemingly where he came from, so sudden was his fame.

Griffith was scraping out a living in 1953 by doing his comedy act in nightclubs across the South, billed as Deacon Andy Griffith. He had a number of monologues, but while he was performing at an insurance convention, someone had the foresight to make a recording of one in which the hopelessly out-of-touch deacon described his reactions to seeing his first college football game. "I have studied about it," he concludes. "I think hit's some kindly of a contest where they see which bunch full o' them men kin take that li'l punkin an' run from one end o' that cow pasture to the other without either gittin' knocked down or steppin' in sompin." The resulting record, *What It Was, Was Football,* was a tremendous smash hit on southern radio stations as soon as it was released just before New Year's Day 1954. It received so much airtime that it attracted the attention of prestigious Capitol Records in Hollywood, which bought the rights to the recording and released it nationally, with side 2 of the record being Griffith's retelling of *Romeo and Juliet* in North Carolina mountain lingo. ("Juliet says, 'Romeo, Romeo, wharfore art thou, Romeo?' An' he pops up an' says, 'I'm right chere.'")

Stand-up comedian Deacon Andy Griffith hit it big nationally with his record, *What It Was, Was Football*, in early 1954.

Capitol continued releasing more Griffith comedy monologues over the next few months. Those familiar with his work only through his later squeaky-clean television image would be surprised to hear some of his material from that period, such as the time he described his first experience with North Carolina moonshine: "I swallered 'er down an' she hit bottom. Mah face turned red an' mah eyes rolled back an' I gagged just a li'l bit, an' then bye an' bye I got over it. Some o' the boys says, 'How are ye?' An' I says, 'Boys, I'm a-doin' fine, gainin' ground all the time, an' I think I've got 'er if she don't jump.'" He also occasionally employed the type of jokes that almost got Bob Burns lynched in Arkansas: "We're really doin' good back home in North Carolina," he reported. "Nearly all of our 'lected officials can read an' write now."

In March 1955, producers were casting a television production based on Mac Hyman's 1953 novel *No Time for Sergeants*, and they chose Griffith for the role of Georgia rube turned draftee Will Stockdale. This obviously was not the first time someone had wrestled comedy out of a country hick joining the military—think back to the Snuffy Smith movies of 1942—but it proved that old ideas sometimes are the most reliable. The television play was such a success when it aired on the *U.S. Steel Hour* that later in the year it was made into a smash Broadway hit, again with Griffith in the lead. The concept of Stockdale confounding his superior officers with his inordinate good humor and practical way of looking at things hit the right buttons with audiences. In one scene, Stockdale completely bumfuzzles an army psychiatrist, played by Don Knotts.

Crowds such as this one turned out to see Andy Griffith whenever he made personal appearances at record stores. By the time his television series began in 1960, he was already a familiar personality.

Griffith and Knotts discovered a facility for working together that would serve both of them well in the future.

It was probably a foregone conclusion that *No Time for Sergeants* would end up as a movie with Griffith as the star, but it was not his film debut. Instead, Griffith's face first appeared on the big screen in a noncomedic role as the star of Elia Kazan's 1957 feature, *A Face in the Crowd.* Griffith's interpretation of Lonesome Rhodes, a hick from the sticks who makes it big in the music world (somewhat like an evil Elvis Presley), only to have success go to his head and turn him into an ego-driven monster, was powerful enough to show that this North Carolina native could handle more than corny comedy lines. The *No Time for Sergeants* film version appeared in 1958, with Griffith back in his usual element (and with Knotts reprising his Broadway role as the psychiatrist who needs his own psychiatrist after dealing with Will Stockdale).

Hillbilly characters might not have been as common on the screen in the late 1950s as they had been in some earlier years, but the cartoon studios still knew how to drag them out whenever a series of shorts needed a surefire plot. We have already seen how Famous Studios put Popeye the Sailor into the hill country in *Silly Hillbilly* (1947), and in 1956 they returned him to that setting for *Hill-Billing and Cooing*.

Popeye and Olive Oyl are motoring through the hinterlands when they are spied by a gargantuan hillbilly gal who is after a man, and Popeye fits her bill, inasmuch as he is breathing. This sets up a battle of brains versus brawn as the formidable female repeatedly snatches Popeye out of Olive's grasp and Olive has to forcibly get him back again. The hillbilly finally gets tired of playing games and hits Olive so hard that her body spins like a drill, at which point the hillbilly allows her to drill herself into a convenient tree stump, immobilizing Olive from the neck down. Watching from the top of a nearby pine, Popeye pulls out his can of spinach, but the hillbilly's sudden shaking of the tree dislodges the can from his grasp. ("Come down from yore nest, mah li'l lovebird!" the romantic ruffian crows.) The spinach lands near the semiconscious Olive, who stretches her already-lengthy neck enough to be able to scoop up the green weed with her tongue. Olive's reinforced Adam's apple splits the stump in twain, and with newly formed biceps bulging, she dashes after her rival. The hillbilly is just approaching the justice of the peace office with Popeye's limp form in tow when Olive grabs her by her Judy Canova–type pigtails, swings her around several times, and then throws the lovestruck lug all the way into outer space, where she hangs by the seat of her dress from a five-pointed star. For the closing, Olive sings, "I'll knock the dame sky high who tries to take my guy / Popeye the Sailor Man, toot toot!"

The Famous Studios staff members obviously thought that their new hillbilly had potential that lay beyond the Popeye series, because the very next year they brought her back for an encore, this time giving her a name and a cartoon of her own, *Possum Pearl* (1957). Possum Pearl has somehow gotten down from outer space and returned to the same mountain setting, where she still dreams of romance. That thought strikes terror into the hearts of all the menfolk in the neighborhood, who dash around in abject fear, shouting, "Possum Pearl's on the manhunt again!" When an escaped bank robber decides to use Pearl's cabin as a hideout, a few minutes of her assault-and-battery brand of lovemaking soon have him fleeing for the nearest jail and locking himself in.

When moviegoers heard that the next installment of the Ma and Pa Kettle series was to be known as *The Kettles in the Ozarks* (1956), the change in the format of the title might have tipped them off that something was going to be different. Indeed it was. Percy Kilbride had grown extremely weary of performing Pa Kettle's routines in film after film at the expense of any other work, so after *Ma and Pa Kettle at Waikiki,* he announced that he was hanging up his black derby hat and quitting. Universal still thought there was green on the Kettle farm, so for this new entry, the writers cooked up a plot device by which Ma and the kids journey to Mournful Hollow, Arkansas, to help Pa's brother, Sedgewick, get his life into some semblance of order. Sedgewick Kettle is played by Arthur Hunnicutt, another in the line of rural actors who were equally at home with slapstick comedy and serious drama. Hunnicutt's portrayal of Sedgewick is so lazy, he makes his brother Pa look like a human dynamo. Before it is all over, Ma has managed to inveigle Sedgewick into marrying his sweetheart of twenty years, Bedelia Baines (no relation to Scattergood, we assume). Taking part in the rambling plot were some familiar faces to rural comedy fans—Robert Easton and ex-Lowizie Sarah Padden. And this time, Pa's first name is given as Egbert, contradicting the previous entry in the series.

Universal had enough sense to know that it was going to be difficult to continue a Ma and Pa Kettle series without a Pa, so the studio took the rather drastic step of recasting the role that Kilbride had made so famous—almost created, in fact. Faced with such a seemingly impossible situation, the folks in the casting department did better than one might expect. For the tenth and final installment in the long-running series, *The Kettles on Old MacDonald's Farm* (1957), into Pa's black derby and mismatched clothes stepped Parker Fennelly. He made no attempt to imitate Kilbride but instead used the same voice he had previously employed in radio as Esley Stebbins, Titus Moody, and a host of other laconic farmers. (Both Kilbride and

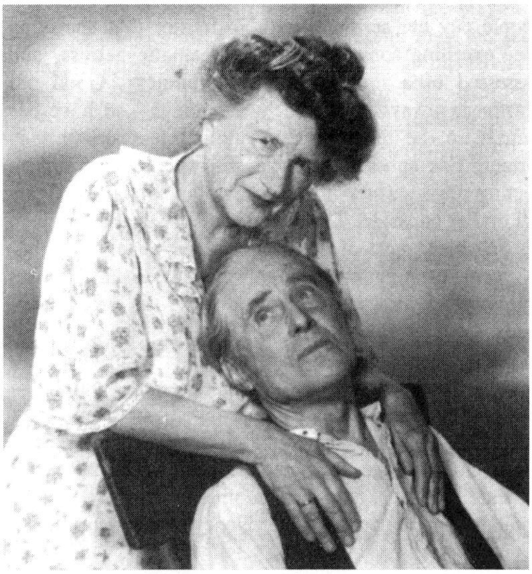

Rustic radio veteran Parker Fennelly became the new Pa Kettle opposite Marjorie Main for the final film in the series, *The Kettles on Old MacDonald's Farm* (1957).

Fennelly started their respective careers by playing New England types but ended up as characters from the opposite end of the North American continent.)

Besides the new voice, Fennelly's version of Pa was somewhat more lively than Kilbride's, and he and Marjorie Main also display far more physical affection toward each other than had been seen in previous entries. The title of the film refers to the fact that the Kettles have finally sold both of their previous homes—the broken-down farm and the house of the future—and moved into a vacant farmhouse previously known as MacDonald Manor. Viewers may have been supposed to infer that this was the farm that Betty MacDonald and her husband (of *Egg and I* fame) had eventually abandoned. In any case, the Kettles took their final bows on the screen and then vanished into entertainment history. Neither Main nor Kilbride made any more movies, although Fennelly continued his career in both television and movies. Kilbride died in an automobile accident in 1964; Main lived until 1975.

Another long-established rural comic made an incredible show business comeback at just about the time the Kettles were put out to pasture. The story goes that on NBC-TV's *Tonight Show* in 1957, host Jack Paar suddenly wondered out loud, "Say, whatever happened to Cliff Arquette?" Well may he have asked, because Arquette had been officially retired for several years by then. You will recall that we last saw him during the closing weeks of the half-hour *Lum and Abner* show in the spring of 1950. Arquette had gotten into television shortly after that, building his reputation around a hayseed character he called Charley Weaver. Arquette, as Charley, had held down his own show for a couple of months in early 1952 and had been a regular on singer Dennis Day's program, but other than that, he had decided to put up his feet and take it easy. That is, until Paar brought up his name. Just a few days later, Charley Weaver ambled onto the *Tonight Show* set, and his appearances (with Paar as his straight man) became one of the program's most anticipated regular features.

Charley Weaver's stock routine was an old vaudeville gimmick, but it never failed to please audiences. Charley would read letters from his Mamma back home in Mount Idy—yes, it is a certainty that he first heard that town's name during his brief time with Lum and Abner or at least from listening to the many stories Ben Withers had told about the place in the earlier days. As for the letter routine, that was obviously a popular gag for vaudeville comedians because it meant they did not have to memorize a script. They could simply read from the letter in their hand and change or alter the material as needed to suit the audience. A typical Charley Weaver letter read,

> Things are fine in Mount Idy. Your father and I spent Sunday with Wallace Swine and his family. My, but their oldest boy is spoiled—a steam roller ran over him. His father put a stamp on him and mailed him to the Mayo brothers. He's coming along fine now. They have to put a bookmark in bed with him, though, to find him.
>
> The entire population of Mount Idy—308 souls in all—was rushed to the Mount Idy Emergency Hospital on Memorial Day, due to a slight oversight on the part of Ludlow Bean. At noon, the old Civil War cannon in the town square was fired, and everybody in town rushed out to the park and dove into our new swimming pool. Ludlow Bean was the only one who didn't go to the hospital. He was also the one who forgot to fill the pool.

After becoming a big star all over again, Arquette was offered another show of his own. During the 1959–60 television season, he starred in *The Charley Weaver Show* on ABC. Describing the show, *TV Guide* reported: "The *Charley Weaver Show* was originally called

Charley Weaver's Hobby Lobby, and, as such, survived for several weeks while its star fenced with Zsa Zsa Gabor, stood still as Maureen O'Hara cracked a bottle over his head, and jumped into a tank full of fish and Gypsy Rose Lee. On his new show, a sort of modified situation comedy, Charley cracks jokes, 'interviews' residents of Mount Idy, and generally just wanders around." One of the residents to whom the article was referring was a doleful, emaciated soul known as beauty pageant winner Miss Mount Idy. This was yet another step in the rural direction for Irene Ryan, who was destined to get there whether she intended to or not. After the series ended later in 1960, Arquette did not make undue haste to find a replacement job. He turned up again later in the decade.

Cliff Arquette's career was rejuvenated when he began making periodic visits to the *Tonight Show* in character as Charley Weaver. His stories about life in Mount Idy were collected into books, including this one.

The end of the 1950s brought the latest and most lavish attempt yet at moving *Li'l Abner* from the funny papers to the funny movies. This time, similar to the situation with the *No Time for Sergeants* movie, the production had already proven itself as a Broadway hit. The stage musical *Li'l Abner* had opened in November 1956 and had been a smash hit, totally eclipsing the disappointments of the 1940 film and Columbia's strange animated cartoons. Since the Broadway show was partially backed by Paramount, it seemed a foregone conclusion that the studio would turn it into a big-screen production, and that version was released in 1959.

In 1959, Paramount released its big-screen version of the hit Broadway play *Li'l Abner*, the only successful translation of Al Capp's comic strip to other media.

Possibly because of his earlier bad experiences with dramatic adaptations of his strip, Al Capp evidenced little interest in putting his stamp on either the play or the movie. The script was concocted by Norman Panama and Mel Frank, two of Bob Hope's former gag writers, who decided to ignore the fact that Li'l Abner and Daisy Mae had finally tied the knot back in 1952 (quite unintentionally on Abner's part). Instead, the writers went back to the strip as most people remembered it, with Daisy pursuing a reluctant Abner against the backdrop of Sadie Hawkins Day. The plot brought together many of Capp's characters from the previous twenty-two years of strips, frequently functioning completely differently than they had in their original appearances.

The basic plot involves the U.S. government looking for the most unnecessary location in the entire country to convert into a new atomic bomb testing site. With the help of the slimy politico, Senator Jack S. Phogbound, the government decides that Dogpatch is the most unnecessary spot of all, and the populace must be evacuated. While trying to discover anything about their community that could possibly be perceived as necessary, they discover that Mammy Yokum's own Yokumberry tonic has given Li'l Abner his superhuman physique and strength and that it will have the same effect on anyone else who drinks it. Since the tonic is made from the Yokumberry tree, which grows only in Mammy's front yard, this formula has the potential to save Dogpatch.

But long before all the play is played, the tonic has become the target of multibillionaire General Bullmoose ("He makes the rules and he intends to keep it that-a-way / What's good for General Bullmoose is good for the U.S.A.!"), who sends his concubine Appassionata Von Climax to Dogpatch to compete in the Sadie Hawkins race, capture Abner, marry him, and then inherit the Yokumberry fortune by doing away with her spouse. His plan fails at just about the same time the government receives the results of its tests: Yokumberry tonic makes men strong, handsome, and muscular but also robs them of any interest in the opposite sex explaining how Abner has managed to avoid Daisy for so long. It would be unfair to reveal just how the problem is solved and Dogpatch is saved from nuclear annihilation, but suffice it to say that Abner and Daisy are married in a foot-stompin' finale, and everyone lives hillbilly ever after.

One of the biggest changes from the strip to the script was the prominent role given to Marryin' Sam, played on both stage and screen by rotund musical comedy star Stubby Kaye. No longer the greedy, grasping Squire Skimp clone of yore, Sam turns out to

Li'l Abner (Peter Palmer) puts it there with Marryin' Sam (Stubby Kaye) in the Paramount film. Sam had been a con man extraordinaire in the comic strip, but for the Broadway play and the movie, his character was softened into a friend to all.

The leading citizens of Dogpatch as seen in *Li'l Abner* (1959): (*left to right*) Pappy Yokum (Joe E. Marks), Mammy Yokum (Billie Hayes), Marryin' Sam (Stubby Kaye), Daisy Mae (Leslie Parrish), and Li'l Abner (Peter Palmer).

be a respected member of the community, and Mammy entrusts him with looking after Abner when the two of them journey to Washington, D.C. Cast as Mammy, also brought over from the stage play, was Billie Hayes. Toward the end of the 1960s, Hayes would achieve television immortality as the daffy Witchiepoo on Sid and Marty Krofft's *H. R. Pufnstuf* Saturday morning series; in one form or another, she would spend the rest of her career playing variations on either Mammy or Witchiepoo. The crucial role of Abner himself was tackled by Peter Palmer, a former college football player who had both the voice and musculature to bring Capp's comic character to life. On Broadway, beautiful Daisy Mae had been played by Edie Adams—best known for her "spend a little dime with me" Muriel cigar commercials—but she was unavailable for the movie, so the role went to a newcomer, Leslie Parrish. Parrish filled what little there was of Daisy Mae's costume to an ample degree.

As part of the promotion for the movie, many of the cast members appeared on an episode of Red Skelton's television program, affording the long-delayed opportunity for radio hick Clem Kadiddlehopper to visit Dogpatch. The story line has Daisy Mae pretending to fall in love with Clem to make Abner jealous; that failing, she visits Nightmare Alice (a character from the strip who appeared in neither the stage play nor the movie) to obtain a love potion. In a development remarkably like that in Abbott and Costello's *Comin' 'round the Mountain,* Clem accidentally drinks the potion intended for Abner and immediately falls in love with the first female he sees—one of Moonbeam McSwine's pet pigs.

> *Abner*: Yo're goin' to marry a PIG?
> *Clem*: If it wuz good enough fer my father, hit's good enough fer me!

All of this flurry of hillbilly humor at the end of the 1950s offered only a preview of the full-fledged craze that would emerge in the coming decade. Now, tune the rabbit ears on your television set and get ready to set a spell and take your shoes off—and enjoy a heapin' helpin' of hospitality. Hillbilly, that is.

Chapter Seven

The Country Broadcasting System

Those sophisticated types who thought the country was going to the pigs with all the rural humor that had taken place over the years could only scream and gnash their teeth after the 1960s arrived. Television was about to experience the biggest hillbilly explosion since Snuffy Smith's still blew up, and it all started almost imperceptibly on the ABC network in October 1957.

The Real McCoys documented the experiences of a family of hill folk who migrated to the more prosperous lands of the West Coast—or, as the theme song described it, "From West Virginny they came to stay in sunny Californi-ay." Patriarch of the clan was Grandpappy Amos (Walter Brennan), a cantankerous old coot who hated everything and everyone who reminded him that he wasn't in West Virginny anymore. Along for the ride was Grandpappy's son, Luke (Richard Crenna), and Luke's wife, Kate (Kathy Nolan), with Luke's younger brother, Little Luke (Michael Winkleman, although why there would be two brothers named Luke in the same family was a mystery), and sister, Hassie (Lydia Reed).

The show had one distinction in that its originator was credited in the opening narration. As Kate rang a dinner bell, an announcer intoned, "*The Real McCoys,* starring Walter Brennan, created by Irving Pincus." Irving and brother Norman Pincus had been trying to pitch their concept to the networks for quite some time before

The Real McCoys, starring Walter Brennan as cranky Grandpappy Amos, became the first of the long-running rural sitcoms when it debuted in October 1957.

ABC took a chance on it, mainly because the "poor stepchild" third network had so little else to offer other than the prestige of Walt Disney's various series.

For six seasons, the McCoy family worked to make their California ranch more profitable than the hardscrabble life they had left behind in the Appalachians. As one might expect, most of the humor came from Grandpappy's conflicts with the world around him; he once railed against the television medium itself: "Hit's jes' pure foolishness, squattin' all day in front of a little black box, starin' bleary-eyed at people who ain't no more'n two inches high." Always ready for a good scrap, Grandpappy carried on a bickering relationship with next-door neighbor George MacMichael, played by Andy Clyde after his Western sidekick career and appearance in the movies with Judy Canova. Since, after all, it *was* California, a hired hand named Pepino (Tony Martinez) spoke suitably fractured English.

When Nolan demanded more money at the end of the 1961–62 television season, the producers reacted in a fashion that was everyday business for soap operas but quite unusual for sitcoms: they killed her off. At about the same time, ABC sold *The Real McCoys* to CBS, which added it to its growing line of rural "corncoms," as some writers derisively labeled them. During one final season on CBS, Grandpappy helped his son pursue other women, but the show's time had passed. Other types of rural comedies had moved into the next hollow, and they took the idea in some completely different directions than the gentle and somewhat moralistic McCoys. (The closing theme song promised, "Week after week you're gonna be showed another human episode / Of Grandpappy Amos an' the girls an' the boys of the family knowed as the Real McCoys.") When it last aired in September 1963, hardly anyone missed it because its neighborhood had become so crowded.

Financing for *The Real McCoys* had come through comedian Danny Thomas's production company, a situation that may or may not have had any direct bearing on what happened at some point in late 1959. Thomas's company was developing an idea for a new series, and company officials decided to test the new series out by making the pilot film an episode of Thomas's show. It was sprung on an unsuspecting public in February 1960 as "Danny Meets Andy Griffith."

Of course, the television audience was already well familiar with Griffith through his many comedy records and the movies we discussed in the last chapter, so seeing him get guest-star billing was not so much of a novelty. What was new was the setting in which Griffith and his low-key humor could be found. Thomas's character, entertainer Danny Williams, en route to appear on a *Person to Person*–type interview show in New York, is driving through the small town of Mayberry, North Carolina, with his family when he is apprehended for running a stop sign. As it turns out, the arresting officer—Andy Taylor, as if you hadn't guessed—is also the town's justice of the peace and the editor of the newspaper. Danny protests,

> *Danny*: There was no road there! Whoever heard of a stop sign where there's no road?
>
> *Andy*: Well now, the town council did vote to put a road in thar, 'bout six years ago I bleave it was. Only trouble is, so far we've just raised enough money fer the stop sign.

The cast also includes young Ronny Howard as the sheriff's son, Opie. Now, where have we heard an unusual name like that before? Oh yes, when putting the script together, Griffith had recalled the drawling bandleader of radio fame, Opie Cates, and decided that his on-air son should carry the same name. (When it comes to rural comedy, "Will the Circle Be Unbroken" is not just a hymn, it is a rule of thumb.) Opie is upset because a lady in the ice cream shop has accidentally stepped on his pet turtle, Wilford. Andy uses the opportunity to deliver a bit of background information on their small family.

Andy: I 'spect it was just Wilford's turn to go. An' we have ta learn ta live with our sorrows. I learned that when you was just a leetle bitty speck of a baby, when I lost yer ma just like you lost Wilford.

Opie: You did?

Andy: That's right.

Opie: Who stepped on Ma?

Other cast members include Frances Bavier as townswoman Henrietta Perkins and Frank Cady as town drunk Will Hoople, who arrests himself and passes out in one of the jail cells. Andy explains that Will became a boozer after the death of his father. "'Fore he passed on, his paw was the town drunk . . . so you see, the position just wasn't open."

Danny becomes even more enraged when Andy spots his large wad of money and immediately raises the five-dollar fine to one hundred dollars or ten days in jail. Thomas sends his family on to New York, choosing to remain behind in the Mayberry jail on sheer principle. He decides to do his television interview direct from the jail to expose the fraud and corruption in the Mayberry legal system, but during the program, Andy delivers a convincing argument that the fine had to be increased in Thomas's case:

Andy: It 'pears to me like a great big entertainer like Mr. Williams here influences a lot o' people. They look up to him, admire him . . . maybe even foller the example he sets. So the way I see it, a big man has got more of a responsibility to obey the law an' respect the fokes who enforce it. Mr. Williams seemed to be in a powerful hurry. That may be why he didn't see that stop sign. Mr. Williams an' a whole lotta people like him seem to be in a big hurry, an' it's

> a pity. 'Cause thar's a whole lotta fine country to be seen 'tween the city he left from an' the city he was a-goin' to. 'Tween them two cities thar's a lotta mighty good fokes to meet, an' a lotta wonderful experiences to be had by a feller that'll take the time to 'preciate it.

The pilot film was enough of a success with the audience that the new *Andy Griffith Show* immediately went into production, debuting on the CBS network at the beginning of the 1960–61 television season. An important addition had come about between the time the Danny Thomas episode had aired and the launch of the weekly series. One of the many viewers watching the Thomas show was Don Knotts, who had made quite a name for himself on *The Steve Allen Show* as a comically nervous gent who always seemed to be in the most dangerous lines of work. Knotts fondly remembered his time working with Griffith in the Broadway and movie versions of *No Time for Sergeants*, and after seeing the pilot film, he called the producers and suggested that sheriff Andy Taylor needed a deputy sidekick. Thus, Knotts's character, Barney Fife, became one of the most renowned and legendary second bananas in sitcom history.

Don Knotts and Andy Griffith had worked together in both the Broadway and film versions of *No Time for Sergeants*, so when Knotts heard that his friend was putting together a weekly television program, he suggested himself for the comic sidekick role.

Calling him a second banana might not be entirely accurate (although the inept Barney might well have slipped on a peel or two). As various members of the staff have explained in recent years, the original concept of the show was that Griffith would be the star funny-man, enlivening the scripts with his trademark yarns as heard on his records. As it turned out, only one of his previously heard monologues made it into the show, and that was an abbreviated version of his "Romeo and Juliet" tale. Instead, after filming the first episode, everyone could see that Knotts needed to be the comic and Griffith more of the wise, all-knowing straight man. Griffith later stated that if the actors had proceeded as originally intended, the show might not have lasted through the end of the first season.

Griffith also disliked the somewhat heavy-handed concept of having him change costume for each of the offices he held in the small town: a uniform when he was serving as sheriff, a robe for justice of the peace, and a green eyeshade as newspaper editor. The end result was a program that was almost realistic enough to be believable but was populated with just enough loony townspeople to keep it from getting dull. Their names and personalities have become such a part of American pop culture that it seems foolish to even try to repeat them here: mother hen Aunt Bee (Frances Bavier); Floyd the Barber (Howard McNear), the fussy tonsorial artist; Ernest T. Bass (Howard Morris), the hillbilly who comes to town periodically to throw rocks at people and things; Otis Campbell (Hal Smith), the town drunk; Briscoe Darling (Denver Pyle), the musically inclined mountain man; and Gomer Pyle (Jim Nabors), the naive service station attendant. Appearing during the first season was our old buddy Dick Elliott, having shed his Marryin' Sam/ Squire Skimp persona for that of Mayor Pike. After Elliott died during production of the second season, the new mayor was played by veteran actor Parley Baer, late of radio's *Granby's Green Acres*. (In the long-running radio version of *Gunsmoke*, Baer had been featured as Chester, while Howard McNear had been heard as Doc. They rarely appeared in scenes together on the Griffith series, but one can only imagine the antics and show biz anecdotes that must have been going on between takes.)

Reams of paper have been used to write about *The Andy Griffith Show* from every conceivable angle. It has been analyzed, dissected, tested, sliced and diced, and still no one can seem to pinpoint just why it was such a hit in its own day and quite probably even more

In Andy Griffith's hometown, Mount Airy, North Carolina, his milestone television sitcom is memorialized in this bronze statue depicting Sheriff Andy Taylor and son Opie (Ron Howard) on their way to their favorite fishin' hole.

popular among television audiences today. The high quality of the writing and acting certainly had much to do with it, but that still does not explain TV buffs' almost fanatical adulation of the program. So familiar are every one of the show's 249 episodes that its staunchest fans can get a chuckle out of such seemingly meaningless phrases as "He was known by two names, one of which was Sport," "Pipe down! This ain't a ball park," "We've got a situation," and "What's the matter? Haven't you ever seen a man take off a dress before?" Taken out of context, they seem totally illogical and irrelevant, but the loyal fans know their context, so to that crowd, they make perfect sense.

While other rural sitcoms never became the cultural touchstone of *The Andy Griffith Show*, things could have turned out a bit differently. During 1959–60, when the elements of the Griffith show were being formulated, Four Star Television was putting the finishing touches on the pilot for another show it hoped would be a hit. Four Star wanted (stop me if you've heard this before) to make a prime-time series out of *Lum and Abner.* This time, however, rather than starring Chester Lauck and Norris Goff, who were busy with their new postradio lives, Four Star decided to cast the show with all new actors, as had been done when radio's *Amos 'n' Andy* made the jump to video. Virtually every tall, lanky actor in Hollywood tested for Lum, and all the short ones were viewed as potential Abners. Just how the final selection was made is unknown, but in the pilot as filmed, Lum was played by Arthur Hunnicutt and Abner by Edgar

Buchanan. As Grandpappy Spears, Andy Clyde moonlighted from his regular *Real McCoys* gig. None of the other characters from the radio show appeared in the pilot, but there were so many other major and minor roles that Lum and Abner themselves were almost lost among the crowd.

The pilot's story line involves Lum's desire to hire an efficiency expert to modernize the Jot 'Em Down Store. This does not sit well with either Grandpappy Spears (whose response to everything is "I'm agin it!") or Abner, who sagely points out, "Lum, the Jot 'Em Down Store is jes' as modern as it wuz the day we bought it forty years ago." Unable to reason with Grandpap, Lum points out, "You can't stop progress; hit'll run right smack over anybody that gits in its way," to which Grandpap responds, "Mebbe so, but at least they'll know there was a bump in the road—me!" Of course, by the time the show winds up, even Lum has had his fill of so-called modern thinking, and the store remains its quaintly outdated self.

Four Star made valiant efforts to sell the new *Lum and Abner* series to a sponsor, but as a resident of either Mayberry or Pine Ridge might have said, the fish just weren't bitin'. The pilot film disappeared into some long-forgotten film vault and has not yet resurfaced despite historians' best efforts to locate it. (Only the script survives.) Had Four Star waited just a year longer, it might have had a bit better chance at selling the series, because television was on the cusp of a country comedy cornucopia (emphasis on the corn) that no one could see coming.

Many chapters ago, we first encountered Paul Henning when he was writing scripts—and performing occasionally—for a Kansas City radio comedy show known as *Happy Hollow.* In the thirty years since, Henning had gone on to write for many different network radio series, most of which had nothing to do with rural humor. By the early 1960s, he had moved on to television writing and was looking to add producing to his bag of tricks, so he started kicking around ideas for a series that might be different enough to attract attention.

Henning later said that it was during a visit to Abraham Lincoln's birthplace that he first began to speculate about how Lincoln would

Few television programs of any type have received the universal condemnation by the critics that greeted the debut of *The Beverly Hillbillies* in 1962. Audiences ignored the critics and made the premiere episode the No. 4 rated show of the week. After only a month on the air, the program was the No. 1 rated show.

react if he were suddenly riding in a car down a busy four-lane tourist highway. He knew that such a premise was too fantastic for television—after all, shows such as *Bewitched* and *I Dream of Jeannie* remained years away—so he thought of ways to bring a similar idea to fruition without going off the deep end into total fantasy. He then remembered the hill country people of southern Missouri, his native state, and how they often reacted violently in the negative when any attempt was made to bring modern roads or other improvements to their backwoods hamlets. He proposed a show about the members of a poor hillbilly family who suddenly became wealthy and had to deal with new surroundings in a big city. At first he thought of having them live on Park Avenue in New York City, but he realized the necessary sets to simulate city streets would be too costly and difficult to replicate on Hollywood's sound stages. Instead, Henning decided, his nouveau riche sharecroppers would move to Beverly Hills, where they (and their show) would be known as *The Beverly Hillbillies.* (To use this title, Henning and his production company had to make a financial settlement with the southern California hillbilly band that had previously used the name.)

When Filmways Television heard that Henning wanted to produce his own series, the company first offered to buy the television rights to the Ma and Pa Kettle characters from Universal. Henning, however, wanted no part of someone else's creation, no matter how successful it had been. He drew up personality profiles for each of his four main characters and then set about the task of casting them as he had visualized. Family patriarch Jed Clampett was fairly easy to cast: Buddy Ebsen had been playing similar roles almost all his life and for that reason was not certain he wanted to get involved in another hillbilly part. He relented when assured that he would be more or less the straight man rather than a buffoon. For the pivotal role of Granny, Jed's cantankerous mother-in-law, Henning tested veteran radio actress Bea Benaderet, but she recommended Irene Ryan. As we have seen, Ryan had brushed up against rural comedy and comedians several times through the years. She was only fifty-nine years old at the time she assumed the role of Granny, but as she told Henning, "You get anyone older and they'll never last through the series." As a reward of sorts for recommending Ryan, Benaderet was cast as the family's wacky Cousin Pearl, who appeared off and on during the early seasons.

The family's two young 'uns were played by relative unknowns. Beautiful but tough as a wildcat Elly May was Donna Douglas, who had made a brief appearance as a Sadie Hawkins contestant in the 1959 *Li'l Abner* film. Idiot nephew Jethro Bodine was Max Baer Jr., son of the famed boxing champ. Jethro and Li'l Abner could have been blood kin, except that Jethro was far more girl-crazy than young Yokum ever was. (Perhaps in an effort to remind viewers of Al Capp's cartoon creation, in the pilot film the Clampetts' nephew was referred to as "Big Jethro.") Beverly Hills bank president Milburn Drysdale, who was in charge of the Clampett fortune, was Raymond Bailey, with Nancy Kulp as his plain Jane secretary, Miss Jane Hathaway, the only character who truly seemed to care about the Clampetts' well-being. Drysdale started out as a relatively straight (if comically greedy) character, but as the series went on, his avarice and lack of even the most basic human morals became increasingly exaggerated until he became almost a cartoon version of himself.

The pilot film for the series aired (with minor alterations) as the first episode in September 1962. It recounts how the O.K. Oil

The chemistry between Buddy Ebsen as Jed Clampett, Irene Ryan as Granny, Donna Douglas as Elly May, and Max Baer as Jethro seemed to hold *The Beverly Hillbillies* together from 1962 to 1971.

Company buys Jed's swamp even though he is convinced the property is worthless. "Too much oil in it," he reasons. Cousin Pearl asks him how much he will receive for his greasy swamp:

Jed: He said it'd run somewheres between twenty-five an' a hundred.

Pearl: Twenty-five an' a hundred?

Jed: I know it don't sound like much—but that Brewster feller seemed to set a great store by the fact that he's goin' to pay me in some new kinda dollars.

Pearl: They AIN'T no new kinda dollars!

Jed: Well, they's new to me. I heard o' gold dollars, silver dollars, paper dollars—but he's payin' me in . . . what'd he call 'em, Granny?

Granny: "Million" dollars.

Jed trusts Cousin Pearl's judgment when it comes to his potential new lifestyle, asking her for advice about whether he should pack up and move away from his ancestral property:

> *Pearl*: Jed, how kin ye even ask? Look around ye . . . Yer eight miles from yer nearest neighbor. Yo're overrun with skonks, possums, coyotes, bobcats . . . You use kerosene lamps fer light, you cook on a wood stove summer an' winter . . . yo're drinkin' homemade moonshine . . . washin' with homemade lye soap . . . an' yore bathroom is fifty feet from th' house, an' you ask should you move?!
>
> *Jed*: [mulls it over] Hmm, reckon yo're right. A man'd be a dang fool ta leave all this.

Each episode thereafter brought viewers up to date on this backstory through the opening theme song, played by Nashville pickers Lester Flatt and Earl Scruggs. (The title sequence did change the background a little by having Jed accidentally uncork a gusher while "shootin' at some food," as the lyrics put it, rather than knowing all along that his swamp contained the greasy kid stuff.)

The critics who reviewed each new television season's offerings for their readers simply could not think of enough derogatory things to say about *The Beverly Hillbillies*. Somehow, the fact that hillbilly comedy had been around for a long time did not seem to faze these reviewers; it was the fact that it was making a comeback that stuck in their craw—that and the overwhelming viewing audience it attracted. The premiere of *The Beverly Hillbillies* snared around 50 percent of the total television viewers during its time slot. By the time the show had been on the air for a month, it was the No. 1 rated program.

Although the critics might not have consciously realized it, what they truly found irritating about the show may have been the fact that for the first time the hillbilly characters were portrayed as eminently likable—much more so than their pseudosophisticated southern California neighbors. There of course had been pleasant rural characters before—as with Lum and Abner and the resi-

The January 1964 *Beverly Hillbillies* episode in which Granny mistakenly thought an escaped kangaroo was a "giant jackrabbit" drew the largest ever audience for a half-hour television show.

dents of Mayberry—but they were not hillbillies in the usual sense of the term. Stretching back to the silent movie days and continuing through the misadventures of Snuffy Smith and Li'l Abner, broadcast hillbillies were usually intended to be laughed at, allowing the audience to feel somewhat superior to them. The Clampetts presented a thoroughly sympathetic image, able to outsmart the city slickers without even being aware of it. The critics—who, after all, were exactly the types the hicks outwitted each week—may have found this particularly irritating.

Another area in which the show's new brand of hillbillies were totally sympathetic was that, especially in the early episodes, the customary slapstick was interrupted by some touching sequences of the members of this simple family trying to adjust to their new life. The second episode aired contains a genuinely moving scene in which Jed tries to explain to Elly why her tomboyish ways will not work for her in California and at the same time fills in some important background information on the characters' lives:

> *Jed*: Y'see, Elly, I raised you like a boy, an' I was wrong to do it. I reckon ever man'd like to have a son, an' you was my only young 'un—When yore maw passed away, I jes' decided to turn you into a boy. By the time Granny come to help out, you was too wild to tame. By thunder, you could outrun, outclimb, outfight, an' outshoot ever boy in them hills.
>
> *Elly*: I still kin, Paw.
>
> *Jed*: Yer purty. I know you don't like it when I say that, but you'll like it when the young fellers around here commence sayin' it—and they will, only they'll probably be usin' fancy words I cain't even understand. But Elly May—ain't nobody can ever tell you how purty you really are 'cept me. Yo're the livin' pitcher of yore maw.

Tender moments like that became less frequent as the series continued, but of course it was meant to be a comedy, and that's what it did best. Some of the show's most interesting (and funniest) sequences came when it deliberately dragged out the traditional hillbilly stereotype and made it ludicrous by contrast. In an early episode, a money-hungry husband and wife "accidentally" back their car into the Clampetts' parked truck and then haul the whole family into court, claiming that the truck rear-ended them, causing life-threatening injuries. As the man and woman relate their version of what happened, the cast acts it out in flashback form, with the truckload of drunken Clampetts careening down the street, firing off their squirrel rifles indiscriminately. Crashing headlong into the car, this perverted version of the family is unperturbed: "Back up an' hit 'em agin!" yells Granny in a moonshine-fueled rage. Of course, back in the courtroom, the Clampetts do not recognize themselves from the couple's fabricated story and in fact are keen to go out and hunt down the sleazy drunkards who have caused the man and woman so much trouble.

In a later episode, Drysdale decides to star the Clampetts in a television commercial to show how banking with him has improved their way of life. (Jane Hathaway's protests that the bank had nothing to do with finding oil on the Clampetts' property fall on deaf ears.) Drysdale sets up the family as hilariously exaggerated versions of what the public expects hillbillies to be: "Shiftless father, dirty grandmother, toothless daughter, and idiot nephew." After being rescued by the Commerce Bank of Beverly Hills, according to the script, Jed emerges in a Brooks Brothers suit, Elly May flashes her pearlies for the camera, Jethro is graduating from college, and Granny proclaims, "I have a date with Mr. Clean."

Petticoat Junction was Paul Henning's second rural-themed hit, premiering at the beginning of the 1963–64 television season. The cast included Bea Benaderet, formerly Cousin Pearl on *The Beverly Hillbillies*, and Edgar Buchanan, who played Abner in Four Star Television's unsold 1962 *Lum and Abner* pilot film.

Regardless of what mud the critics threw at the show, CBS was as happy as a pig in slop with the phenomenal ratings *The Beverly Hillbillies* drew. So happy were network officials that they begged Henning to come up with another series. Sticking with what worked, he decided to continue with the rural theme, but this time the stories would take place in a small community far away from the Clampetts' Beverly Hills lifestyle in both locale and flavor: a farming town known as Hooterville.

Paul Henning's wife, Ruth, claimed that she had given her husband the basic idea for his new show by relating anecdotes about her grandparents, who ran a hotel near the railroad depot in Eldon, Missouri. When Henning had to come up with something to appease the salivating suits at CBS, he cooked up the concept of the Shady Rest Hotel, run by Kate Bradley and her three beautiful daughters. Because the girls liked to swim in the railroad's water tank with their unmentionables draped over the side, the hotel's neighborhood and the title of the show became *Petticoat Junction.*

Hotel Guest: I don't suppose you get television out here.
Kate: No, but I saw it once in Greenville. I didn't get it then, either.

Bea "Cousin Pearl" Benaderet was Henning's first choice to play Kate, with growly voiced Edgar Buchanan (after his *Lum and Abner* pilot did not sell) as lazy Uncle Joe, always on the make for a fast buck. Kate's three daughters, Billie Jo (Jeannine Riley), Bobbie Jo (Pat Woodell), and Betty Jo, kept the casting directors in a whirl, as the roles seemed to change actresses every couple of seasons or so. Only Betty Jo, played by Henning's daughter Linda, remained constant until the end of the series. As the operators of the broken-down Cannonball locomotive that served as Hooterville's only link to the outside world, Henning cast two well-worn Western comedy sidekicks, Smiley Burnette as engineer Charley Pratt and Rufe Davis as conductor Floyd Smoot. Seemingly the only other business establishment in Hooterville was the general store run by Sam Drucker (Frank Cady, the town drunk in the 1960 Danny Thomas/Andy Griffith pilot), which carried on the tradition established by the Stebbins Boys and Lum and Abner.

For some reason—perhaps because *Petticoat Junction* did not rely so heavily on the Hooterville townsfolk outsmarting the city slickers

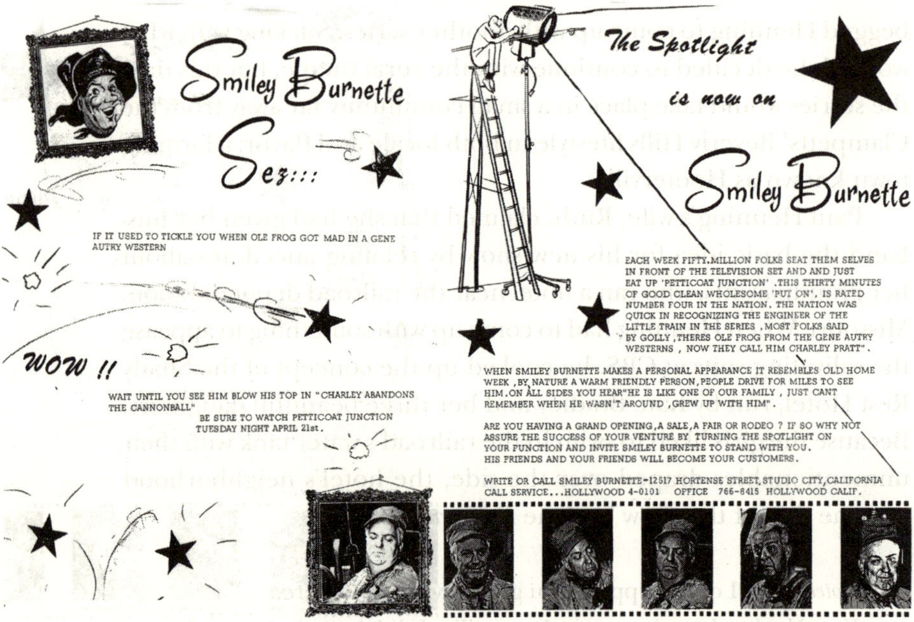

Ex-Western movie sidekick Smiley Burnette was cast as engineer Charley Pratt on *Petticoat Junction*. As evidenced by this handout sheet, he was not adverse to using the show to drum up personal appearances.

Petticoat Junction was unique among rural sitcoms in at least one way: it loaned its name to a small amusement park in Panama City Beach, Florida, where a replica of the Cannonball carried tourists around the property.

(about the nearest the show got to that was a running battle with cranky Homer Bedloe [Charles Lane], a railroad official who constantly schemed to have the Cannonball converted into scrap iron)—the critics were a bit kinder to the premiere of *Petticoat Junction* in September 1963 than they had been with *The Beverly Hillbillies* a year earlier. Some viewers assumed that since *Petticoat Junction* sprang from the same creative well as *The Beverly Hillbillies,* the new show represented the people "back home" on the Clampetts' former turf, but in fact several seasons passed before the characters from the two shows encountered and got to know each other.

The 1964 television season arrived without a new Henning series, but by 1965 the network brass was begging him to give them a third show. CBS made him the unprecedented offer of a half hour with no questions asked: he would not even be required to produce a pilot film. Henning was flattered but realized that he was already burning his candle not only at both ends but dangerously close to the middle as well. He remembered that one of his *Petticoat Junction* writers had been thinking about getting into producing and decided that this might be his protégé's big chance. When Henning approached the writer, Jay Sommers, with the opportunity to create and produce a rural comedy, Sommers responded by dragging out the thirteen scripts of his *Granby's Green Acres* radio series of fifteen years before and set to work adapting the premise and characters for television.

The basic idea remained the same—a born-and-bred city feller buys a farm and tries to make a living in the rural countryside—but John and Martha Granby became Oliver and Lisa Douglas (Eddie Albert and Eva Gabor). The hired help, Eb, remained on the job but was now a young man (Tom Lester) rather than Parley Baer's middle-aged duffer. In the radio series, Mr. Kimball had been the absent-minded general store owner; since *Green Acres* was set in Hooterville, that position was already filled by Frank Cady as Sam Drucker, so addlepated Hank Kimball (Alvy Moore) became the county agent, theoretically on hand to help Douglas improve his farm but generally dispensing useless advice.

Pat Buttram (*right*) had already been a radio star on the *National Barn Dance* and a movie personality in Gene Autry's films, but his role as con man Mr. Haney on *Green Acres* assured him of immortality. Oliver Douglas (Eddie Albert) never stopped falling for Haney's harebrained schemes.

Of the new characters invented for the television series, by far the most important was Hooterville's all-purpose con man, Mr. Haney. According to those who were there, Haney was intended to appear only in the premiere episode, in which he sold the Douglases his run-down farm. However, when Pat Buttram was cast as Haney, he brought with him so many funny ideas—plus that distinctive voice—that Haney became an indispensable part of the series. Like Squire Skimp and Marryin' Sam before him, Haney was prone to appear whenever he got the faintest whiff of money to be made, and he did not particularly care how much he had to exaggerate (or lie) to sell anything to anyone.

Other major new characters included the brother and sister carpenters, Alf and Ralph Monroe (Sid Melton and Mary Grace Canfield)—Ralph was the sister. Then there was the elderly farm couple, Fred and Doris Ziffel (Hank Patterson and Barbara Pepper) and their son, Arnold. The fact that Arnold was smarter than either of his parents yet looked nothing like either of them did not seem to bother anyone in Hooterville except Oliver Douglas. The even more overlooked fact that Arnold was a pig rendered the whole situation even more ludicrous. He performed all sorts of wonders when out of camera range—driving a car, going to school, flying a plane, writing letters—but his favorite pastime was watching television at the Ziffels' farmhouse.

Elements such as Arnold immediately set *Green Acres* apart from the two Henning shows that had preceded it. In fact, while people tended to think of the three series as a unit, Paul Henning went so far as to take out advertisements in the Hollywood trade papers correcting the misconception and giving Jay Sommers full credit as the fertile brain behind *Green Acres.* Although the product of two different creative geniuses, *Petticoat Junction* and *Green Acres* continued to share characters throughout their respective runs. At times story lines began on one show and were continued on the other.

Green Acres's bizarreness extended to the opening theme; whereas *The Beverly Hillbillies* featured the guitar and banjo pickin' of Lester Flatt and Earl Scruggs and *Petticoat Junction* had the railroad-style harmonica melodies of Curt Massey, the *Green Acres* theme was composed and conducted by Vic Mizzy, who gave it a more than little offbeat sound by utilizing eccentric instruments such as the fuzz guitar. (Historian Steve Cox has compared the sound to a "harmonized musical grunt.") Other surreal touches included having the opening credits of each episode appear in unlikely places, such as the toast Lisa Douglas was preparing for breakfast. Of course, Oliver—pragmatist that he was—was the only character who could not see them.

The Henning shows were not the only ones qualified to spawn spinoffs. In addition all of this activity in Hooterville, some changes had occurred out in Mayberry, too. In the last *Andy Griffith Show* of the 1963–64 season, the simpleminded gas station attendant, Gomer Pyle (Jim Nabors), had enlisted in the U.S. Marines, and sheriff Andy personally delivered him to the nearby camp. These events were intended to prepare audiences for the new series that would premiere in the fall of 1964, *Gomer Pyle, USMC.*

Gomer Pyle had the distinction of eventually outlasting the original series that had inspired it, and it became yet another of CBS's hits that caused critics to refer facetiously to the network as the Country Broadcasting System. Gomer's ongoing battles with the apoplectic Sergeant Carter (Frank Sutton) were reminiscent of the newspaper comic pages' long-running *Beetle Bailey,* but more people felt that it was inspired by Andy Griffith's Broadway/motion picture smash, *No Time for Sergeants.* That fact seemed to be reemphasized when ABC debuted its own sitcom version of *No Time for Sergeants*

At the beginning of the 1964–65 TV season, simpleminded Gomer Pyle (Jim Nabors) was spun off from the *Andy Griffith Show* into his own series, *Gomer Pyle, USMC*. Gomer gave his commanding officer, Sergeant Carter (Frank Sutton), apoplexy until 1970.

the same week that Gomer's starring vehicle began. (The television networks obviously engaged in quite a bit of espionage—how else could one explain the fact that CBS dug up *The Munsters* and ABC resurrected *The Addams Family*, a cartoon feature in the *New Yorker* since the late 1930s, for fall 1964 debuts?)

No Time for Sergeants expired after a single season, while *Gomer* lasted the rest of the decade. A true measure of its success was when other actors began appropriating imitations of Nabors's Gomer for various cartoon characters: Robert McFadden used it as the basis for his voice of the title character in *Milton the Monster* (1965), and to a certain extent Gomer's inflections could also be heard (via actor Lennie Weinrib) as Sid and Marty Krofft's friendly dragon on *H. R. Pufnstuf* (1969).

Gomer's departure from Mayberry for the Marines left a gaping hole in the familiar *Andy Griffith Show* cast, and it was filled by bringing in the character of Gomer's cousin, Goober, who had previously been mentioned but not seen. The Griffith producers must have had a fondness for casting actors from Alabama in the show's "village idiot" role; Jim Nabors was a native of Sylacauga, while Goober was played by former Jasper citizen George Lindsey. Like Nabors, Lindsey had arrived in Hollywood in the early 1960s and was immediately saddled with hillbilly roles, although many of his early parts were dramatic or even frightening in nature. Assuming Goober's trademark hat with the crown-shaped brim, similar to that worn by Jughead in the *Archie* comic books, was a terrific step for Lindsey as far as visibility went, but Goober's ghost haunted him for the rest of his life.

As had been the case to a limited extent in radio, the newfound popularity of rural shows affected other comedy programs. During the 1960s, few sitcoms failed to build at least one episode around hillbilly gags. Even earlier, Jack Benny employed such routines in his television programs, just as he had in radio. One 1957 episode features Benny's fictitious manager supposedly relating the story of how he first discovered Jack as a performer in a small-town theater in Arkansas. (Sam Hearn, whose rube voice was often used on the Benny radio show, makes a cameo appearance as the master of ceremonies at the theater.) Billed as Zeke Benny and His Ozark Hillbillies, Jack and a group of imbecilic-looking musicians twang their way through "You Are My Sunshine" and "Fascinating Rhythm." The other member of the act is a tiny girl with a deadpan expression (Valerie Scott) whom Benny introduces proudly as "mah wife."

Benny returned to the same theme seven years later, by which time the hillbilly television programs were firmly entrenched. His 1964 skit chronicled the doins of the Skinner family: Lem (Benny), wife Em (singer Connie Francis), son Clem (Dale White), and Uncle Shem (announcer Don Wilson).

> *Connie*: Lem, Ah think it's high time yuh talked to Clem about th' facts o' life. He's goin' on twenty-eight.
>
> *Jack*: Well, he don't have to learn about that 'til he starts school.

Connie: Well, when's he gonna start?
Jack: When Ah git through.

The routine ends with Francis belting out "I'm Gonna Sit Right Down and Write Myself a Letter" in a hillbilly accent.

In an early 1965 episode of *The Munsters*, Herman tries to straighten out his niece Marilyn's college tuition problems and instead gets mistaken for the school's expected new basketball star. (Don't bother asking how all of this happens; you'd never believe it.) The real basketball player, Moose Mallory, is described as a "big lug from the hills of Kentucky," and sure enough, when Mallory and his Paw show up at the terminal on the latest bus from Nashville, he is played by the ever-luggish Robert Easton, with Paw in the guise of Pat Buttram (who uncorked Mr. Haney the following season). A funny commentary on the state of rural comedy, especially considering that *The Munsters* was another CBS show, comes when Paw and Moose first stick their heads into the basketball coach's office: "Sorry, the class in acting for television is down the hall," says the coach dismissively.

Lucille Ball and Tennessee Ernie Ford were reunited in a February 1967 episode of *The Lucy Show*, thirteen years after Ford's memorable guest shots on *I Love Lucy*. The new program ignored the background of those shows, presenting Ford as Henry Higgins, a country singer who has recently made it big and comes to Los Angeles with copious amounts of money stuffed into cardboard boxes. (Lucy historian Geoffrey Mark Fidelman got it right when he stated that this show "steals generously from *The Beverly Hillbillies*.") When Lucy and boss Mr. Mooney (Gale Gordon) go to see Higgins about opening an account at their bank, they are introduced to Higgins's wife, Effie (Carole Cook), and her oafish brother, Iffie (Robert Easton again). They explain Iffie's odd moniker: "They named him that 'cause iffie'd been a gurl they was gonna name him Effie."

Lucy and Mooney discover that Higgins distrusts "big city bankers" and will do business only with those he considers "down-home country folk." Lucy plays along by getting Mooney dressed in an ill-fitting Duke of Paducah–type suit, insisting that he is as rural as they come and that his middle initial, *J*, stands for Joshua:

> *Mooney*: All my friends call me "Josh."
> *Higgins*: Well, now, you LOOK like a Josh.

Lucy and Mooney fail to mention that Gale Gordon once owned a farm on *Granby's Green Acres*, but they finally convince Higgins of their sincerity by having the bank stage an elaborate hoedown after hours, where Higgins/Ford performs a rousing hillbilly tune:

> *Thar's gonna be singin', thar's gonna be dancin',*
> *Thar's gonna be banjo pickin' an' the fiddler will be there*
> *You'll like our cornbread an' sweet molasses*
> *An' purty gals with ribbons in their hair.*

At the end, Higgins announces that he has decided exactly where he wants to put his money—he's going to build a bank of his own so he can have entertainment like this every night. Mooney is not amused:

> *Lucy*: Well, now—ain't that a knee-slapper?
> *Mooney*: No, that's a NOSE-PUNCHER!

Yes, such routines were popping up everywhere, no matter how loudly the critics protested. Even the mop-topped quartet who starred on *The Monkees* (described by some as the Beatles run through a photocopying machine) got into the act in October 1967. Passing through some indeterminate mountain settlement, they encounter an Elly May Clampett/Daisy Mae duplicate (Melody Patterson) who is hot to marry one of them, and she doesn't particularly care which one. The supporting cast is made up of rural humor veterans; the girl's Paw is Dub Taylor, while her boyfriend's mother is Billie Hayes doing her traditional Mammy Yokum shtick. To give it that extra air of authenticity, the background music is supplied by Lester Flatt and Earl Scruggs, taking a breather from their *Beverly Hillbillies* duties.

In a September 1968 installment of *I Dream of Jeannie*, the titular cutie of a jinni (Barbara Eden) accidentally causes her astronaut pals (Larry Hagman and Bill Daily) to crash-land their test spacecraft in yet another vaguely defined hill country setting, where they are all captured and held under suspicion of being Martians. The hillbilly Paw this time around is J. Pat O'Malley, a British actor known largely for his many voices in Walt Disney animated features but who carved out a second career playing American rustics in television.

This trend toward television-style hillbilly humor even spilled over into movies of the 1960s, although most of them had only limited release—and limited appeal. A pair of them, *Las Vegas Hillbillies* (1966) and *Hillbillies in a Haunted House* (1967), were somewhat inaccurately named, since their only connection with hillbillies was that they starred a parade of Nashville country music stars. What little plots the films had would frequently stop cold for several minutes to allow one or another of these stars (Bill Anderson, Wilma Burgess, Del Reeves, Connie Smith, Merle Haggard, and others) to perform their hit songs. *Las Vegas Hillbillies* even featured one of the few big-screen appearances by the Duke of Paducah, who normally stuck with radio and television.

Another country music superstar, Ferlin Husky, appeared in both films and was featured in another of the most oddball examples of the genre, *Forty Acre Feud* (1965). The slim plot, which could probably have played out in fifteen minutes if not for the many musical numbers, concerns political wrangling in the forgotten community of Shag Bottom. It turns out that when the state's congressional districts were recently redrawn, somehow the forty acres comprising Shag Bottom were left out, so now the town has to elect its own representative to be sent to the State Capitol. The cast reads like a compendium of rural comedians of the day; in addition to Husky's starring role as his goofy alter ego, Simon Crum (with crooked baseball cap and moronic laugh), the roles of Ma and Pa Culpepper are played by Minnie Pearl and monologist Bob Corley, best known for his hit single about a family vacation to Florida, "Number One Street." ("We seen this sign that said 'Free picnic tables, one mile.' So Ah said, 'Let's stop an' git us one!' Well, hit

Forty Acre Feud (1965) was part of a string of movies made primarily to feature musical numbers by Nashville stars. Its cast featured veteran comedians Minnie Pearl and Bob Corley, with singer Ferlin Husky in his dimwitted Simon Crum persona.

wuz awful hard ta git inta the car, hit bein' made outa concrete an' all.") The requisite lineup of Nashville singing stars (Skeeter Davis, Roy Drusky, Loretta Lynn, George Jones, and other luminaries) is dragged in by the heels because a television show known as *Smoky*

As Charley Weaver, Cliff Arquette began his final successful string of television appearances as one of the celebrities on *Hollywood Squares* in 1966.

Mountain Jubilee is broadcasting from the town during the election. Husky performs a pair of songs as himself, with cutaway shots of Simon Crum watching from the audience.

All of these films not only spotlighted Nashville talent but were filmed in Tennessee. At first glance, *Saturday Night in Apple Valley* (1965) would appear to have sprung from the same mold, but in fact it was a West Coast production notable for our discussion only because it features Cliff Arquette in dual roles: as Charley Weaver, mayor

An animated Charley Weaver, still hanging out in his beloved Mount Idy, appeared in a public service announcement for the American Heart Association.

of Apple Valley, and as Mama Coot, using the old-lady characterization that had served him so well since radio days. By the time this movie was released, Arquette's regular appearances on the *Tonight Show* had long been put to bed, and the next year he would begin his most lasting television work, as a panelist on *The Hollywood Squares.*

> *Question*: What do most dentists say you should do with your dentures when you go to bed?
>
> *Charley*: Out at the home we throw 'em into the center of the room an' have a swap party.

Arquette/Charley became one of the most durable staples of the game show during its first several years. Occasionally, just to break things up a bit, Arquette would drag out his drag act and appear as Charley's Mamma, still relating stories about things back home in Mount Idy. (During this period, Arquette used the same persona in a series of well-remembered commercials for Mrs. Butterworth syrup, where he did bear an uncanny resemblance to the figural bottle in which the sticky, sweet substance was sold.) He also provided his own voice for an animated version of Charley in a public service announcement for the American Heart Association.

Arquette suffered a stroke in the early 1970s, and those who knew him said he was never quite the same afterward. *Hollywood Squares* host Peter Marshall related that the members of the show's cast and crew were shocked to see him when he returned to the show, as he had lost so much weight that his Charley Weaver costume simply hung on him like rags on a skeleton. Arquette also seemed disoriented, merely going through the motions of reading what was on the prepared answer cards he received. Improving somewhat as the months went by, good old Charley Weaver held down the lower-left-hand square until his death on September 23, 1974. (His show business legacy lives on in the successful careers of his grandchildren, David, Rosanna, and Patricia Arquette, none of whom have evidenced the slightest interest in reviving their grandfather's Mount Idy stories.)

As we are about to see in our next chapter, by the time Arquette died, television had changed so much that there would hardly have been a place for him and his Mount Idy memories anyway. Some bright spots remained to ignite and then burn out before that happened, though, and we shall now turn our attention to those.

Chapter Eight

From Cartoon Alley to Kornfield Kounty

Since animated cartoons had always been right out in front when it came to employing hillbilly humor during the 1930s and 1940s, it should have been no surprise that they would continue that tradition after theatrical shorts had given way to television. The silent Farmer Al Falfa cartoons were among the first to be made available to local stations, although the prints seen on television frequently had the star rechristened Farmer Gray. When the first country-flavored character created especially for the new medium appeared in 1958, he too had his roots in the world of theatrical cartoons.

In the early 1950s, Tex Avery, one of the directors at MGM's cartoon studio, had fallen in love with a particular voice supplied by a young actor named Daws Butler. Butler had been plying his vocal talents around Hollywood since shortly after World War II; in fact, when *Lum and Abner* had made its ill-advised transition to a weekly half-hour show in 1948, Butler was one of the aspirants who auditioned for a role in the new series, using approximately the same voice he would perfect for Avery a few years later. Under Avery's direction, Butler's southern drawl was affixed to a shuffling, droopy-eyed wolf character who faced all manner of mayhem with a stolidly deadpan expression. When a tree the size of a sequoia fell on his head, the wolf would look at the audience and state the obvious: "Man, that thar wuz a right heavy tree."

When MGM closed its cartoon studio, Tex Avery went on to work in commercials, but the studio's other primary directors, Bill Hanna and Joe Barbera, set up their own studio to produce new animated series for television consumption. Remembering Butler's seemingly bottomless voice box, they built much of their early success around him. He gave a more energetic version of the wolf voice to the second half of the cat-and-dog team Ruff and Reddy, but it truly got attention when the original lackadaisical voice became the basis for the star of Hanna-Barbera's first big breakout successful series, *Huckleberry Hound.*

At the time, many people assumed that Huck Hound and his voice were meant as a spoof or parody of Andy Griffith. This assumption was only natural, since many cartoon characters were based to some degree on established live-action stars; during the 1960s, most of Hanna-Barbera's characters fell into that classification. In the case of Huck, though, his voice had been around since before Andy Griffith had emerged from the North Carolina hills, although most people would not have known that. Huck was not exactly a hillbilly character, but his slow speech and constant off-key warbling of "Clementine" would have rendered him perfectly at home with Bob Burns or Judy Canova in the early days (even if Butler and that voice ultimately did not make the cut for *Lum and Abner*).

Hanna-Barbera's success with *Ruff and Reddy* and *Huckleberry Hound,* followed by *Quick Draw McGraw* (1959) and *Yogi Bear* (1961), soon convinced other cartoon producers that television was the new frontier for animation. Paul Terry, Farmer Al Falfa's creator, had sold his Terrytoons studio to CBS in 1955 and had retired, leaving others to carry on the production of films for both theaters and television. One of the Terrytoons TV cartoons that debuted in 1960 seemed to be more than a little inspired by the popularity of Huckleberry Hound. *Deputy Dawg* presented the misadventures of a slow-talking, slower-thinking lawman in a vaguely defined backwater setting. Several animation historians have identified the locale as southern Mississippi, but the scenery certainly contained more mountains than one would find in that region. At any rate, Deputy Dawg was surrounded by a menagerie of swamp-

Deputy Dawg premiered in TV markets across the country in the fall of 1960.

land critters, including Muskie the Muskrat, Vincent Van Gopher, Ty Coon, and other vermin. The only human figure was the sheriff, who seemed not to notice that he was consorting with a gang of humanized beasts. All of the voices were provided by former Steve Allen sidekick Dayton Allen, who saddled Deputy Dawg with a braying laugh based on Frank Fontaine's character, Crazy Guggenheim, from Jackie Gleason's variety show.

Deputy Dawg appeared in the television logs off and on throughout the 1960s and early 1970s and in 1965 produced a spinoff series of sorts, made especially for theatrical distribution. *Possible Possum* was set in what was apparently the same neighborhood as *Deputy Dawg* but featured a whole new set of characters strongly reminiscent of both the Uncle Remus tales by Joel Chandler Harris and Walt Kelly's popular comic strip, *Pogo*. As in *Deputy Dawg*, all the voices in *Possible Possum* were supplied by a single actor, in this case Lionel Wilson. He imparted an astonishing range of tones to the regular cast, which included not only the title marsupial but also Owlawishus Owl (who sounded like Walter Brennan) and Billy Bear (who supplied the brawn, if not the brains, of the group).

Even though television cartoons were the new breed, at least some demand for theatrical shorts remained, so you could bet your patched britches that the studios would return to the hillbilly comedy that had sustained them in the past. In 1959, Bugs Bunny appeared in *Backwoods Bunny*, a sort of remake of the earlier (and much funnier) *Hillbilly Hare.* In the new film, Bugs is once again visiting the Ozarks, but instead of human hillbillies he runs into two buzzards with empty stomachs and heads to match, Pappy and Elvis (both voiced by Daws Butler, who had more than one variety of rural accent up his sleeve—er, in his throat). Bugs, of course, has no difficulty in staying out of their clutches. At the finish, he arranges to have Elvis blast his Pappy with a shotgun every time he hears someone say the word *Four.* Naturally, Bugs strolls off singing, "I'm looking over a *four* (BANG!) leaf clover that I overlooked be*fore* (BANG!), be*fore* (BANG!), be*fore* (BANG)."

Woody Woodpecker joined the crowd with *Ozark Lark* (1960) and *Canned Dog Feud* (1965), pitting him against a pair of *Hillbilly Hare*–type twin mountaineers; for a change of pace, in *Feudin', Fightin-n-Fussin'* (1968), Woody's adversaries were a husband-and-wife couple greatly resembling Walter Lantz's long-gone Maw and Paw characters. Once again, Dal McKennon and Grace Stafford supplied the voices.

Meanwhile, back on the boob tube, King Features Syndicate, a powerhouse in newspaper comics since the days of William Randolph Hearst, had noticed the blossoming popularity of television animation. The company had watched helplessly as stations across the country reaped pile after pile of green stuff out of the two-hundred-plus *Popeye* cartoons that had been made for theaters between 1933 and 1957. While King Features owned Popeye and his supporting players lock, stock, and spinach can, the company made no residuals off Paramount's sale of these old short subjects. King Features not surprisingly decided to invest in its own new Popeye series, which went into production in 1960. (As we have seen, the original theatrical cartoons had paired Popeye with hillbillies only twice; the made-for-TV cartoons added an episode titled *Hillbilly Dilly*, but it broke no new ground.)

Once the new Popeye cartoons had set sail, King Features tried to adapt some of its other newsprint properties for animation. The result was fifty episodes based on Mort Walker's saga of army life, *Beetle Bailey*; fifty more derived from George Herriman's pioneering humor strip *Krazy Kat*; and, to the point of our discussion here, another fifty representing the latest adaptation of *Barney Google and Snuffy Smith* (although, reflecting the strip's changed focus, the new cartoons reversed the two characters' billing).

The *Snuffy Smith and Barney Google* TV toons suffered from some of the same problems that plagued King Features's Popeye series: hasty production, awkward animation, and stories that could have been summarized on the back of a cereal box. A lot could be said for the voice casting, though. Cartoon legend Paul Frees played both Snuffy and Barney, while the dual roles of Loweezy (Fred Lasswell had changed Billy DeBeck's original spelling, Lowizie) and nephew Jughaid were handled by Penny Phillips.

For the 1963 series of made-for-TV *Snuffy Smith* cartoons, the designs of the comic strip characters had to be somewhat simplified. This new streamlined look even made it into a few toys and other pieces of merchandise released at the time.

The cartoons' story lines roamed far from anything seen in the newspaper strips. In *Beauty and the Beat*, a pair of beatniks arrive in Hootin' Holler ("Like, man, what part of Greenwich Village is this?") and are wowed by Snuffy's recitations of simple nursery rhymes, which they mistake for, like, far-out poetry, man. They outfit the old coot with wig and goatee and open a coffee house with Snuffy and Loweezy as the featured entertainers, talking the lyrics to "Old MacDonald Had a Farm" in beatnik style. *Jughaid for President* has Barney Google counseling the coonskin-capped kid that if he will be more diligent in his schoolwork, instead of a "lazy, no-good varmint" like his uncle, Snuffy, he could someday become president. Google uses the example that Abraham Lincoln started out as a poor farm boy, and Jughaid overdoes the analogy, dressing in a battered stovepipe hat and oversized frock coat, annoying his neighbors and relatives with his wood-chopping, "rasslin'," and "speechifyin'." In the Christmas installment, *It's Better to Give,* Jughaid wants Santa to bring him a bicycle, so instead of a stocking he hangs up a pair of Aunt Loweezy's long johns. "Thar's room enough in thar fer ten bicycles an' a hay wagon besides," Snuffy observes.

This 1963–64 series of cartoons ran on locally hosted children's shows for the next twenty years and marked the final attempt—at least to date—at dramatizing the venerable comic strip. The Snuffy characters were animated only once more, in a 1972 Saturday morning special, *The Man Who Hated Laughter.* In that story, Snuffy and Loweezy (along with Spark Plug, who was for some reason portrayed as belonging to them rather than to Barney Google) are part of a huge group of King Features comic characters that is kidnapped by a mad scientist who wants to remove all laughter from the world. With such a large cast, the Smiths have very little screen time of their own, but it is interesting to see them interacting with Blondie and Dagwood, Little Iodine, Hi and Lois, Maggie and Jiggs, and all the rest.

Since Hanna-Barbera built a major part of its reputation on its television cartoons following current trends in entertainment, when the rural sitcoms of the early 1960s really began to bear their fermented fruit, the studio was quick to respond. During the same period, *The Flintstones* was airing as a weekly prime-time show and got quite a lot of footage out of satirizing contemporary trends in movies and television. Thus, January 1964 brought an episode, "Bedrock Hillbillies," in which Fred inherits property in the state of Arkanstone and has to contend with his family's ages-old feud with the neighboring Hatrocks. Exactly one year later, the Hatrocks returned for another episode, this time foisting their unwelcome presence on the Flintstone homestead in Bedrock.

Unlike *The Flintstones,* in which each episode was a self-contained half hour, most Hanna-Barbera series came in threes. That

Hanna-Barbera's *Punkin Puss and Mushmouse* cartoons began in 1964 as one segment of the *Magilla Gorilla Show*. The orange feline and the floppy-hatted rodent battled it out in episode after episode, with neither coming out as the clear winner.

is, a half-hour show would comprise three individual short cartoons featuring different characters. At the same time the Flintstones were finding out that hillbillies were more dense than Neanderthals, the studio also introduced *The Magilla Gorilla Show.* The three short segments that made up this series included the escapades of the title ape, of course; the Western adventures of sheriff Ricochet Rabbit and his phlegmatic deputy, Droop-a-Long; and yet another hillbilly team, Punkin Puss and Mushmouse. The orange feline's voice was supplied by Allan Melvin, who was doing double duty as the star of the show, Magilla Gorilla; the voice of Mushmouse was no stranger to hillbilly dialects, as Howard Morris was concurrently making his occasional appearances in Mayberry as rock thrower extraordinaire Ernest T. Bass.

The series took the standard hillbilly feud clichés and translated them into cat-and-mouse terms. Unlike most such antagonistic animated pairings, where the big character is perceived as the villain and the little one as the hero, Mushmouse harbored a nasty streak of his own. Neither combatant was precisely a paragon of virtue, and the cartoons frequently ended with Punkin Puss enjoying revenge.

In the first episode, "Calling All Kin," Mushmouse decides to even out the feuding score by bringing in his dozens of look-alike cousins to help bedevil his adversary: "What's th' matter, Punkin Puss, ain't you nevah seed a mess o' Mushmouses before?" Punkin Puss retaliates by hauling in his own mob of identical cousins to vanquish the Mushmice. In "Catch as Cat Can Day," we learn that their community has its own version of Sadie Hawkins Day: the female cats are allowed to capture the male ones with the purpose of matrimony. (*Punkin Puss*: "I don't hafta worry about th' weddin'; I ain't gonna live through th' courtship!") "Hyde and Shriek" has Mushmouse concoct his own "Dr. Jackal" formula that transforms him into a snarling, fanged fiend. In the highly implausible finish, Punkin Puss decides to try out the stuff himself "since Ah'm ornery already!" Instead of changing his personality, the potion simply creates a second, more vicious Punkin Puss with fangs and claws. Punkin No. 2 chases Punkin No. 1 into the middle distance as Mushmouse enjoys a good laugh out of it all.

As if one hillbilly series were not enough, Hanna-Barbera did it again in 1965 as one of the three segments of *The Atom Ant Show*. This time around, the adventures of the superpowered insect (in the title segment) and the machinations of the inappropriately named Precious Pupp (in the second segment) were joined by a quartet of bruins known as the Hillbilly Bears. Designer Iwao Takamoto recalled for animation historians Jerry Beck and Amid Amidi,

> Sometimes a name, like "The Beverly Hillbillies," would start a design. Joe Barbera comes up with this great title, "Hillbilly Bears." Everybody loves it. So he comes in and says he's going to New York and asks if I can give him a family of bears—a mother, a father and this time a teenage girl and a little kid brother. All I know is that they're bears and they're hillbillies. So I do a lineup on that and he grabs it and takes it to New York, comes back and says, "I'm in trouble." I ask, "Why?" and he says, "Because they loved it. They loved the title, concept and designs. And we got the show. Now I don't know what the hell to do with it."

That little problem aside, the studio tackled the project and made the bears into the Rugg family. Paw Rugg (voiced by Henry Corden) was lazy, had notoriously poor posture, and mumbled all of his dialogue in a mostly unintelligible noise. Maw Rugg wore a kerchief around her head like Snuffy Smith's wife, Loweezy, and usually had to translate what her lazy husband was saying. Her voice was provided by Jean VanderPyl, a veteran radio actress whose most lasting role for Hanna-Barbera was Wilma Flintstone. (Like Daws Butler, VanderPyl had auditioned for a role on *Lum and Abner* in 1948, using the same world-weary voice that would later find a home in Maw Rugg's larynx.) The two Rugg young 'uns, Floral and Shag, could hardly have been more different. Floral (also played by VanderPyl) was the hillbilly equivalent of a mid-1960s teenager, with her own record player and Beatles posters on her walls. Shag (voiced by the studio's oft-used second banana, Don Messick) was a fraction of the size of the rest of the family but had inherited his Paw's slouch.

The Hillbilly Bears would have had a hard time making it in today's world of children's programming, if for no other reason than Paw's habit of blasting anyone and everyone with his shotgun. As it was, Maw got pretty tired of it herself. In one episode, "Stranger Than Friction," she makes Paw promise to be nice to the next stranger who wanders onto their property. "Now remember, that's a promise," she tells Paw, "an' us hillbilly folks never breaks a promise." Naturally, the first stranger who shows up is a trained gorilla that

The Hillbilly Bears (1965) depicted the backwoods adventures of the Rugg family, Paw, Maw, Floral, and Shag.

has escaped from a nearby circus, and the ape soon has Paw tied up in knots.

> *Maw*: Now, Paw, count ta ten afore you lose yer temper.
> *Floral*: Shucks, Maw, you know Paw cain't count!

Another episode, "Detour for Sure," could have been inspired by Paul Henning's anecdote about the hill folk who objected to a new highway being put through their region. Paw has the same opinion about the highway crew attempting to build a road across his property, and this time Maw seems to be on his side. When a burly worker tries to serve the eviction papers on the family, Maw brains him with a skillet: "Durn pesky salesmen! We gotta whole mess o' them eviction gadgets already! We don't want none!"

In "Goldilocks and the Four Bears," the Ruggs go for a walk while their bowls of grits are cooling. (Shag comments that he has heard of a similar situation in a certain fairy tale.) While they are away, who should show up but blonde Hollywood starlet Tuesday Goldilooks, who eats the grits and then takes a nap in Paw's bed. She foils all of Paw's forcible attempts to enter the house, but after nearly chasing the Ruggs into the next county, she has a better idea. Her next movie will be *Goldilooks and the Four Bears,* and during the filming she reenacts all of the gags she pulled on Paw, including clobbering him with a frying pan as he sticks his head through the window.

Paw: Mumble grumble mutter mumble.

Director: What did he say?

Maw: He said, "Air you shore this is the way Marlo Brandon got started?"

Paw: Grumble mumble mutter mumble ouch.

After their original run, the studio largely forgot about the Hillbilly Bears until 1972, when they were included, along with most of the studio's other characters, in an hour-long special, *Yogi's Ark Lark.* While hanging wet clothes during freezing weather, Maw is exasperated when a pair of icy trousers shatters like glass. "Them overhauls only lastid forty years," she complains. "They jes' don't make 'em like they used to." When the special gave birth to a weekly Saturday morning series, *Yogi's Gang,* the bears continued to make occasional appearances. (At least a few episodes featured a mail-delivering pelican whose voice was an imitation of Percy Kilbride as Pa Kettle.)

Some animation histories have erroneously reported that the Hillbilly Bears were a part of Hanna-Barbera's 1968 series, *Wacky Races,* which was unashamedly based on the 1967 feature film *The Great Race.* An unlikely crowd of racers in even more unlikely vehicles made up the cast of the cartoon show; one of the entries in the weekly race was a rattletrap heap known as the Arkansas Chug-a-Bug, driven by humanoid hillbilly Luke, who spent most of his time on the road asleep at the wheel, using his bare feet to steer. His companion was the cowardly Blubber Bear, who had one conniption fit on top of another at the slightest danger. Thus, Blubber Bear was a hillbilly bear, but not one of the Hillbilly Bears. Get it? Aw, never mind.

The *Beverly Hillbillies* cast members appeared in commercials for Kellogg's cereals, and the products were often worked into the show's story lines.

This explosion of cartoon hillbillies, in combination with all of the live-action sitcoms, even spilled over into the world of advertising—the commercials that interrupted all shows, whether comedies, dramas, or cartoons. As those viewers of a certain age will recall, the casts of various shows commonly appeared in character for the commercials as well, making the ads seem like miniature extensions of the story line. *The Andy Griffith Show* was sponsored by Post cereals (as was its spinoff, *Gomer Pyle, USMC*), and sheriff Andy and deputy Barney filled time between scenes by plugging Grape Nuts ("A Grape Nuts breakfast fills ya up, not out"). Griffith proved he was not adverse to advertising even later in his career, when he starred in a long-running series of commercials for Ritz crackers ("Gooooooood crackuh!").

Probably the show that achieved the most seamless connection with its sponsor was *The Beverly Hillbillies.* The program has been in syndicated reruns for so many years now that most people probably do not realize that the opening credits sequence has been truncated. As it appears today, the final shot is the head-on view of the Clampetts driving through Beverly Hills in their ramshackle truck, and the picture (and theme music) fade just after creator/producer Paul Henning's on-screen credit. During the original CBS run, however, that was not the end. Immediately after the Henning credit, the truck continued on its way, as did the music and lyrics:

Now come along an' visit with the Clampett family
As they learn the simple pleasures of the hills of Beverly;
An' that includes the products of your sponsor of the week,
The cereals of Kellogg's, Kellogg's of Battle Creek.
K, E, double L, O, double good, Kellogg's best to you!

The final shot of the complete opening was a Kellogg's billboard showing a giant box of Corn Flakes. With the critics frothing at the mouth about how corny the show was, no better sponsor could have been chosen. The cast appeared in the customary commercials for Kellogg's, but the products were also frequently incorporated into the main body of the show. Numerous episodes managed to work in a scene where one character or another (usually Jethro, whose stomach was described as a bottomless pit) was snacking on cereal between meals, and there was a running gag about Jed's attempts to enjoy a bowl of Corn Flakes, only to be interrupted before he ever got the first spoonful into his mouth.

When the Clampetts themselves were not selling Corn Flakes, the job was handed over to another rural comedy team we encountered earlier in this book, Homer and Jethro (no relation to Jethro Bodine). The veteran musical satirists participated in a series of commercials in which the tag line was always the same:

Homer: Waiter, give me coffee without cream.
Jethro: We're outta cream, sir.
Homer: Well, make it without milk, then.
Both: Ooooh, that's corny!

Or,

Homer: My uncle crossed a raccoon with a kangaroo.
Jethro: A raccoon with a kangaroo? What'd he git?
Homer: A fur coat with pockets.
Both: Ooooh, that's corny!

Had enough of that? The audience couldn't get its fill, so Kellogg's even offered Homer and Jethro joke books as Corn Flakes premiums.

For the first few years, Kellogg's alternated with Winston cigarettes as *The Beverly Hillbillies* sponsor, and the cast appeared in commercials for that product as well. In one of them, Granny and Cousin Pearl were discussing the virtues of smoking Winstons and put their own spin on the famous "Winston tastes good, like a cigarette should" jingle:

Pearl: Remember, Granny, Winston tastes good . . .
Granny: . . . Like a cigarette had oughta!

After the U.S. surgeon general's initial warning about the possible health hazards of smoking was issued in 1964, there was a general feeling that the family-oriented show might receive bad publicity from being associated with such a controversial product, so the cast commercials stopped. Winston's parent company, R. J. Reynolds tobacco, pulled its sponsorship in 1965, leaving Kellogg's to find its own way through the corn alone.

(For reasons unknown, Kellogg's chose not to flake off into the other Henning-produced sitcoms. *Petticoat Junction* was sponsored by Prell shampoo, which had the benefit of Kate Bradley's three knockout daughters demonstrating its quality, while Kellogg's archrival, Post, somehow snatched up *Green Acres*.)

Kellogg did so well with *The Beverly Hillbillies* and Homer and Jethro pitching its cereals to prime-time audiences that the company and its ad agency, Leo Burnett, decided to add a hillbilly character to its established lineup of animated mascots: Tony the Tiger; Toucan Sam; Snap, Crackle, and Pop; and the rest of the gang. Stars (sometimes All-Stars or Sugar Stars) had been twinkling around the cereal aisle for several years without any long-running character of its own; Huckleberry Hound had pushed Stars for a while, as had a magician known as the Wizard of Oats. Finally, in 1965 the Stars brand was given over to a character known as Hillbilly Goat. In his commercials, he ate the alarm clock that awakened him for breakfast, then went for a box of Stars (eating the box along with the contents), while singing,

Shore do love those crunchy oats,
Brand-new Stars with caramel coats;
Good fer kids an' hillbilly goats . . .
Human kids, that is!

Perhaps encouraged by its successful sponsorship of *The Beverly Hillbillies*, Kellogg's introduced a new character, Hillbilly Goat, as the spokesperson—er, spokesmammal—for Sugar Stars cereal in 1965.

After Pepsi-Cola bought the national marketing rights to the soft drink Mountain Dew, the product was promoted with clever animated commercials featuring comical hillbillies who shouted "Ya-hooo! Mountain Dew!" and "It'll tickle yore innards!"

Although Kellogg's tried hard to make Hillbilly Goat and Stars into stars, neither the character nor the brand ever really caught on. However, another product that relied on animated hillbillies certainly did well for a number of years. Mountain Dew, that citrus flavored soft drink, had been around in one form or another since the late 1940s, but not until Pepsi-Cola purchased the national bottling and distribution rights in 1964 did the advertising shift into high gear. Pepsi decided to capitalize on the drink's name with the slogans "Thar's a bang in ever' bottle o' Mountain Dew," "It'll tickle yore innards," and most famously, "Ya-hooo! Mountain Dew!"

The animated commercials depicted humorous hillbilly vignettes set to new lyrics for Grandpa Jones's trademark tune, "Mountain Dew":

Beautiful Sal was a stone-hearted gal,
Refusin' to bill or to coo;
But Clem was right smart, he appealed to her heart
With that gal-gittin' good ol' Mountain Dew.

The accompanying cartoon showed the undeniably lovely Sal rejecting all of her would-be suitors' advances (and if anyone thought it was impossible for a hillbilly gal to wear less clothing than Daisy Mae, they had another think a-comin'). When pint-sized Clem offers the coquette a bottle of the product, gunshots

Mountain Dew's successful advertising campaign soon inspired imitators, including Hill Billy Brew and Kickapoo Joy Juice.

fire from Sal's ears as she yells, "Ya-hooo! Mountain Dew!" and then growls like a wild varmint moving in for the kill as she grabs Clem and smothers his runty frame with kisses.

Mountain Dew used its mostly nameless hillbilly cast in all forms of advertising aside from the animated commercials, and as one might expect, inspired some imitators, including Hill Billy Brew and Kickapoo Joy Juice (which used the Li'l Abner characters in its advertising). Having established itself through these methods, Mountain Dew began to gradually eliminate the hillbillies from its packaging and advertising during the late 1960s, although some of its later slogans ("Get that barefoot feeling") continued the tradition at least somewhat.

While all of these words from our sponsors were taking place, rural sitcoms experienced some changes in the latter half of the 1960s. Most notably, Andy Griffith had grown so tired of playing the Andy Taylor character that he announced that he would leave his own show at the end of the 1967–68 season. General Foods (and Post cereals) was still the sponsor, and company officials did not want the show to end. The question became how to do *The Andy Griffith Show* without Andy Griffith? The answer: prepare a new series, *Mayberry, RFD,* that would retain as much of the original setting and characters as possible and hope that no one would notice Andy's absence. (At the time, George Lindsey was telling reporters that the Griffith producers were preparing a Goober Pyle spinoff series, as had happened with Jim Nabors as Gomer, but apparently nothing ever came of those plans.)

Knowing what was going to happen ahead of time enabled the writers and performers to come up with a smooth transition between the two series. The final episodes of *The Andy Griffith Show* introduced dancer Ken Berry as townsman Sam Jones; when the new fall season arrived, the first episode of *Mayberry, RFD* featured Andy Taylor marrying his longtime sweetheart, teacher Helen Crump (Aneta Corsaut), then taking Opie and his new bride and moving to Charlotte. From that point, the series continued with Berry as the star, supported by Griffith veterans Lindsey, Frances Bavier, Jack Dodson (as Howard Sprague), and Paul Hartman (as Emmett Clark, the inept fix-it man). Even the *Mayberry, RFD* theme song was a piece of background music, the "Mayberry March," that had been featured in episodes of the original series since the beginning.

The Beverly Hillbillies, Petticoat Junction, Gomer Pyle, USMC and nearly all of the rest of CBS's programming switched from black and white to color at the beginning of the 1965–66 season. The change necessitated refilming the opening title sequence for each of the shows; in the case of the *Beverly Hillbillies* cast, it gave them a chance to make a permanent record of Jed's oily discovery, as the black-and-white opening titles had used scenes originally shot for the pilot film. *Petticoat Junction* took the opportunity to recast two of the three girls, bringing in Gunilla Hutton as Billie Jo and Lori Saunders as Bobbie Jo. Since *Green Acres* was premiering that fall and was in color from the beginning, it got to keep its original opening all the way to the end.

The biggest challenge facing *Petticoat Junction* came when star Bea Benaderet died of cancer on October 13, 1968. Her declining health had been obvious in the shows in which she had appeared; her final one aired on October 26, and featured only Benaderet's voice, with a stand-in seen from the rear. The story line's excuse for Kate Bradley's sudden absence was that she had gone off to another city to care for an ailing relative. No sooner had Kate (and Benaderet) departed than the show started a crossover story line with *The Beverly Hillbillies*, no doubt in an attempt to keep the ratings from sagging. During the period between Thanksgiving and Christmas 1968, the Clampetts and the Hooterville denizens moved back and forth between their respective shows; the plot line included a Thanksgiving dinner featuring the casts of both programs plus *Green Acres.* (One reason Jed and Granny had never previously visited the Shady Rest Hotel presumably was that in their world, Benaderet was Cousin Pearl instead of Kate Bradley—an' thar jes' ain't no tellin' what sorta tribulations woulda takened place iffen those two separate worlds hadda collided!)

Petticoat Junction rolled along for two more seasons by introducing June Lockhart as Dr. Janet Craig, who took over operation of the hotel. Edgar Buchanan, as Uncle Joe, was promoted to star billing in the new opening titles. (And yes, by that time Gunilla Hutton was out as Billie Jo and Meredith MacRae was in, making *Petticoat Junction* have the most-often-revised opening of any of the rural comedies.)

The 1969–70 season of *The Beverly Hillbillies* opened with the cast traveling to the Silver Dollar City theme park near Branson, Missouri. The show previously had offered no real hints about exactly where the Clampetts had lived before moving to California other than the fact that Granny was from the Smoky Mountains of extreme eastern Tennessee. Inasmuch as Silver Dollar City was now given as their home, viewers were free to assume that the Ozarks of southern Missouri were the clan's original stompin' grounds.

With all of these shows still thriving in variations of their original forms, one would think the airwaves were quite crowded with corny comedy, especially on CBS. Oh, yeah? The next big project proved once again that rural humor did not necessarily have to be southern in origin—and in this case, it did not even have to come from the United States. In October 1968, Canadian comedians Gordie Tapp and Don Harron began a north-of-the-border show, *Hot Diggity.* It followed the traditional variety show format, mixing music and extended skits with quick jokes, much like NBC's phenomenally successful *Rowan and Martin's Laugh-In,* which had premiered in January of that year. One of the first *Hot Diggity* episodes featured

In the late 1960s, Grandpa Jones was still performing the same aged character he had begun in 1935. In October 1968, he appeared as a guest on a Canadian rural comedy show, *Hot Diggity*, that was the basis for the long-running U.S. program, *Hee Haw*.

Grandpa Jones and Minnie Pearl as its guests, and Jones described it in his autobiography: "The set was made up to look like a barn, and different ones of us would sit around on hay bales or barrels. A string band would play 'May the Bird of Paradise Fly Up Your Nose' and they would cut to me, and I'd say something like, 'Twenty years ago the girls wore bathin' suits that looked like Mother Hubbards; now they wear ones that look more like her cupboard.' Then the music would go on for another chorus, and they would cut to Minnie for a joke. And Gordie would tell a gag at the end of every segment and slap his leg and say, 'Hot diggity!'"

The Canadian producers, Frank Peppiatt and John Aylesworth, proved that rural humor was international in its scope, but good old reliable CBS (who else?) brought the format to U.S. viewers. In the summer of 1969, the network began its own answer to *Laugh-In*, puzzling audiences with its title, *Hee Haw*. The program initially was thrown onto the air as a replacement for a recently canceled variety show starring the Smothers Brothers, whose endless references to touchy political issues had kept nervous CBS executives biting their fingernails all the way up to their elbows. *Hee Haw* would offer no such social commentary. Filmed in Nashville and set in Kornfield Kounty, which made Hooterville look like Times Square, the series made use of most of the surviving *Grand Ole Opry* comedians from the early days, including Grandpa Jones, Minnie Pearl, and Stringbean Akeman, but it also provided exposure for some humorists who had come along in the years since the Opry's network radio run had run out.

Chief among this new group was Archie Campbell, who had joined the Opry in 1959, initially as a replacement for the recently

Archie Campbell had joined the *Grand Ole Opry* in 1959 as a replacement for Rod Brasfield. However, his greatest fame came from his television exposure on *Hee Haw* beginning in 1969.

deceased Rod Brasfield. According to his son, Phil, Campbell somewhat shocked the Opry management at first by refusing to wear the same type of ill-fitting duds that Brasfield had used; in fact, said Phil, his dad was the first performer to wear a tuxedo on the Opry stage. Campbell's jokes were of the reliable if not always original type, but what would become the signature of his act came about quite against his wishes.

According to Phil Campbell, one day an aspiring comedy writer came to Archie Campbell with a routine that took the well-known story of the Three Little Pigs and transposed the letters into a smorgasbord of spoonerisms. He offered to sell the routine to Campbell, but the comic thought it was the dumbest, most ridiculous thing he had ever heard and was convinced that no one would think it was funny. Other heads prevailed, and Campbell did his best with the story of the "Pee Little Thrigs." For once, his comedy judgment must have been off, because audiences ate it up as if it were pork sausage and then held out their plates for more. The transposition of the letters frequently produced material that was slightly naughty without veering off course into adults-only territory: "I'll puff an' I'll huff an' I'll hoe your blouse down!" Once "Pee Little Thrigs" had taken off, Campbell came up with some sequels, and along with his other material, all of them became staples of the new *Hee Haw* series. He tackled "Beeping Sleuty," and of course there was the immortal "Rinderceller." ("If you wanna go to a bancy fall an' meet a pransome hince, don't fergit to slop your dripper.")

Another talent introduced on *Hee Haw* would have seemed to be even more unlikely than Campbell and his fractured fairy tales: Junior Samples of Cumming, Georgia. As an entertainer he made a terrific sawmill hand—his actual profession—but he shot to stardom on country music radio stations in 1966, all because of a fish story. More as a joke than anything else, Samples started spreading the story around his neighborhood that he had caught a world record bass but instead of preserving the body or having a photo taken, he had eaten the whole thing. The tall tale brought out Jim Morrison of the Georgia Game and Fish Commission, who recorded an "interview" with Samples, although Morrison obviously realized that the whole thing was a big put-on. The resulting recording was augmented with some plodding background music to match Samples's molasses-slow enunciation and released to radio stations under the title *World's Biggest Whopper.* Other records followed, until it seemed natural that Samples would be added to the *Hee Haw* cast as the resident moron. Much of his humor on the show stemmed from his real-life personality:

> *Judge*: Junior, you've been brought in here fer drinkin'.
> *Junior*: Well good, let's git started then.

Stringbean Akeman's routines involved his reading letters from home, which sounded suspiciously like he might have picked up one or two of Charley Weaver's former writers. Stringbean was still performing regularly on both *Hee Haw* and the *Grand Ole Opry* in November 1973, when he and his wife were brutally murdered in their home during a botched robbery attempt. The producers of *Hee Haw* wisely decided to continue utilizing the film footage already in the can, giving people a fitting way to remember the lanky banjo plucker.

Others in the large *Hee Haw* cast included hosts Buck Owens and Roy Clark; *Hot Diggity* alumnus Don Harron as newscaster Charlie Farquharson, whose accent was that of a Scots-Irish farmer from southern Ontario; Gordie Tapp, who had started the whole thing; chubby Lulu Roman; Misty Rowe, a buxom blonde with a squeaky little-girl voice; former *Petticoat Junction* cuties Jeannine Riley and Gunilla Hutton; girl next door Cathy Baker; and of course, Jimmie Riddle and Jackie Phelps, who provided occasional bursts of their specialty, "eephing and hamboning." (If you don't know what that is, you obviously never saw the show.) In later seasons, other cast members were added, including George Lindsey, still playing Goober Pyle, and those two ex-Western sidekicks who had gone to the hillbillies, Dub Taylor and Slim Pickens.

If anyone thought the television critics had savaged *The Beverly Hillbillies* when it debuted, they had not seen anything until those same critics started braying about *Hee Haw*. In a cover story less than a year after the show's premiere, *TV Guide* kindly pointed out some of the comments that had been made by reviewers in the more sophisticated parts of the country:

"It is so bad, it's an insult to the intelligence of a nursery school dropout."

—Eleanor Roberts, *Boston Herald Traveler*

"Possibly the worst show I've ever seen."

—Ann Hodges, *Houston Chronicle*

"For the life of me I can't realize any entertainment value or enjoyment out of this obvious put-on."

—Rex Polier, *Philadelphia Bulletin*

Just as the earlier critics seemed to be consciously or subconsciously reacting to the fact that *The Beverly Hillbillies* made their class of citizen look like the dumb ones, the critics of *Hee Haw* seemed especially irked that the vernacular variety show had, as *TV Guide* phrased it, "come to life over the dead bodies of the Smothers Brothers, who were always making those terrific jokes about racial tensions, the Vietnam war, Congressional ethics, air pollution and the military-industrial complex." Probably demonstrating just what type of comedy the general audience preferred, *Hee Haw* was such a smasheroo as a 1969 summer replacement that it was soon added to CBS's regular schedule for the 1969–70 season.

As if the advent of *Hee Haw* were not enough to send the critics screaming from their comfortable chairs in front of the tube, the number of rural shows on television appeared about to get even more out of control. It was natural that someone would try to come up with a *Li'l Abner* series, and try they did—not once, but twice. The first pilot aired in September 1967, starring Sammy Jackson as Abner and *Petticoat Junction/Hee Haw* eye candy Jeannine Riley as Daisy Mae. Jerry Lester, who had been a big comedy-variety TV star in the 1950s, handled the role of Pappy Yokum, and who played opposite him as Mammy? Would you believe Judy Canova? You're tellin' I!

(Around this same time, Canova put up her hair in the familiar pigtails for a commercial plugging the new "country style" Shake 'n' Bake mix. "Makes chicken as good as country fried without fryin',"

The first two seasons of *Hee Haw* aired on CBS, but in 1971 the network decided to purge itself of all country-themed programming, and the happenings in Kornfield Kounty were one of the casualties. The show began producing new episodes for syndication and remained on the air in that form until 1992.

During its original network run, *Hee Haw* even made it into comic books, with reasonable facsimiles of the show's core cast.

In 1970, one final aborted attempt occurred to bring *Lum and Abner* to television, this time in animated cartoon form. An unidentified animator prepared these sketches of how the characters might look. They in no way resembled their appearance in earlier publicity photos and movies.

she spieled. "Take it from this country chicken, try new Shake 'n' Bake country style!")

The second *Li'l Abner* pilot appeared in April 1971, this time with Ray Young as Abner and relative unknown Nancee Parkinson as Daisy Mae. (Remember Ray Young's name, because you'll meet him again in the next chapter.) The producers of this version did not take any chances when it came to Mammy Yokum, bringing in Billie Hayes to do her thing one more time. Pappy was a bit more unusual casting: Billy Bletcher, a short actor with a deep voice who was best known for his many animated cartoon villain roles (including Disney's Big Bad Wolf). These two *Li'l Abner* pilots came along at about the time a theme park called Dogpatch USA opened near Harrison, Arkansas, and its operators and the television bigwigs clearly hoped that the series would help the park and vice versa. However, when there were no takers for the pilots, the idea of a weekly *Li'l Abner* series fell off a precipice and vanished into Bottomless Canyon.

(Even a year after Al Capp discontinued the newspaper strip in November 1977, some newspapers carried a story announcing that NBC would be airing a one-hour *Li'l Abner* special featuring Polly Bergen, Kaye Ballard, and Louis Nye. If this program ever made it to the air, no concrete evidence indicates the fact.)

If *Li'l Abner* was trying to make it to television, could Lum and Abner be far behind? In 1970, CBS producer Ace Ochs contacted Chester Lauck and Norris Goff about producing *Lum and Abner* as an animated cartoon and sent an unidentified cartoonist's sketches of possible ways the characters could be depicted. They in no way resembled any previous visual portrayal of the Pine Ridge storekeepers. Dal McKennon and Daws Butler were recruited to supply the voices, but that was as far as the project went. Longtime *Lum and Abner* writer Roswell Rogers recalled that around the same time, there was talk of licensing the characters as a running feature on *Hee Haw,* and this concept eventually blossomed into the idea of a new series. Archie Campbell was to have played Abner, but no one could remember which cast member was the potential Lum. Rogers was preparing to move lock, stock, and typewriter to Nashville to begin composing scripts for the series when it was suddenly called off.

All of the rural comedy mainstays felt that something strange was happening during the 1970–71 television season, especially on their comfortable old home network, CBS. Programming executives had begun to use the dreaded term *demographics* to determine the most desirable audiences for television sponsors; experts found that young, urban dwellers were far more valuable than older, rural residents. CBS's schedule was still loaded down with rural shows and stars in the fall of 1970 when the network premiered *The Mary Tyler Moore Show,* a direct appeal to this more appealing audience. That bombshell was followed in January 1971 by *All in the Family,* which took edgy, urban humor in directions no TV viewer had ever before gone—not even with those darlings of the intelligentsia, the Smothers Brothers.

The ratings pulled in by both new shows, combined with their desirable demographics, meant that rural comedy was on the chopping block. *Petticoat Junction* and *Gomer Pyle, USMC* had ended at the close of the 1969–70 season, but Jim Nabors had quickly returned to the air in a variety series. CBS was still airing new episodes of *The Beverly Hillbillies, Green Acres, Hee Haw,* and *Mayberry, RFD,* and Andy Griffith himself had launched a new show, not surprisingly called *The New Andy Griffith Show.* CBS, emboldened by the success of its hip humor and completely fed up with its "Country Broadcasting System" nickname, took a deep breath and canceled all of those shows, along with the Jim Nabors variety series and the legendary *Red Skelton Show.* (Even though Skelton was not necessarily a rural comedian—the character of Clem Kadiddlehopper notwithstanding—studies found that his audience comprised primarily that highly undesirable older, rural demographic, so he got the axe along with all the hillbillies. The same fate awaited the venerable *Lawrence Welk Show,* whose audience was more elderly than rural.)

Some of the canceled shows and their stars fared better than others. *The Beverly Hillbillies* was probably headed for the retirement home anyway, as its story lines had been getting rather "out there" during its final seasons. In one of the best-remembered episodes from the late years, Granny had fallen in with a group of hippies who were positively giddy with anticipation when she told them she smoked crawdads—especially after she added, "but first I'll need a little pot." When the Clampetts had to start dealing with drug abuse, the women's lib movement, and geisha girls, it was time to pack up and head back to the hills. At any rate, Irene Ryan died in April 1973, and it is unlikely that the show could have survived without Granny.

Hee Haw got the best of the deal, as its production company never lost stride. New episodes continued to be produced for the burgeoning syndication market, and in that format the show eventually reached an even larger audience than it had enjoyed on CBS. (Lawrence Welk followed the same pattern, and his syndicated show produced new episodes for years after its network cancellation.) As we have already seen, George "Goober" Lindsey found himself without a home when *Mayberry, RFD* was vacated, so he simply shuffled over to *Hee Haw* and continued playing the same character there.

So, within the space of one television season, the face of rural comedy on the small screen not only changed but was obliterated entirely. Quite a few years passed before anyone else attempted to revive the genre, and when they did so, it took a drastically different form.

Chapter Nine

They're in a Heap o' Trouble

In the early 1970s, the hills were not alive with the sound of music. In fact, with every trace of a rural situation comedy consigned to the junkyard, them thar hills were as quiet as a cemetery. The performers who had been enjoying steady work found that their talents provoked nowhere near the same demand as they had during the preceding ten years. However, a few remnants still hung around like autumn leaves in November.

Except for the "Martins and the Coys" segment in *Make Mine Music*, the Walt Disney studio had evidenced very little interest in rural humor during the years when Walt was still alive. After his death in December 1966, some observers doubted whether the company could continue turning out successful animated feature films, so *The Aristocats* (1970), the first Disney animated feature to be produced totally without Walt's input, aroused quite a bit of interest. The movie started a trend of using rural comedians for several of its voices, a practice that would persist for the rest of the decade.

The main plot of *The Aristocats* need not concern us here, except to say that it involves a family of pampered felines in Paris who become the target of a dastardly kidnapping—er, make that cat-napping—scheme. (The mother cat, Duchess, was played by Eva Gabor, and a horse was voiced by Nancy Kulp, both of whom knew more than a little about working with rural comics.) Partway through the

Pat Buttram found a whole new career by providing voices in four animated Disney feature films released between 1970 and 1981, *The Aristocats*, *Robin Hood*, *The Rescuers*, and *The Fox and the Hound*.

story, the audience is introduced to two farm hounds, Napoleon and Lafayette, who speak in the immediately familiar voices of Pat Buttram and George Lindsey. If anyone stopped to wonder what two dogs with Alabama accents were doing in the French countryside, they would have been even more surprised to find where these voices turned up next.

In 1973, Disney released *Robin Hood*, a retelling of the famous English legend with an all-animal cast. Along with a smattering of British voices were a crowd of others that made Sherwood Forest sound more like the Okefenokee Swamp. The evil Sheriff of Nottingham (a wolf) was played by Pat Buttram in his best Mr. Haney tradition, gleefully extracting every bit of tax money possible from the poverty-stricken villagers ("Th' family that stays together PAYS together!"). His two bumbling deputies (vultures) were voiced by George Lindsey and Ken Curtis, who was then appearing as Matt Dillon's hillbilly deputy Festus on CBS's *Gunsmoke.* Portly Friar Tuck (a badger) was *Lum and Abner* alumnus Andy Devine. And, as if all of these hick voices were not enough, the film was narrated by Nashville music star Roger Miller as the troubadour of the Merrie Men, Allan-a-Dale (a rooster).

People were getting used to hearing the same voices turn up over and over again, so when *The Rescuers* (1977) came along, it seemed natural that a good portion of the film was set in the Louisiana bayou country, where those familiar voices would at least sound at home. A posse of critters known as the Swamp Volunteers played a crucial part in the finale, with Pat Buttram returning, this time as lazy, shiftless Luke the muskrat. George Lindsey was also back, although as Deadeye the Rabbit he was little more than background noise. The same could be said for Dub Taylor's dubbing the voice of Digger the Mole. The major character of Orville the Albatross was brought to life by the voice of Jim "Fibber McGee" Jordan, who, as we know, started out as Luke Gray, the *Smackout* storekeeper, so many decades earlier. (Former Hooterville resident Eva Gabor returned as Miss Bianca the mouse, one of the rescuers of the title.)

Even the talented artists and staff responsible for making the Disney features felt that they were getting into something of a rut, so the next film, *The Fox and the Hound* (1981), was going to bear a new scent by being a much more serious and emotional story. Unable to completely let go of the past, however, studio officials again brought in Pat Buttram, returning him to the form in which he had started in *The Aristocats* eleven years earlier—a farm dog.

Despite the relatively dismal state of rural humor in the early 1970s, a new stock character emerged in what remained of the genre. As we have gone along, we have repeatedly seen how certain character types turned up over and over again: the big, handsome, but dumb oaf (Li'l Abner, Cedric Weehunt, Jethro Bodine); the cutie who makes men fall all over themselves with passion (Daisy Mae, the *Petticoat Junction* girls, much of the *Hee Haw* cast); the con man (Squire Skimp, Marryin' Sam, Mr. Haney); the general store owner (Lum and Abner, Eb and Zeb, Luke Gray, Sam Drucker); and so forth. Suddenly, as if out of nowhere, these familiar figures were joined by an even larger one—the redneck southern sheriff or state trooper, always ready to throw his considerable weight around and terrorize his victims.

Now, the concept of a hick sheriff in and of itself was not necessarily new. Even in movies of the 1930s, character actors such as former Keystone Kop Slim Summerville turned up as somewhat bungling rural lawmen, usually providing comedy relief alongside whatever crime drama was being enacted. These characters frequently made up their minds about who was guilty, regardless of any evidence or lack thereof, only to be shown up at the end by Charlie Chan or whoever the starring detective might be. A radio show broadcast from San Francisco, *Blue Monday Jamboree* (on which Eb and Zeb were a feature), included the character of a half-deaf southern sheriff who shouted everything he said and repeated everything he shouted. (The name of the actor who played this sheriff has apparently been lost somewhere in radio's history, but his characterization would later inspire both Kenny Delmar's performance as Senator Claghorn and in turn Mel Blanc's imitation of the voice as Foghorn Leghorn.) And, of course, Deputy Dawg was not exactly the type of constable one would want in charge of securing the neighborhood.

These earlier comedic cops were of a different breed than the type that suddenly burst onto the scene in the late 1960s, however. It has been said that it is nearly impossible to burlesque a concept unless audiences have seen it played straight first, and that rule would seem to apply here. After years of being taught unquestioningly to obey authority, the public was suddenly exposed to the appalling personalities and activities of police chiefs such as Birmingham's Bull Connor and Mississippi's Lawrence Rainey during the civil rights upheaval of the early 1960s. People suddenly realized that law enforcement could sometimes be on the wrong side of the law, a situation that set the stage for more movie and television portrayals that presented the dark side of rural—especially southern—law officers.

Historians have concluded that the model on which all future southern sheriffs, comedic or dramatic, was based was Rod Steiger's performance as the bigoted lawman in the feature film *In the Heat of the Night* (1967). There was certainly nothing funny about Steiger's role, but when people had been exposed to it, it became so familiar that it could be spoofed without further explanation. The actor who probably should get credit for bringing the Steiger-style sheriff from drama into much lighter fare is Joe Higgins.

You don't recognize that name, do you? That is because Joe Higgins was one of that class of actors who become so familiar by playing a certain character that everyone instantly knows them by sight, yet their names remain relatively unknown. In the case of Higgins, he first donned his khaki state trooper uniform and tinted

Joe Higgins (*left*) popularized the image of the comical redneck southern sheriff in his commercials and guest appearances beginning in 1968. Here, while visiting Birmingham, Alabama, he inspects the police station on the local kids' show hosted by Neal "Sergeant Jack" Miller.

glasses over his portly frame for a series of television commercials for Dodge automobiles. You remember them—it seemed that each opened with Higgins stopping a sporty Dodge for some imagined infraction or another, always trying to intimidate the driver with a bellowed "You in a heap o' trouble, boy!" Of course, by the end of each spot, the sheriff would be mollified, never resorting to physical violence.

Higgins became so popular as the Dodge sheriff that he carried the same character and personality with him to work in various continuing series. In 1970, he played the sheriff on a summer replacement series, *Johnny Cash Presents the Everly Brothers,* and three years later he turned up on one of the many Sid and Marty Krofft Saturday morning shows, *Sigmund and the Sea Monsters.*

(The Kroffts had one other brush with rural comedy of the past. Their 1970–71 series *The Bugaloos* starred Martha Raye as Benita Bizarre, who constantly schemed to one-up the talented musical group of the show's title. In one show, she disguised herself as a country music performer, Hattie Hoedown, who greatly resembled Minnie Pearl. Lost on nearly everyone was the fact that Raye had been teamed with Bob Burns for a couple of his late 1930s movies. See what we mean about the circle being unbroken?)

Now, back to Joe Higgins. He had clearly made the loudmouth sheriff/trooper a comedy staple, with other actors imitating him without really being aware of who they were impersonating. On *Hee Haw,* Gailard Sartain added a redneck sheriff to his vast repertoire of characters, and no one seemed to care that he was a substitute instead of the original. When the Disney folks were preparing the animated *Robin Hood,* some character designers initially discussed depicting the Sheriff of Nottingham as a Higgins-model highway trooper type, which would have seemed even more bizarre in Sherwood Forest than the eventual experience of hearing Pat Buttram's voice coming out of a medieval wolf.

Warner Bros. was still in the business of producing cartoon shorts for theatrical release in the late 1960s, even though the quality of this work had taken a definite downward spin since the halcyon days of Bugs Bunny and Porky Pig. The stereotyped sheriff shtick found its place there, too, in two cartoons that were parodies of Warner's hit 1967 feature *Bonnie and Clyde.* (*Bonnie and Clyde* was almost as famed for its musical sound track as for its story; the frantic guitar and banjo "Foggy Mountain Breakdown" that accompanied the chase scenes was the work of Lester Flatt and Earl Scruggs, and one of their many visits to *The Beverly Hillbillies* was built around that fact.) The cartoon studio answered with *Bunny and Claude* (1968) and *The Great Carrot Train Robbery* (1969), which had virtually the same plot. As if you couldn't guess, Bunny and Claude were two rabbits who stole carrots; Claude was voiced by Mel Blanc and Bunny by Pat Woodell—those ex–*Petticoat Junction* girls certainly knew how to get around. Blanc was also the bombastic sheriff who unsuccessfully pursued the larcenous long-eared pair, only to be outsmarted in the end. One of the final cartoons the studio produced before shutting down was *Feud with a Dude* (1968), in which the forgettable (and forgotten) character Merlin the Magic Mouse mixed it up in the mountain country. If the studio could start out with hillbilly gags in the early 1930s, there was no reason it could not bow out with them more than three decades later.

When television arrived, radio had almost been given up for dead. In fact, when all of its drama and comedy stars had either made the transition to TV or to retirement, there was almost nothing left except news, music, and disk jockeys. In 1974, Minnesota Public Radio began *A Prairie Home Companion*, which in many ways was a sort of Upper Midwest tribute to/parody of the *Grand Ole Opry*. Not everything about the show was rural, but even a casual observer would have noticed that host Garrison Keillor's weekly stories about the happenings in fictional Lake Wobegon bore more than a little resemblance to the Mount Idy tales formerly spun by Ben Withers and Charley Weaver. The show was a huge hit and has continued in one form or another for nearly thirty-five years.

An event that took place in national politics during the late 1970s seems to have been the catalyst for the next big revival of rural comedy, although most people probably did not think there was a connection. Jimmy Carter's November 1976 election as president signaled (perhaps coincidentally, perhaps not) a new wave of productions in both movies and television that seemed to reflect the mood of his term. Even during his campaign, newspaper cartoonists and other satirists had a cornfield day with Carter's background as a peanut farmer, his toothy grin, and his soft-spoken middle Georgia drawl, and when he became the nation's top official, rural humor seemed to rub off on popular culture as a whole.

In motion pictures, this revived interest manifested itself in a somewhat new and different way. The 1960s and early 1970s had ushered in the era of the antihero, or at least the concept of a heroic character who was, to put it simply, a lawbreaker. The aforementioned contempt for corrupt law enforcement authorities probably had quite a bit to do with this development, but as far as it applied to rural-themed movies, it first appeared in noncomedic action/adventure stories such as *White Lightning* (1973), *Macon County Line* (1974, in which the evil sheriff was none other than ex-Jethro Max Baer Jr., trying his best to reinvent his acting career), *Moonrunners*

(1975), *Moonshine County Express* (1977), and others of that type. Combining this formula with good-old-boy humor produced the first such hit of its type, *Smokey and the Bandit* (1977).

Since the film's star, Burt Reynolds, was originally from Waycross, Georgia (the Okefenokee Swamp's backyard), at least he did not have to work very hard at putting on a southern accent. More surprising was the casting of the sheriff who spent the entire film pursuing him, Jackie Gleason. Those who knew Gleason only as Ralph Kramden the New York bus driver must have gone into shock after seeing him as the sweaty, profanity-spouting sheriff Buford T. Justice. Gleason went on to play the same character in two sequels, establishing that personality so well that some casual viewers might have decided Joe Higgins was imitating Gleason instead of the other way around.

The Carter presidency was even responsible for the first new rural sitcom to hit the TV airwaves since the wholesale purge of such "trash" in 1971. In September 1977, the ABC network debuted *Carter Country,* distinguished as the first situation comedy to have the name of a sitting president in its title. In hindsight, what is even more remarkable is the name given to the town, reminiscent of Plains, Georgia, where the humor took place: Clinton Corners. (It is unlikely that the producers had ever heard of Opie Cates's home of Clinton, Arkansas, so where they came up with that prophetic name is anyone's guess.) *Carter Country* was not a huge hit in the overall history of television comedy; it lasted for only two seasons and even then attracted little attention while it was airing. The cast of characters read like an encyclopedia of rural stereotypes: the sheriff and his deputy, the dumbbell mayor, the mayor's wisecracking secretary, and so on and so forth. After its short ABC run, the show went into syndication and proved inordinately popular in southern television markets. It became a running gag among radio and TV personalities in Birmingham, Alabama, where ABC affiliate WBRC-TV seemingly aired *Carter Country* reruns in place of any number of other highly promoted, much-anticipated network offerings.

Carter Country only slightly hinted at what was to come. There had been some talk of turning the 1975 movie *Moonrunners* into a

After eight years of wanting nothing to do with rural comedy, in January 1979 CBS took a deep breath and braced itself for the critical onslaught that greeted the debut of *The Dukes of Hazzard*.

weekly series. The movie had told the story of an old-time moonshiner, Uncle Jessie (Arthur Hunnicut), and his two nephews fighting to protect their family hooch business from both competitors and revenooers. With the popularity of the Burt Reynolds/Jackie Gleason movies, it seemed the time just might be right to translate that comedy/action/adventure/car chase format to the small screen. Gy Waldron, who had helmed the *Moonrunners* feature, had his doubts as to whether such a basically serious story could be turned into a comedy, but the resulting show almost seamlessly blended the two disparate approaches.

The Dukes of Hazzard premiered on CBS—yes, CBS!—in January 1979. The network was leery about putting the show on at all, especially since several officials still in power remembered smarting from the "Country Broadcasting System" appellation. Their worst fears were realized when the first reviews came out. It looked like it was becoming a tradition: the same critics who had earlier lambasted *The Beverly Hillbillies* and *Hee Haw* as the dregs of television were leaping for the thesaurus to find terminology scathing enough for the *Hazzard* gang. *TV Guide* branded the show "moron heaven," and a writer for one of the Los Angeles papers spewed his venom in more detail: "The worst thing to happen to the South since Appomattox," he declared. "Video historians may well study it as an astounding example of how to fill an hour of prime time with no visible signs of acting, writing or direction." Well, thankee kindly, Suh.

The critics were fond of pointing out that the show embodied every previous stereotype of southern/rural character in existence. Of course, if those same critics had had this book as a reference, they would have seen that *Hazzard* was nowhere near the first show to assemble such a collection. The only *Moonrunners* character who survived the transition to the series intact was Uncle Jesse (the spelling was changed), patriarch of the Duke clan, now played by former musical Mayberry resident Denver Pyle. The nephews—the antiheroes who made the law look like fools, not that the law in Hazzard needed much help—were John Schneider as Bo and Tom Wopat as Luke. Their beautiful cousin was straight from the Daisy Mae mold except that she was a brunette: Catherine Bach as Daisy Duke, the only reason a lot of fellows even tuned in to the show. Bach was credited with coming up with the ultrashort cutoff blue jeans that she wore in most episodes, but such attire had in fact been a staple of many previous backwoods beauties, including but not limited to the girls on *Hee Haw.*

As the nominal heroes of the piece, the members of the Duke family had to be played relatively seriously, with the comedy left to the supporting cast. Chief among these boffo buffoons was Sorrell Booke as Boss Hogg, the ultimate country con man, who could have taken Squire Skimp, Marryin' Sam, and Mr. Haney to the cleaners and gotten them to pay the laundry bill. His partner in grime was James Best (remember when he showed up in one of the Ma and Pa Kettle movies many pages back?) as sheriff Roscoe P. Coltrane. Sheriff Roscoe perfectly combined the two previous most common types of rural lawmen, the incompetent brand and the corrupt version, into a single character. In the early episodes he leaned much more toward the corrupt side, but as the series went along and found its style, Sheriff Roscoe was softened to the point of being a friendly enemy for the Dukes. Nearly everyone (except the critics, of course) agreed that his scenes with Boss Hogg had all the elements of a brand-new classic comedy team.

The narrator for the series was also in on the comedy: Nashville singer Waylon Jennings performed the theme song and was heard throughout each episode, commenting on the action with such down-home remarks as, "Did ya ever have one o' those days when you couldn't even hit the ground with yer hat?" And of course, most viewers considered the Dukes' car, a Dodge Charger painted bright orange and named the General Lee, as much a cast member as anyone else. No, the car had no funny lines, but it came close with its horn that played "Dixie" as a sort of way of sticking its tongue out at the sheriff and Boss Hogg.

Unlike most earlier television "corncoms" that left their locations vague, the Dukes explicitly lived in fictional Hazzard County, Georgia. Its exact geographic placement was left open to speculation, but it was near enough to Atlanta for the characters to venture there occasionally. Considering that the first few episodes were filmed on location in Covington, Georgia (before production moved to a Hollywood back lot for the rest of the series), that is probably as close to a real Hazzard as anyone is likely to find. Weathering occasional cast disputes and the never-ending critical scorn, the show survived until 1985 and, like many of its predecessors, has subsequently lived on in syndication.

It also found added life on Saturday mornings. Hanna-Barbera brought out an animated version of the show known simply as *The Dukes,* with the cast supplying their own characters' voices. That was not the first time the studio had revisited the rural landscape since the days of the *Hillbilly Bears* and *Wacky Races.* One of Hanna-Barbera's offerings for 1976 was *Clue Club,* another in its long line of *Scooby Doo* rehashes, but with the twist of having not one but two canines on the team, Woofer (a bloodhound) and Wimper (a basset hound). Their southern drawls, supplied by Paul Winchell and Jim

MacGeorge, respectively, made it appear that they were more than a little inspired by the Buttram/Lindsey farm dogs in *The Aristocats.* In 1977, *Scooby's All-Star Laff-a-Lympics* created a sports competition between three teams made up of seemingly every previous Hanna-Barbera character. The bad guy group, the Really Rottens, counted among its unworthies the cutoffs-clad Daisy Mayhem and her swine of an accomplice, Sooey Pig. (Defying all previous rules of cartoondom, in this series the villains were allowed an occasional victory.) Daisy's Judy Canova–like cackle was supplied by versatile voice artist Marilyn Schreffler.

While all of these pretenders to the throne were coming and going, reliable, corny old *Hee Haw* continued to produce new episodes for syndication year after year. The show looked almost the same in 1979 as it had in 1969, with the noticeable absence of a few cast members who had died (such as Stringbean) or otherwise moved on. One addition during the late 1970s was Baptist minister Grady Nutt, who was best known for his recordings and personal appearances but who fit seamlessly into the Kornfield Kounty proceedings. Nutt would probably have remained with the show indefinitely had he not been killed in an airplane crash in 1982.

(A rural comic whose career closely paralleled that of Grady Nutt was Mississippi native Jerry Clower. Like Nutt, Clower's primary fame came from his record albums and personal appearances, not broadcasting. He joined the cast of the *Grand Ole Opry* in 1973, but again, his established reputation made his radio appearances seem almost as if they were afterthoughts. Clower's style could best be described as a stereotypical southern Baptist preacher, and in fact much of his material was heavily Christian in its nature. Otherwise, he could be considered a latter-day equivalent to Uncle Josh, even though Clower's drawn-out stories about life in the Mississippi backcountry tended to be much longer than Uncle Josh's brief monologues.)

With its *Laugh-In*–style format, *Hee Haw* might have seemed the least likely rural show to produce a spinoff series. That it did, although not a very successful one. The 1978–79 television season saw the syndication of *Hee Haw Honeys,* featuring several of the cast members in what amounted to half-hour-long skits revolving around a truck stop run by Lulu and Kenny Honey (Lulu Roman and Kenny Price, who were a good match in the physical size department). Shades of *Petticoat Junction*, the waitresses in the café were Misty Honey (squeaky-voiced Misty Rowe) and Kathie Honey (Kathie Lee Gifford, the only cast member not with the original series). Gailard Sartain, *Hee Haw*'s man of a thousand faces, used face No. 1001 as Willie Billie Honey, the chief cook and bottle washer-outer. The show was a notable attempt to expand *Hee Haw*'s reach into true sitcomland, but after a single season it deflated like a flat tire in the truck stop's parking lot. The original series marched onward until 1992, when the final new episode was filmed.

The late 1970s and early 1980s even saw a resurgence of hillbillies in commercials, though nowhere near as many as the Corn Flakes/Mountain Dew/Hillbilly Goat days of the mid-1960s. The Odom's sausage company used a Huck Finn–type barefoot boy as the logo for its Tennessee Pride brand; in animated commercials, he crowed, "Pick up a package o' Tennessee Pride!" in a voice that sounded like Roy Acuff as a youngster. Nothing goes with sausage as well as biscuits, so Pillsbury's Hungry Jack commercials featured an actress who looked and sounded as much like Marjorie Main as could reasonably be expected, bellowing "Hun-GREEE! HUNGRY JACK!" at the top of her considerable voice. Sears used a pair of Lum and Abner–like general storekeepers for a spot in which they went to a modern mall store to return a Craftsman brand hammer they had purchased decades earlier, thereby demonstrating the store's lifetime warranty. Tennessee Ernie Ford was still appearing in commercials for Martha White flour, attesting, "Goodness gracious, hit's pea-pickin' good!" Even Parker Fennelly, whose career as a radio rube went back further than that of nearly anyone else, was seen regularly in his usual deadpan New England farmer character for Pepperidge Farm cookies. Fennelly died in 1988 at the age of ninety-six.

A common practice among commercials of that time was to have a certain set of characters and scripts that could be adapted to fit local or regional sponsors in many different areas of the country.

We wonder if "Granny's secret recipe" used in these biscuits came from a still. At any rate, they no doubt tasted better if eaten with your shoes off.

Jim Varney made himself a star as the irritating neighbor Ernest (actually more of an urban trailer-park-style redneck than a rural one), sticking his face into the camera and pestering his buddy (with the viewer as a surrogate) by shouting "Hey, Vern!" Varney performed these routines for companies ranging from dairies to local television stations, becoming so popular that he starred in his own series of slapstick comedy feature films.

Another series of adaptable commercials featured the team of Pearl 'n' Paw. These spots were based in Birmingham, Alabama, and featured veteran radio personality Jack Voorhies as Paw (practically an Arthur Hunnicutt look-alike) and ad agency executive Edie Hand as daughter Pearl (whose appearance was deliberately modeled after Elly May Clampett). The pair began making commercials for various northern Alabama businesses in the mid-1980s, but their biggest exposure outside the state came from their ads for Sunshine pet foods. For these, they were frequently joined by Hand's young son, Linc, as (who else?) Cousin Linc and bodybuilder Tom Owen as Pearl's lunkheaded boyfriend, Maynard, the latest escapee from the mold that produced Li'l Abner and Jethro Bodine. With a limited amount of time to be funny and sell the product, the jokes usually took the form of wheezes that had proven themselves classics:

> *Pearl*: I like yer cat, Maynard. Whut's her name?
> *Maynard*: Her name's Woodrow, Miss Pearl.
> *Paw*: Whut ye feed Woodrow?
> *Maynard*: Sunshine cat food . . . That's why she's so good at what she does.
> *Pearl*: Whut does Woodrow do?
> *Maynard*: She keeps the elephants away from the henhouse.
> *Paw*: They ain't no elephants around here, Maynard.
> *Maynard*: I know it, Mr. Paw. Jus' proves how good Woodrow is.

With the Dukes and the Hee Haw Honeys and Ernest and Pearl 'n' Paw all crawling out of their backwoods bailiwicks, it seemed that perhaps the world was safe for humorous hicks despite the travails of the early 1970s. A 1988 sitcom, *Empty Nest*, featured in a supporting role an actress with the remarkable name of Park Overall as an Arkansas-born an' -bred nurse named LaVerne. She delivered the kind of lines that might have had Bob Burns swingin' from the nearest white oak tree if the residents of his state had gotten hold of him: "Datin' wuz simple back home. Ya warshed yer hair ever' Sairdee night an' then when ya wuz fourteen ya married yer cousin."

Jimmy Carter's election as president had ushered in one wave of country humor, but Bill Clinton's election in 1992 had an even wider influence. Carter, from middle Georgia, projected a friendly, country image that induced chuckles, but the fact that Clinton had served as governor of Arkansas, the butt of the nation's hillbilly japes since the days of the infamous *Slow Train through Arkansaw* joke

Sunshine pet food was one of the companies that featured the humorous television commercials of Pearl 'n' Paw (Edie Hand and Jack Voorhies). Hand's young son occasionally appeared as Cousin Linc.

book, made him an even easier target. Cartoonists and media types loved to draw parallels between Clinton and *Li'l Abner*, *The Beverly Hillbillies*, and even the noncomedic backwoods thriller *Deliverance*, conveniently ignoring the fact that many of them had nothing to do with the state of Arkansas.

This onslaught of new rural characters might make it seem that audiences would forget about the pioneering TV sitcoms that brought these figures into living rooms. (From the critical reaction, some of these personages obviously were not exactly welcome.) But never fear, the same era that produced a new breed of country comedians also spawned a unique form of video known as the reunion movie.

Shows as diverse as *The Addams Family*, *Leave It to Beaver*, and *Gilligan's Island* had reassembled surviving members of their original casts in made-for-TV movies, and it looked like high time for the rural variety to see what sort of ratings could be gotten by "exhuming the corpses of old shows," as one former actor phrased it. The first of them to do so aired the result on October 6, 1981, *The Return of the Beverly Hillbillies.*

In retrospect, most of those involved felt that this project was doomed from the start. Of the original core cast, only Buddy Ebsen, Donna Douglas, Max Baer, and Nancy Kulp were still living. That meant the reunion would have to be done without the two principal comic characters, Irene Ryan as Granny and Raymond Bailey as Mr. Drysdale. Then, there was the not-so-little matter of Baer refusing to return to the role of Jethro even for old times' sake. He had struggled so hard to overcome that typecasting that he wanted nothing to do with any reunion, so that cut the original cast down to three. Paul Henning came up with a script that even he had to admit was rather halfhearted, but the whole thing was pushed through production despite its many faults.

Kulp, as Jane Hathaway, delivers the opening narration to explain the events that have occurred in the decade since the final *Beverly Hillbillies* episode: "I know the last time we saw Mr. Clampett, he was living in a magnificent mansion in Beverly Hills. But after Granny 'went to her reward,' as they say, he divided his enormous fortune between Elly May and Jethro and moved back to his beloved hills." The real reason for this turn of events was that it would have been prohibitively expensive to rebuild the Clampett mansion's sets for a single movie, so some excuse had to be devised to get the plot back to the backwoods, which would be much easier to depict.

While the movie acknowledged up front that Granny was dead and gone, it made no reference to Mr. Drysdale or his eventual fate. Instead, Jane Hathaway was teamed with C. D. Medford, a Washington bureaucrat played by Werner Klemperer (unrecognizable to those who remembered him as Colonel Klink in *Hogan's Heroes*). As the plot unravels, the duo decides that Granny's "white lightnin'" just might be the solution to the nation's energy crisis and dependence on foreign oil, and they set out to uncover the formula. They first visit Jethro, who has used his share of Uncle Jed's money to become head of a large movie studio. Uh, wait. . . didn't we say

The ill-begotten TV movie *The Return of the Beverly Hillbillies* (1981) purported to show the lives of the Clampetts ten years after their show ended. The strangest piece of casting was Imogene Coca as Granny's Maw.

that Max Baer had refused to come back for this reunion? Yes, that's right. So, instead of doing the logical thing and writing Jethro out of the story, as with Granny and Drysdale, the producers recast the role. The "new Jethro" was Ray Young, who, you will recall, we last saw as Li'l Abner in the failed 1971 TV pilot. In another link to the past, Jethro's secretary was played by Linda Kaye Henning, the only constant among the *Petticoat Junction* girls. (There was apparently never any consideration of doing a *Petticoat Junction* reunion, inasmuch as none of the cast was still living except Frank Cady and the many girls who between them had made up the three Bradley daughters.)

Anyway, Jethro (regardless of who is playing him) does not know what went into Granny's moonshine, and besides, he is too busy directing his latest blockbuster, *Jaws and the Godfather Make Star Wars on Superman while the Empire Strikes Back with Rocky*. "With a title like that, who needs actors?" reasons the muddled mogul. Next, Miss Jane and Medford go to see Elly May, who now operates her own petting zoo as a tourist attraction. Donna Douglas looks virtually unchanged by ten years, nailing the Elly voice perfectly and still fitting into her blue jeans with the rope belt. After failing to procure Granny's formula from Elly May, too, Jane and Medford head into the hills to see whether Jed can help. They find him living in a somewhat larger and more comfortable cabin than the one he left behind in 1962, but he admits to not knowing the secret recipe either. This sets the scene for what would be the most inane and universally condemned concept of this whole misguided effort:

Jed: That wuz one family secret that wuz handed down from mother to daughter.

Jane: Then the secret died with Granny?

Jed: No, her Maw still makes it.

Jane: [incredulous, as is the audience by this point] Granny's MOTHER is still ALIVE? How OLD is she?

Jed: I'm not shore that she knows. . . an' if she did, she wouldn't tell ya.

Jane: Would you say that she's a hundred?

Jed: Not in front of her, I wouldn't.

Yes, the writers got around the absence of Granny by bringing in the unlikely character of Granny's Maw, played by Imogene Coca in what might have been the unfunniest role of her long television career. Maw is the warden of the Happy Hollow Old Ladies' Home, where the unmarried old maid residents range in age from eighteen to twenty-one. (It is probably no coincidence that Paul Henning gave the home the name from his long-ago radio series on KMBC in Kansas City.) Miss Jane learns that Maw stirs up a batch of her potent potion only for gala occasions such as weddings, so she and

Medford reluctantly agree to get married to procure a sample for the government. Jed realizes that this is a marriage of convenience, so he arranges for the ceremony to be performed by a fake judge so it will not be legally binding. Elly May and Jethro fly in from California by helicopter just as the phony wedding is ending; this is another blunder that renders the whole "reunion" pointless, as they appear with what remains of the original cast for only the final seven minutes of the film, and even then in only a few brief scenes. For a finish, the coveted sample of moonshine is lost when Maw pours it into the gas tank of her car to avoid being snagged by revenooers.

Weaving in and out of this story—and not just from drinking Maw's brew—were as many actors as possible who had played supporting roles in the original series. Among these were Shad Heller and Shug Fisher, who had been part of the Silver Dollar City episodes; Charles Lane, not as *Petticoat Junction*'s Homer Bedloe but as the chief revenue officer; and King Donovan, in a dual role as both the inept revenooer trying to capture Maw and his aged father, who tried before him. Even Earl Scruggs, whose partner, Lester Flatt, had died in 1979, returned with his band to play a couple of numbers. A two-foot-tall wood carving of Granny, created by Silver Dollar City artisan Peter Engler, appeared in several scenes as a memorial of sorts.

Fortunately, this misbegotten mishmash did not discourage other producers. With fan hysteria for *The Andy Griffith Show* showing no signs of abating, all of the elements were put in place for *Return to Mayberry*, broadcast by NBC (not CBS!) on April 13, 1986. The cast and crew had always been somewhat more protective of their show and its heritage than some others, so Griffith made absolutely sure that if they were all going to get together again, they were going to avoid the mistakes made by other reunion debacles. Unlike *The Beverly Hillbillies*, nearly all of the Griffith show's original cast was still alive and well, except Howard McNear, who had suffered a stroke while the original series was still on the air and died soon thereafter, and Frances Bavier, who was alive but was too debilitated to appear. A quiet scene early in the movie showed Andy Taylor visiting Aunt Bee's grave, simply acknowledging her absence.

The former cast members of the *Andy Griffith Show* got together one more time for the reunion movie *Return to Mayberry* (1986).

In the story, Andy and his wife, Helen, come back to Mayberry for the first time in nearly twenty years. Andy is now a postal inspector in Cleveland, Ohio, and has returned to his hometown for the dual purposes of being present for the birth of his first grandchild (Opie's son) and running for sheriff again. The first order of business is dealt with during a certain amount of confusion, as the expectant parents and grandparents do not reach the hospital in time and Andy has to deliver his grandson in the backseat of the car. "I've done it before," he reasons. "There must be a half dozen people in this town who saw me before they saw their mothers." Opie does not get through the ordeal with nearly as much aplomb as his dad and his wife.

The other half of Andy's reason for returning is complicated when he learns that Barney is already running for sheriff against Ben Woods, who is conducting the worst type of mudslinging campaign. The townspeople are divided as to whether Barney has a fighting chance against Ben; Gomer Pyle remarks that Barney ought to do well since "he hasn't done nothin' stupid fer at least a month now." (After getting out of the Marine Corps, Gomer has opened his own garage in partnership with cousin Goober.) The old familiar faces are reintroduced one by one: Ernest T. Bass is still throwing rocks and acting like an idiot, Howard Sprague is still dapper and worrying about aging, Briscoe Darling is still leader of his musical family, and Otis Campbell has given up drinking and is now the ice cream man. (While the original show was always timeless, the producers of the reunion movie realized that in 1986 it was no longer acceptable to make alcoholism a topic for humor; thus, Otis received the most dramatic transformation of any of the original group.)

All of this becomes entangled with a publicity stunt engineered by a young businessman who has opened a restaurant and motel on the outskirts of town. To attract more tourists to Mayberry, he arranges to have a Loch Ness Monster–type creature show up in Myers's Lake, and Barney swallows the story hook, line, and stinky sinker. He nearly becomes the laughingstock of the town until Andy, in his usual wise way, solves the mystery and makes it appear that Barney should get all the credit. In the windup, Barney tells everyone to vote for Andy as sheriff when they go to the polls, and then he and his longtime sweetheart, Thelma Lou, finally get married. At the wedding reception, Andy makes a speech that is probably intended to apply to the show's real-life cast as much as the characters they portrayed:

> *Andy*: The feeling around here is that these two were always meant to be married, just like it was always in the cards for Helen and me to come back home and for Barney to be my deputy again. But not everybody's movin' in. Opie and his little family will be leavin' for a big new job out of state. But I wouldn't be surprised at all if some day they'll be comin' back. There's somethin' about Mayberry and Mayberry folk that never leaves you. No matter where life takes you, you always carry in your heart the memories of old times and old friends. So, here's to all of us . . . old friends!

As the closing credits roll over the Mayberry town square—or, actually, the town of Los Olivos, California, standing in for North Carolina—we see Andy back in his traditional sheriff's uniform for

Oliver and Lisa Douglas (Eddie Albert and Eva Gabor), along with Arnold the Pig and the other offbeat denizens of Hooterville, came out of retirement for *Return to Green Acres* (1990).

the only time in the film, as he and Barney lower the U.S. flag at sundown and walk together down the street, and into television history.

As we said earlier, there were not enough surviving cast members from *Petticoat Junction* to make entertaining the idea of a reunion worthwhile. However, the population was still hale and hearty over at the other end of Hooterville, so in May 1990, CBS broadcast *Return to Green Acres.* The opening scenes demonstrate not so much how the characters have changed in nearly twenty years but how much they have stayed the same. In the opening dialogue, we find Oliver Douglas ecstatic over the success of the alfalfa he has bought from Mr. Haney, apparently never having learned any better in all those decades. Soon enough he finds that the lush greenery in his field is poison ivy instead of alfalfa.

In rapid succession we are reintroduced to Alf and Ralph Monroe, still as incompetent at carpentry as ever; Hank Kimball, still absent-minded but holding down his job as county agent anyway; Eb Dawson, no longer the Douglases' handyman but the father of a huge brood of children; Sam Drucker, whose general store looks so much the same that it could now be an antique shop; and feisty Daisy Ziffel, niece of the late Fred and Doris, who now owns their former farm and shares it with Arnold the Pig. (No explanation is given as to why Arnold is the same size he was two decades earlier.)

The main story gets under way when Oliver and Lisa decide that the time has come for them to sell the underproducing farm and return to their former lives in New York. Not-so-coincidentally, a real estate developer named Armstrong and his slimy son arrive in Hooterville, in cahooters with Mr. Haney to buy up all the farms in town and turn the whole area into a suburb with strip shopping centers and fast food restaurants where fields and white picket fences now stand. Haney is only too happy to buy the Douglas farm back at a cheap price, since he can use it as leverage to get others to sell out to him. He spreads rumors that the Douglases know that a major disaster is about to befall Hooterville and thus decided to get out, and his ruse tricks everyone else into selling their property.

Oliver and Lisa get wind of Haney's plot at just about the time they discover that the New York of 1990 is not nearly as glamorous as the city they left in 1965. They return to Hooterville to help the townspeople fight and end up giving Haney a dose of his own snake oil by staging an earthquake right in his living room. The developer calls it quits, and the Douglases decide to stay on the farm. Oh, and Daisy Ziffel marries the developer's son, who sees the error of his ways.

Return to Green Acres was hampered by the fact that Jay Sommers, who had been the sole creative force behind the original show (as well as its radio predecessor, *Granby's Green Acres*), had died in 1985. Having other writers handle his characters gave the movie a considerably different flavor, but it helped that the original cast members slipped so easily back into their familiar roles. Except for gray hair and wrinkles, they all even looked about the same—and, befitting her legendary family, Eva Gabor had taken pains to not be caught with either of those physical attributes.

Paul Henning and his longtime associates still felt that the 1981 *Beverly Hillbillies* reunion movie had been a total mistake, so 1993 saw an attempt of sorts to rectify that. In May of that year, CBS presented *The Legend of the Beverly Hillbillies*, which was not so much a movie as a retrospective of vintage film clips woven into a mock documentary about what had happened to the Clampetts in their later lives. All those involved apparently preferred to forget the first reunion, because the details were completely different. At the beginning of the show, host Mac Davis explains that Jed lost the biggest part of his fortune through Mr. Drysdale's embezzlement of funds from his bank's various depositors. Jane Hathaway turned him in to the authorities and is now living under a new identity somewhere under the witness protection program. (Nancy Kulp had died in 1991.) Mixed in with the excerpts from the original series, various celebrities, including Reba McEntire, Ray Charles, and Hoyt Axton, give bogus reminisces about their association with the Clampetts. Eddie Albert and Eva Gabor make an extremely brief cameo appearance in a special remote direct from Hooterville.

A roving reporter catches up with Jethro, now a doctor (although he still has just a sixth-grade education). To everyone's surprise, Max Baer returned to the role he had refused to even mention for so many years. He had finally decided to embrace the character, especially since he had big plans to build a *Beverly Hillbillies*–themed casino in Las Vegas, complete with giant oil derrick spouting fireworks from the roof. In the program, he demonstrates that he can still assume Jethro's accent and goofy grin when needed; he shows the reporter his wall of framed photos of his numerous children:

> *Jethro*: This is mah youngest daughter Daisy . . . an' over here is Ulysses, an' Clem . . . that's li'l Norbelle . . . o'course th' triplets, William, Bill an' Billy . . . an' then Amelia, Li'l Jed, Maude, Robin, an' Granny Junior . . . an' then Mike an' Teena an' Eddie . . . an' over here's mah li'l angel an' mah li'l punkin.
>
> *Reporter*: And what are their names?
>
> *Jethro*: Angel an' Punkin. An' then we got Lorie an' Pixie an' Dixie.

Next, the reporter finds Elly May living in a modest home with a yard full of her beloved critters, including a talking bear.

> *Reporter*: It's amazing the way that bear can talk.
>
> *Elly May*: Yessir, hit shore is . . . would you believe, when I first met him, he stuttered.

Donna Douglas had aged considerably since the 1981 film but still put on her best Elly voice. Her attempt to re-create Elly's trademark whistle did not come out so well, though. Finally, the reporter ventures deep into the hills to find the aged Jed Clampett himself (Buddy Ebsen was eighty-five years old by this time), sitting on a bench and whittling contentedly. They talk about his drastic change in fortune due to Drysdale's chicanery, but Jed assures his visitor that he holds no grudges, although he does admit wistfully that he misses Granny more than anything else from his previous life. When it comes to the fact that Drysdale is now incarcerated, Jed proves to be philosophical:

> *Jed*: The way I look at it, I jes' lost some money. But Mr. Drysdale lost his freedom. I think I came out purty good on th' deal.

As they finish their conversation, Jed sticks his whittling knife into the ground, and more oil begins spouting forth. It looks like we will be "listenin' to a story about a man named Jed" for some time to come.

Practically the only series with a reasonable number of surviving cast members that had not staged a reunion movie was *The Dukes of Hazzard*, and that oversight was remedied in April 1997 with a film titled, creatively enough, *The Dukes of Hazzard: Reunion*. The dozen years since the end of the original show represented the shortest time before a reunion of all of these shows except the ten-year *Beverly Hillbillies* attempt. Those dozen years were enough to cause a few changes among the cast members, most notably the death of Sorrell "Boss Hogg" Booke. The story repeatedly acknowledged his passing, especially since he left his entire lineup of crooked business interests to Sheriff Roscoe. As Daisy, Catherine Bach did not feel she still had quite the physical attributes to squeeze into her trademark cutoffs, so would-be voyeurs had to content themselves with the rest of her. Denver Pyle was extremely ill at the time the reunion was filmed, but he gathered enough strength to give one final performance as Uncle Jesse. His breathing was labored and at times he seemed to be in a fog, but the rest of the cast was just thankful to have him there. Pyle died later that year.

The story was typical of the series. All of the Duke family members and their friends gather in town for the annual Hazzard Homecoming and find that Uncle Jesse is a social pariah. Bo is now a NASCAR driver, Luke is a firefighter, and Daisy is a divorcée taking graduate courses at Duke University (where else?). They learn the reason for the family misfortune is that a company is planning to build a theme park on the site of Hazzard Swamp, with no concern for the ecological disaster such a project will create. Since the only access to the swamp is across Uncle Jesse's property, he refuses to grant said access, and the rest of the town is down on him because of the lost potential revenue.

As one might expect, "Boss Roscoe" is mixed in with the developers, and the Duke boys agree to a race to determine who will get the swamp. They drag their General Lee out of storage, where it has been collecting dust and chicken droppings for the past twelve years, and no one gets a prize for guessing whether they save the day (and the swamp). Three years later, and without the departed Denver Pyle, the remaining cast members got together for a second reunion, *Hazzard in Hollywood,* which attracted little if any media attention—perhaps because one reunion had already taken place.

The Dukes pretty much closed the book on rural comedy reunions, especially since so few performers from the earlier shows remained alive and/or active. As the 1990s lurched into a new millennium, the face of rural humor was changing with it. We will conclude this protracted discussion in the next chapter with a quick look at how the farmers and general store owners and hillbillies of old have seemingly been put out of business for good.

Chapter Ten

Still Fertile Ground

One danger in trying to be too current is that the definition of *current* changes daily. For this reason, this book is concerned with rural comedy of the twentieth century; we are not far enough into the twenty-first to ascertain where it will go from here. In this closing, however, we can make a few observations and wrap up a few loose ends.

When people speak of "country comedy" today, they are usually referring to the acts of stand-up comedians such as Jeff Foxworthy, Bill Engvall, Ron White, Dan "Larry the Cable Guy" Whitney, and Etta May (whose publicity describes her as "Minnie Pearl with a migraine"). A close dissection of their routines reveals that while they do have some similarities with what has come before, their humor is not so much rural as it is redneck. Many people probably cannot distinguish between the two, but those who have struggled this far have probably noticed that quite a definite difference indeed exists.

"Rural," as exemplified by the shows and characters profiled in the past nine chapters, usually took the form of hillbillies in the mountains, with their cabins, moonshine stills, battles with revenooers, and distrust of anyone from the outside world. The second-most-common strain was the genteel small town of *Lum and Abner*'s Pine Ridge, *Scattergood Baines*'s Coldriver, or *The Andy Griffith Show*'s Mayberry, just to name a few. These locales were rural simply by virtue of being located well outside the influence of any large city, but the residents were not necessarily as barbaric as the feudin' and fightin' hillbilly image. Other series, such as the Ma and Pa Kettle films, fell somewhere in between.

Now, take another look at those redneck comedians. They try to project the background of the low-income suburban trailer park rather than that of the hills or farms or idyllic small towns. The comics are far more likely to be found with a beer from Wal-Mart in hand than a jug of homemade corn squeezins. We could get into an even deeper discussion of the frequently controversial and even scatological topics of their jokes, but that point might not necessarily be valid, since these redneck humorists operate in a media world with far less censorship than the earlier comedians encountered. (Some of the old-timers possessed a sense of humor as raunchy as anyone's, but their acts were squeaky clean as a consequence of the attitudes of the time. Would they have performed off-color material if they had been allowed to do so? There is no way to know for sure.)

That said, programmers occasionally have attempted to bring old-time rural sitcoms into the present, and not just in the form of the reunion movies, which by their very nature had to strive to duplicate the style of the original shows. No, the trend in big-budget theatrical films such as *The Beverly Hillbillies* (1993) and *The Dukes of Hazzard* (2005) has been to completely reimagine the premise as if the original source material had never existed. Reaction from critics and the even-more-important paying audiences has been mixed, to say the least.

As part of the fallout from the same emphasis on a more youthful culture that doomed CBS's rural sitcom lineup in 1971, these new theatrical films generally end up with the characters appearing much younger than their television predecessors. In the *Beverly Hillbillies* feature, for example, Jed Clampett was portrayed by Jim "Ernest" Varney. Although Varney was the same age Buddy Ebsen was when he assumed the role, Ebsen's makeup was designed to make him look much older. Established screen villain Dabney Coleman was suitably avaricious as Mr. Drysdale, but again, Coleman lacked Raymond Bailey's patina of seniority. The true triumph of the film was Cloris Leachman's performance as Granny, which nearly everyone agreed was so similar to Irene Ryan that it bordered on eerie. *Hillbillies* creator Paul Henning wanted it made perfectly clear that he was in no way connected with the feature film—his involvement went no further than his licensing of his characters. He especially wanted to distance himself from the added touches such as having the Clampetts stop their truck to pick up roadkill to eat for lunch, or the infamous gag in which they mistake the middle-finger gesture of the other freeway drivers to be a "Californy howdy" and cheerfully return the salute.

(In the story, Jed narrowly escapes an arranged marriage designed to separate him from his millions. As if to illustrate how little the jokes about Arkansas had changed since the days of Opie Read and Thomas W. Jackson, one quick scene features a shot of the White House with an imitation of Bill Clinton's voice: "Hillary, have you seen mah invitation to Cousin Jed's weddin'?")

The *Dukes of Hazzard* feature employed some stunt casting of its own, particularly when it came to redefining Boss Hogg. That name was singularly appropriate for Sorrell Booke's balding, swinelike appearance, but when the suave, mustachioed Burt Reynolds took on the role in 2005, a less likely transformation could hardly have been imagined. Ditto for the casting of Willie Nelson as Uncle Jesse, although at least his age and whiskers worked. Television starlet Jessica Simpson took on the persona of Daisy, with cutoff bluejean shorts that climbed to dizzying heights, but her blonde mane of hair put the Duke darling right back to where Daisy Mae and most of her hillbilly companions had been many years earlier.

Those hillbillies from Beverly Hills made headlines once again in late 2002 and early 2003 when CBS announced that it would air a new "reality show" to be called *The Real Beverly Hillbillies*. Producers planned to find an actual backwoods family from the hills and valleys of Appalachia, transplant them to a southern California mansion, and then let the cameras roll as the newcomers tried to make sense of it all. The idea met with condemnation from all parts of society, although both supporters and opponents of the project seemed completely to miss the point of the original show. The would-be producers huffed that their "real hillbillies" would not be made to look like fools, since the Clampetts always outsmarted those who were out to cheat them. But these television executives failed to mention that scriptwriters had always made sure that the Clampetts came out on top—a "reality" show would lack that safeguard. The main argument against the new show ran along the lines of "the original show was a bad enough reflection on the southern mountains without dredging it up again." They too missed the point: for all their lack of sophistication, the Clampetts were by far the show's most lovable characters. The idea eventually was dropped.

Meanwhile, the original shows just seem to keep going and finding new audiences. Old-time radio programs first became available on cassette tapes in the 1970s and have now been converted into the MP3 format, meaning that anyone who desires to hear the approximately fifteen hundred existing episodes of *Lum and Abner* can do so for just a few dollars. Virtually all other radio series of the 1930s and 1940s are available in the same form; it is likely that more people have heard *Si and Elmer* in the last few years than listened to the show when it originally aired.

The vintage rural comedy movies have a more hit-and-miss record when it comes to modern media. Some, such as the entire Ma and Pa Kettle collection, have been lovingly restored and issued on officially licensed DVD sets, looking better than they have since their original theatrical release. Others, including most of the Bob Burns, Judy Canova, and Scattergood Baines epics and the 1940 *Grand Ole Opry* film, exist only as privately sold (bootlegged) DVDs and VHS tapes, with wildly varying picture quality. The seven Lum and Abner movies are available in both video formats but have yet to receive the painstaking restoration work that the Kettles have enjoyed.

Most of the television sitcoms, by contrast, are enjoying great success in official DVD releases, usually including generous bonus material such as the original cast commercials and behind-the-scenes documentaries. One of the biggest surprise hits was when the original *Hee Haw* shows were first offered on DVD; the demand was so great that the manufacturer could not turn out DVDs fast enough.

Not to be overlooked in the preservation of these programs is the influence of the fans themselves. A Web search for nearly any of the shows and personalities covered in this book will turn up multiple sites, some official, some operated by surviving members of the performers' families, and some merely amateur fan projects. There are also officially sanctioned organizations such as the National Lum and Abner Society (www.lumandabnersociety.org) and *The Andy Griffith Show* Rerun Watchers' Club (www.mayberry.com) that have worked to preserve and document the history of specific programs.

This is a most useful resource tool, inasmuch as the vast majority of the performers, writers, and others who created the classic rural comedy of the past are now deceased. A roll call of the departed legends of rural humor includes (but is not limited to) Phillips H. Lord (died in 1975), Parker Fennelly (1988), Chester "Lum" Lauck (1980), Norris "Abner" Goff (1978), Al "Eb" Pearce (1961), Jim Jordan (1988), Marian Jordan (1961), Clarence Hartzell (1988), Will Rogers (1935), Bob Burns (1956), Judy Canova (1983), Roswell Rogers (1998), Sarie and Sallie (1994 and 1967), Pat "Uncle Ezra" Barrett (1959), the Duke of Paducah (1986), Minnie Pearl (1996), Grandpa Jones (1998), David "Stringbean" Akeman (1973), Pat Buttram (1994), Red Skelton (1997), Andy Devine (1977), Opie Cates (1987), Irving Bacon (1965), Granville Owen (1995), Martha O'Driscoll (1998), Grady Sutton (1995), Dick Elliott (1962), Guy Kibbee (1956), Dink Trout (1950), the Weaver Brothers and Elviry (1950, 1967, and 1977), Bud Duncan (1960), Dub Taylor (1994), Slim Pickens (1983), Arkansas Slim Andrews (1992), Andy Clyde (1967), Marjorie Main (1975), Percy Kilbride (1964), Gale Gordon (1995), Parley Baer (2002), Tennessee Ernie Ford (1991), Walter Brennan (1974), Richard Crenna (2003), Dorothy Shay (1978), Stubby Kaye (1997), Cliff Arquette (1974), Don Knotts (2006), Howard McNear (1969), Arthur Hunnicutt (1979), Buddy Ebsen (2003), Irene Ryan (1973), Nancy Kulp (1991), Raymond Bailey (1980), Paul Henning (2005), J. Pat O'Malley (1985), Homer and Jethro (1971 and 1989), Jay Sommers (1985), Bea Benaderet (1968), Edgar Buchanan (1979), Smiley Burnette (1967), Rufe

Davis (1974), Eddie Albert (2005), Eva Gabor (1995), Hank Patterson (1975), Barbara Pepper (1969), Paul Frees (1986), Daws Butler (1988), Jean VanderPyl (1999), Ray Young (1999), Archie Campbell (1987), Junior Samples (1983), Joe Higgins (1998), Jackie Gleason (1987), Denver Pyle (1997), and Sorrell Booke (1994). Many performers died before their careers received any attention (Arthur Allen, Perry "Si" Crandall, William "Elmer" Reynolds, Bill "Zeb" Wright), and their dates of death are not available. The list could easily be twice as long.

In the end, though, the work of these talented actors outlasts their mortal existence. As long as those old recordings, tapes, and films can be transferred to whatever audio or video medium is invented next, their hilarious performances will continue to be rediscovered and enjoyed by future generations. As George D. Hay, the "Solemn Ole Judge" of the *Grand Ole Opry,* recited at the close of each week's program (in words that came close to making no sense at all but are somehow comforting nonetheless),

That's all for now, friends,
Because the tall pines pine
And the pawpaws pause,
And the bumblebees bumble all round;
The grasshoppers hop
And the eavesdroppers drop,
While gently the ol' cow slips away.
George D. Hay sayin', so long fer now!

Bibliography

Acuff, Roy, and William Neely. *Roy Acuff's Nashville: The Life and Good Times of Country Music.* New York: Perigree, 1983.

Adams, T. R. (pseud.). *The Flintstones: A Modern Stone Age Phenomenon.* Atlanta: Turner, 1994.

Adamson, Joe. *Tex Avery: King of Cartoons.* New York: Popular Library, 1975.

Allen, Fred. *Treadmill to Oblivion.* Boston: Little, Brown, 1954.

Andrews, Bart. *Lucy and Ricky and Fred and Ethel: The Story of I Love Lucy.* New York: Dutton, 1976.

"Arkansas: Prejudice and Pride." *Time,* July 27, 1942.

"The Arkansas Traveler." *Time,* October 31, 1938.

Austin, Wade. "The Real Beverly Hillbillies." *Southern Quarterly* 19 (Spring–Summer 1981): 83–94.

Baker, Ruth. "In Memory of Mr. Haney." *Jasper (Ala.) Daily Mountain Eagle,* April 22, 1994.

Beck, Jerry, and Will Friedwald. *Looney Tunes and Merrie Melodies: A Complete Illustrated Guide to the Warner Bros. Cartoons.* New York: Holt, 1989.

Blevins, Brooks. *Hill Folks: A History of Arkansas Ozarkers and Their Image.* Chapel Hill: University of North Carolina Press, 2002.

Bresee, Frank, and Bobb Lynes. *Radio's Golden Years.* Hollywood, Calif.: Bresee, 1998.

Bruce, Scott, and Bill Crawford. *Cerealizing America: The Unsweetened Story of American Breakfast Cereal.* Winchester, Mass.: Faber and Faber, 1995.

Cox, Stephen. *The Beverly Hillbillies: A Fortieth Anniversary Wing-Ding.* Nashville: Cumberland House, 2003.

———. *The Hooterville Handbook: A Viewer's Guide to Green Acres.* New York: St. Martin's, 1993.

———. *The Munsters: A Trip down Mockingbird Lane.* New York: Back Stage, 2006.

DeLong, Thomas A. *Radio Stars: An Illustrated Biographical Dictionary.* Jefferson, N.C.: McFarland, 1996.

Dunning, John. *On the Air: The Encyclopedia of Old-Time Radio.* New York: Oxford University Press, 1998.

Ebsen, Buddy (obituary). *Los Angeles Times,* July 8, 2003.

Ely, Melvin Patrick. *The Adventures of Amos 'n' Andy: A Social History of an American Phenomenon.* New York: Free Press, 1991.

Escott, Colin. *The Grand Ole Opry: The Making of an American Icon.* New York: Center Street, 2006.

Evanier, Mark. "Li'l Abner in Hollywood." In *Li'l Abner: 1959.* Northampton, Mass.: Kitchen Sink, 1997.

"Exhibit Shows Hillbilly Roots of Mountain Dew." Associated Press wire service story, August 19, 2001.

Fidelman, Geoffrey Mark. *The Lucy Book.* Los Angeles: Renaissance, 1999.

Furmanek, Bob, and Ron Palumbo. *Abbott and Costello in Hollywood.* New York: Perigree, 1991.

Gerome, John. "No Joke, Larry the Cable Guy, Other Comedians Hot on Charts." Associated Press wire service story, August 6, 2006.

———. "Southern Humor Applies Elsewhere, Too." Associated Press wire service story, November 27, 2005.

Grabman, Sandra. *Pat Buttram: The Rocking Chair Humorist.* Boalsburg, Pa.: BearManor, 2006.

Grant, John. *The Encyclopedia of Walt Disney's Animated Characters.* New York: Harper and Row, 1987.

Gumfudgin, Ormly (pseud.). "I Remember One Time Back in Van Buren, Arkansas." *SPERDVAC Radiogram,* June 2004.

Hagan, Chuck. *Country Music Legends in the Hall of Fame.* Nashville: Nelson, 1982.

Harkins, Anthony. *Hillbilly: A Cultural History of an American Icon.* New York: Oxford University Press, 2004.

Hickey, Neil. "Who's Laughing Now?" *TV Guide,* March 7, 1970.

"Hillbilly: A Local Bazookist Makes Good in Some Big Cities." *Newsweek,* December 14, 1935.

Hinds, Julie. "Hazzard Duty." Knight Ridder Newspapers wire story, June 9, 2005.

Hirschhorn, Clive. *The Universal Story.* London: Octopus, 1983.

Hofstede, David. *The Dukes of Hazzard: The Unofficial Companion.* Los Angeles: Renaissance, 1998.

Hollis, Tim. *Florida's Miracle Strip: From Redneck Riviera to Emerald Coast.* Jackson: University Press of Mississippi, 1994.

———. *Hi There, Boys and Girls! America's Local Children's Television Programs.* Jackson: University Press of Mississippi, 2001.

———. *The Land of the Smokies: Great Mountain Memories.* Jackson: University Press of Mississippi, 2007.

Hollis, Tim, and Greg Ehrbar. *Mouse Tracks: The Story of Walt Disney Records.* Jackson: University Press of Mississippi, 2006.

Hurst, Jack. *Nashville's Grand Ole Opry: The First Fifty Years.* New York: Abrams, 1975.

Jewell, Richard B., and Vernon Harbin. *The RKO Story.* New York: Arlington House, 1982.

Jones, Louis M., and Charles K. Wolfe. *Everybody's Grandpa: Fifty Years behind the Mike.* Knoxville: University of Tennessee Press, 1984.

Josefsberg, Milt. *The Jack Benny Show.* New Rochelle, N.Y.: Arlington House, 1977.

Keats, Robin. *TV Land: A Guide to America's Television Shrines, Sets, and Sites.* New York: St. Martin's, 1995.
Keenum, Andy. "Good Ol' Boy of Mayberry." *American Profile,* January 14, 2007.
Kelly, Richard. *The Andy Griffith Show.* Winston-Salem, N.C.: Blair, 1981.
Kirby, Jack Temple. *Media-Made Dixie: The South in the American Imagination.* Baton Rouge: Louisiana State University Press, 1978.
Kloer, Phil. "Prime Time TV Show Moves Country Comedy Out of Sticks." Cox News Service wire story, May 19, 2005.
Knotts, Don, and Robert Metz. *Barney Fife and Other Characters I Have Known.* New York: Berkley Boulevard, 1999.
Kosser, Michael. *How Nashville Became Music City* USA. Milwaukee: Leonard, 2006.
Lawson, Tim, and Alisa Persons. *The Magic behind the Voices.* Jackson: University Press of Mississippi, 2004.
Lenburg, Jeff. *The Encyclopedia of Animated Cartoons.* New York: Facts on File, 1991.
Lovullo, Sam, and Marc Eliot. *Life in the Kornfield: My 25 Years at Hee Haw.* New York: Boulevard, 1996.
MacDonald, Betty. *The Egg and I.* Philadelphia: Lippincott, 1945.
Mackaym Harvey. "Eddie Albert Made His Life the Greenest of Acres." *Huntsville (Alabama) Times,* June 26, 2005.
Malone, Bill C., and Judith McCulloh, eds. *Stars of Country Music: Uncle Dave Macon to Johnny Rodriguez.* Urbana: University of Illinois Press, 1975.
Maltin, Leonard. *The Disney Films.* New York: Disney, 2000.
———. *The Great Movie Comedians.* New York: Harmony, 1982.
———. *Movie Comedy Teams.* New York: Plume, 1985.
———. *Of Mice and Magic: A History of American Animated Cartoons.* New York: Plume, 1980.
Marshall, Peter, and Adrienne Armstrong. *Backstage with the Original Hollywood Square.* Nashville: Rutledge Hill, 2002.
"Master of the Paunch Line." *TV Guide,* January 16, 1960.
McCabe, John, and Al Kilgore. *Laurel and Hardy.* New York: Ballantine, 1975.
McLeod, Elizabeth. "Amos 'n' Andy Imitators: Minstrels, Etc. on Early Radio Programs." *Radio Recall,* June 2002.
Miles, Jim. *Weird Georgia.* New York: Sterling, 2006.
Mitz, Rick. *The Great TV Sitcom Book.* New York: Marek, 1980.
"A New Capp to Feather." Unidentified newspaper clipping in the author's collection, November 15, 1978.
Ohmart, Ben, and Joe Bevilacqua. *Daws Butler: Characters Actor.* Boalsburg, Pa.: BearManor, 2005.
Parish, James Robert. *The Slapstick Queens.* New York: Castle, 1973.
Parish, James Robert, and William T. Leonard. *The Funsters.* New York: Arlington House, 1979.
Pearl, Minnie, and Joan Dew. *Minnie Pearl: An Autobiography.* New York: Simon and Schuster, 1980.
Peterson, Elmer T. "Bob Burns, Real Human Being." *Better Homes and Gardens,* February 1939.
Poindexter, Ray. *Arkansas Airwaves.* North Little Rock, Ark.: Poindexter, 1974.

Price, Michael H., and George E. Turner. "Abner Goes Hollywood: Gets Lost in Shuffle." In *Li'l Abner, 1940.* Princeton, Wis.: Kitchen Sink, 1989.

"Professor Doesn't Tire of 'Andy Griffith Show.'" Associated Press wire service story, February 10, 1985.

Rhodes, Joe. "*The Beverly Hillbillies*—The Movie, That Is." *Atlanta Journal-Constitution,* July 11, 1993.

Robinson, Jerry. *The Comics: An Illustrated History of Comic Strip Art.* New York: Putnam's, 1974.

Rothel, David. *Those Great Cowboy Sidekicks.* Waynesville, N.C.: World of Yesterday, 1984.

Sennett, Ted. *The Art of Hanna-Barbera.* New York: Viking Studio, 1989.

Short, Dale. "An Emotional Time of It in Nashville." *Jasper (Ala.) Daily Mountain Eagle,* undated newspaper clipping in author's collection.

Simon, Richard. "Congressmen Criticize 'Hillbillies' Proposal." *Los Angeles Times,* February 26, 2003.

Smith, Ron. *Comic Support: Second Bananas in the Movies.* New York: Citadel, 1993.

Spears-Stewart, Reta. "Weaver Brothers and Elviry." *Springfield! Magazine,* undated clipping in College of the Ozarks collection.

Staten, Vince. "Heavens! It's the Hillbillies." Gannett News Service wire story, May 24, 1993.

Story, David. *America on the Rerun.* New York: Citadel, 1993.

Stumpf, Charles, and Tom Price. *Heavenly Days! The Story of Fibber McGee and Molly.* Waynesville, N.C.: World of Yesterday, 1987.

Svokos, Heather. "The Real Beverly Hillbillies." Knight-Ridder Newspapers wire story, undated clipping in author's collection.

Truman, Cheryl. "Redneck Lit Big Enough Now to Fill a Double-Wide." McClatchy News Service wire story, July 30, 2006.

Von Doviak, Scott. *Hick Flicks: The Rise and Fall of Redneck Cinema.* Jefferson, N.C.: McFarland, 2005.

Walker, Brian. *Barney Google and Snuffy Smith.* Wilton, Conn.: Comicana, 1994.

Wertheim, Arthur Frank. *Radio Comedy.* New York: Oxford University Press, 1979.

"Wilbur and Ezra." *Radio Digest,* April 1932.

Williamson, J. W. *Hillbillyland: What the Movies Did to the Mountains and What the Mountains Did to the Movies.* Chapel Hill: University of North Carolina Press, 1995.

Zafft, Bruce, and Tim Tromp. *Mountain Dew Collectibles.* Paducah, Ky.: Image Graphics, 2001.

Other sources include the author's thirty-plus-year accumulation of audio and video recordings, all archived in the museum he laughingly calls a home.

Index

Page numbers in **bold** refer to illustrations and/or captions.